Reflections From The Mountains

Helton Creek Falls, Blairsville, GA

An Anthology
by
Georgia Mountain Writers
Club

REFLECTIONS FROM THE MOUNTAINS

ISBN: 978-0-9849099-0-2

First Edition ~~~ Published 2012 by
Georgia Mountain Writers Club
P.O. Box 374
Blairsville, GA 30514

Book cover photograph by Ellie Dobson
Title page photograph by Rhonda Kay Brigman

Produced by Straub Publishing
Blairsville. GA

Manufactured in the United States of America

INTRODUCTION
to
GEORGIA MOUNTAIN WRITERS CLUB

Some of our members have lived in these mountains all their life. Many of us claim these mountains as our home now.

These reflections are from the authors' individual lives now and from their past. You will find stories about hauntings, legends, UFO's, one-room school houses, picking cotton, war stories, and the death of FDR. Also Queen Elizabeth, illegal gambling, the everglades, a pioneer aviator, narrow escapes, and the mishaps of growing older.

Rather than editing our stories to the point of losing the uniqueness of each member's special way of depicting their tale, we have let each of the thirty authors have a final say on the content.

We are celebrating our tenth year in existence by publishing our first book. In these pages you will find Poems, Short Stories, Personal Essays', Fiction and Nonfiction. Their entries will show what a diverse group of people we are, having come from all walks of life and having settled into these Georgia and North Carolina mountains. Over these last ten years we have watched at least twenty members become published authors.

We hope you will find this book enjoyable, funny, and thought provoking.

MISSION STATEMENT

This club was formed in 2001 by a group that had taken writing classes at the OASIS program. When these classes were completed we were not finished with our writing, so this club of seven members was co-founded by Larry Casey and Ellie Dobson. We now have approximately forty-five members.

The mission of our club is to offer support, encouragement, and motivation to each member. Members may read their work and then obtain wise critiquing, help and information. We keep in mind that everyone has a right to express their opinions in their written work and you may respectfully disagree.

Occasionally we will have guest speakers that share their journey on getting published. We are of a kindred spirit because we LOVE to write. Each of the thirty authors has shared their love of writing in their own personal experiences of life. It is hoped that all of the above will help the members to become more disciplined and productive writers. Over these last ten years we have watched at least twenty members become published authors.

We meet on every second Wednesday of each month, right now at the St. Francis of Assisi Catholic Church on S.R. 515, at 10:00 am to 12:00 noon. Come by and visit with us and find out for yourself what we are all about. For information please feel free to call Ellie Dobson @ 706-745-0678. Our mailing address is: P.O. Box 374, Blairsville, GA. 30514 or e-mail us at **gmwc@windstream.net or jldobson@windstream.net**

ACKNOWLEDGEMENTS

Special thanks go out to everyone that was on a committee. Starting with the **Genesis/Steering committee**, we appreciate and thank Sylvia Turnage, Sonny and Laurie Boyer, Eleanore McDade, Rhonda Kay Brigman, and Ellie Dobson.

Editing and Proofreading:
Laurie Boyer, Chairperson; Zadie McCall; Judy Abercrombie; Idell Shook; Benetta Cook; Jean Nethery; Leeann Wildman; Anna Stone.

Layout and Printing:
Sonny Boyer, Chairperson; Rick Straub.

Cover and Title:
Juanita Schneider, Chairperson; Lorraine Orth; Idell Shook.

Editors:
Ellie Dobson, Chairperson; Sylvia Turnage; Rhonda Kay Brigman.

Marketing and Promotions:
Ralph Kwiatkowski, Chairperson; Phil Gatlin; Eleanore McDade; Ellie Dobson; Rhonda Kay Brigman.
.

Final Editing by Ellie Dobson and Rhonda Kay Brigman.

Contents

Old Times

Animal Stories

Paul and Christy Goings, Living with Multiple Sclerosis

Idell M. Shook, Our Resident Poet

Poetry

Experiences

Biographies

Local Stories

Blairsville, GA Courthouse

Can't Get Too Much of a Good Thing, Living in The Georgia Mountains
by
Ralph Kwiatkowski

We discovered the area several years ago when we drove home to Atlanta after visiting my mother-in-law in a nursing home in Robbinsville, North Carolina. A friend had told us about a scenic route through the mountains and we found it more relaxing than the four-lane we had been using. In the process, we discovered Union and Towns Counties in North Georgia.

Blairsville and Hiawassee, Georgia share the Georgia-North Carolina state line with the towns of Murphy and Hayesville, North Carolina. All contribute to the richness of the area, and except for the signs on the highway, you wouldn't know that you were crossing a state line.

We visited the area several times before moving. We met friendly, neighborly people wherever we went. Making conversation with strangers was like meeting old friends. It wasn't long before we were sold on the small town atmosphere surrounded by the mountains, clear lakes, fresh air and good mountain water.

Several lakes and numerous mountain vistas break the landscape as we drive through the countryside. Cool starry nights light the night sky and warm summer days linger after a hike or visit to a local waterfall. While hawks and eagles soar above; bear, deer and coyotes roam the fields and forests. Natural wonders of creation abound here and all is shared with good friends and neighbors always ready to lend a helping hand.

Originally settled by the Scots, the North Georgia Mountains grew in proportion to that of the city of Atlanta. The area became a weekend retreat or vacation destination for city folks. Today, nearly a third of the population are retirees who share their ethnic backgrounds and heritages contributing to the cultural diversity of the region. Many have come from Florida trying to escape the long hot summers; others came from the city to escape the rat-race, searching for a slower pace of life.

Local talent abounds in the mountains. Artisans, musicians and singers share their talents in the theater, hoedowns, blue-

2

grass concerts and art festivals. The Georgia Mountain Chorus presents two concerts each year, as well as several performances by the Young Harris College Chorus. Three theaters in the area, the Peacock Playhouse in Hayesville, the Blue Ridge Community Theater, and the Young Harris College Theater annually bring more than a dozen plays to the stage.

The Scottish, Butternut and Green Bean Festivals highlight the summer fare while the Georgia Mountain Fair and the Sorghum Festival kicks-off the fall season. All are well attended by local folks as well as visitors from as far away as Atlanta.

The Anderson Music Hall in Hiawassee is home to Country Music Superstars from May through October. Top country music entertainers such as George Strait, Reba McEntire, Glenn Campbell and the new stars of today, bring their tours to this little bit of heaven. The DeKalb Symphony performs at Young Harris College annually presenting works from the great masters. Blairsville is also home to the Mountain Bluegrass Festival, and on the rowdy side, there is the Celtic Concert during the Scottish Festival.

The visitor's center on Brasstown Bald, the highest point in Georgia, sits upon the top of the "bald" like a chimney and can be seen from miles around. On a clear day, four states and the Atlanta skyline can be seen. The area also includes many waterfalls, hiking trails, and trout streams. Nature lovers never lack for something to do in the North Georgia Mountains. Helton Creek, Duke's Creek, and Desoto Falls are easy rewarding hikes. High Shoals Scenic area is a bit more strenuous but the hike leads to spectacular falls at the bottom of the trail.

Many educational opportunities abound for the beginner as well as the accomplished artisan. Classes are offered by area colleges and folk schools promoting arts and crafts taught by area masters. There is something here for everyone. The Institute for Continuous Learning, hosted by Young Harris College in Young Harris, Georgia, sponsors more than fifty seminars each year covering topics of interest for the inquisitive mind. Attended generally by "senior citizens", the program is open to the public. Classes are taught by experts in their field; many of whom are former teachers and professionals eager to share the love for their favorite subject.

Another program called OASIS (Older Adults Sharing In Service) is sponsored by the First United Methodist Church of Union County. The program offers instruction in a variety of programs from basket-weaving, chair caning, yoga, computers, and beginning French, to painting, music and creative writing. Other classes are also offered based on interest and availability of instructors.

The Lapidary School in Young Harris, GA., and the John C. Campbell Folk School in Brasstown, NC. are both known countrywide for their specialty programs for the serious craftsman. Artisans from all over the country come here to vacation while learning more about their specialty as they participate in week long classes.

The towns of Blairsville, Young Harris, and Hiawassee are ideal sizes; large enough to offer the necessities of life and small enough to have a friendly small town atmosphere. Meeting and making friends, slowing down the hurried pace of life, and enjoying the moment are all part of everyday living here in the mountains.

We also enjoy having four seasons. Winters are short and not too cold; summers can be warm but bearable. The spring and fall seasons are very comfortable. Mountain Laurel in the spring and fall colors in Autumn are highlights of the year, and is the best time for hiking and photography. While visitors may come through for an afternoon drive or stay a day or two, those of us who live here enjoy these beautiful vistas daily.

Like grandma's apple pie, homemade chocolate chip cookies, and mouth-wateringly Bar-B-Q, life in the mountains is good. It's better than good! It is terrific! There is something for everyone! So whether you are visiting or already live here, you'll soon discover that there is no such thing as "getting too much of a good thing" in the North Georgia Mountains.

Reflection:

Contentment is not the fulfillment of what you want but the realization of how much you already have.

Author Unknown

Haunting Tales
By
Ralph Kwiatkowski

In Burke County, near Morganton, North Carolina, the Brown Mountain Lights as they are known can best be seen at Wiseman's View on Highway 105. A reddish colored light appears on a hillside only to disappear, and reappear further along the mountain. Sometimes it reappears going in the opposite direction. The lights have been investigated by the US Geological Department, and like UFO's, no one has found any real explanation for the mystery. Some have thought they were a reflection of car lights from a nearby mountain; however, these lights have been around since before cars were invented. Others thought that moon-shiners were firing up their stills; however, moon-shiners have been gone for many a year but the lights remain. There's a rumor that a man murdered his wife, and a few years later he mysteriously disappeared. The lights were gone for a time, but then the body of a murdered female was found in the area. The lights returned and are still there today.

In 1831, Burke County, Georgia, was the scene of another famous murder. Frankie Silver, age nineteen, was hanged for the murder of her husband Charles. Frankie hacked her husband to death with an ax, supposedly in self defense, and scattered the pieces around the countryside. Since his remains were not all found at the same time, each discovery was buried separately. Today, his dismembered body lies in three separate graves, with one head stone. Frankie's body lies in an unmarked grave behind Buckthorn Tavern, a few miles west of Morganton.

The mystery of the Brown Mountain lights may very well hinge on the man who murdered his wife, but then again, Frankie Silver was a woman who murdered her husband. Opposites attract. Were the families related? Could there be a connection? If you are passing through Burke County, it may be wise not to stay too long!

Backpackers trekking from Springer Mountain, GA, to Mount Katahdin, Maine, may well encounter unexpected travelers. The Appalachian Trails (AT) 2,175 miles are filled with Indian lore and spirits of Union and Confederate dead. All along the AT, apparitions of murder's ghosts and the spirits of mother's looking for their sons lost in the Civil War are frequently experienced. It is a "deathly" part of our country with many tales of fighting, murder and war. Stories of wars between Indian tribes, and between settlers and Indians abound. Many Civil War battles were fought on these ridges and the Trail of Tears began here.

Most hikers are not adequately prepared for the endurance required for the through-hike nor the encounters that await them on the trail. The southern portion of the trail is some of the most rugged and challenging. Many give up after a few days, some after a week or two; some quit for a very different reason.

Hikers have reported hearing weird noises in the night, sounds of crying children, and unexpected sightings. Their experiences have lead to many a sleepless night. Some say that these were "terrifying experiences"! Others say *"Ghostly"*! Whatever you call it, the experience has been the demise of more than a few attempting the entire journey.

Area natives have many stories not accounted here, but these are written for posterity. Handed down for generations, tales are told of the spirits of the Indians, long driven from their land as well as the spirits of civil war soldiers slain in the name of freedom. Thousands of soldiers, both Union and Confederate, died in these mountains. Their spirits still wander through the hills and battle fields. It has been reported that on a clear night, a light can be seen flickering like a star on a nearby ridge. It is said to be the lantern of a lost soldier in search of his unit. On foggy nights, the dim light of the lantern fades into the wispy clouds as they drift between the ridges. Many *skeptics* have come to appreciate these apparitions after spending a night or two camping under the stars. They come back knowing that they were not alone!

There are also tales of mysterious happenings in the lodge at Amicalola Falls State Park in Georgia. The falls are located near Spencer Mountain, the southern most point of the Appalachian Trail. As the story goes, young Indian braves climbed this mountain seeking a vision and praying to the spirits that lived there. As one of the Indians' most sacred mountains, it is considered a place of peace. Rowdiness in and around the Amicalola Lodge is not welcomed. On occasion, when tempers flared between workers in the kitchen, a frying pan or pot would come flying across the room. No one has ever seen the thrower either, but it sure got their attention! They say the spirits do this in order to keep the peace. This has happened many times; luckily no one has ever been hurt.

Further up the trail, hikers are reluctant to stop near Big Willow, North Carolina, where a menacing spirit relentlessly pursues anyone on the trail at night. It is said to be the spirit of an old woman in search of her son who went off to fight in the Civil War and never returned. She wanders up and down the trail near Big Willow, still waiting and searching for the son.

For backpackers, sections along the AT have camp sites maintained by local hikers. Most camp sites are open shelters about a days hike apart where hikers can set up camp in a dry shelter out of the weather. A shelter near the North Carolina-Virginia line is haunted by a "hungry" spirit. Campers have said that they have tied off their food supplies high off the ground safe from bears, mountain lions and other scavengers as recommended. However their back packs have been opened and some even "moved" to a different tree. No one knows who or why their backpacks were opened or moved. No sounds were heard, and no sign of any human or animal was noted.

In the Shenandoah Valley of Virginia, the AT trail descends and runs along several farms. It runs through the woods and along a community cemetery. At one time there were two cemeteries, one either side of a sacred Indian burial ground. The government took possession of the cemeteries for a short time but later returned the cemetery to the Native Americans. The government had promised to relocate the graves of the pioneers, removing them from the Indian burial ground. Legend has it that instead of going through the expense of relocating the graves, only the headstones were moved. The souls of these pioneers and Indians have not rested. Their spirits, still in turmoil, are not the friendliest!

The Southern Appalachian Mountains and the Appalachian Trail hold more secrets that we may ever know. Recent murders and bodies found in the mountains will undoubtedly be the cause for more spirits to be searching for peace and a final resting place. If you're camping in the hills or hiking on the trail, don't be surprised if a cool wind gives you a chill and spirits dance around your camp fire. If this happens to you, welcome your guest and set another plate for dinner. Your best bet for a good nights' rest is to invite your guest to join you. The welcomed spirit will be grateful for your hospitality!

If you're a *doubter*, just beware! The unknown can be a powerful force. Many a "*doubter*" has not returned. Some never found. I hope you enjoy your hike and live to tell the tale!

Reflection:

It's your road and yours alone. Others may walk it with you but no one can walk it for you!

Author Unknown

Brasstown Bald, The Top of Georgia
by
Sylvia Dyer Turnage

You see it silhouetted against the sky with lesser mountains trailing its sides, its watchtower perched like a feather on a fancy lady's hat. Georgia's highest mountain, Brasstown Bald, stands at a majestic elevation of 4,784 feet. The Cherokee Indians gave it the name *Itse'yi*, meaning "new green place" or "place of fresh green." There were several early English translations of the Cherokee word—Echia, Echoee, Etchowee and Brasstown. The translation of "Brasstown" appears to have occurred as a result of confusing *Itse'yi* (place of green) with *Untsai'yi* (place of brass).

There was once an Indian camping ground approximately where the present parking lot is located, near a clear, cold spring. A Cherokee legend says that a great flood occurred years ago. All of the people living in the area died except a few Cherokee families that found refuge in a large canoe. The canoe finally ran aground at the top of this mountain. The Cherokee had no wild game to hunt and nowhere to plant their crops, so the Great Spirit killed all of the trees on top of the mountain so the surviving people would have a place to grow their food. They lived there and planted their crops until the water subsided.

We really don't know if there is merit to the Cherokee legend, but some of the more recent history is verifiable. In the early 1900's, the Pfister and Vogel Company owned much of the land on and around Brasstown Bald and engaged in extensive logging of the area. A wooden lookout was built on the mountaintop to help detect fires on their lands. In 1934, Pfister and Vogel deeded the site to the State of Georgia, and the Civilian Conservation Corps erected a 33-foot high stone and wood structure that was manned by the U. S. Forest Service. By this time, much of the logging company's land had been acquired by what was then known as the Cherokee National Forest.

In 1947, the State of Georgia deeded the one-quarter acre of land upon which the tower sits to the United States of America. By Act No. 162 (Senate Bill No. 92) the State approved transfer of 0.13 acres in Union County and 0.12 acres in Towns County for "construction thereon of a Lookout Tower or observatory for use in detecting and suppressing fires and for other purposes in preventing forest fires and other damage to national and state forests in the State of Georgia." The tower is located approximately in the center of the tract.

Brasstown Bald is part of the Appalachian mountain range. Geologists estimate the age of rocks found in these ancient mountains to be as much as 600 million years old. Unlike the higher Rockies, which are younger and still in the upward thrust stage, Brasstown Bald and surrounding mountains are remnants of lofty peaks that have be worn down through the effects of time and the elements. The rounded shoulders, wooded slopes and fertile valleys of the Appalachians are what remain from this once mighty range.

Access to the mountaintop is provided by way of a spur off Georgia Highway 180, "Micajah Clark Dyer Parkway." The observation tower commands a panoramic view of the surrounding mountains and valleys across four states. One can hardly be blamed if the mountain's splendor inspires a poem.

Ode to Brasstown Bald

I stand in Choestoe
And look toward mountains high
Brasstown Bald is standing
So tall it scrapes the sky.
Its tower is overlooking
The valley far below,
Keeping watch o'er all of us
As on our ways we go.
It stands there so majestic,
My heart is filled with awe.
What a work of creation
God did on Brasstown Bald!

She's beautiful in Autumn,
Her leaves are all aglow;
Then comes the winter season
And she's lovely in the snow.
Spring then breaks upon her,
The flowers start to bloom.
Summer rounds the corner—
In green she stands well groomed.
No matter when you find her,
She'll make a hit with you.
This grand and glorious mountain
Will thrill your heart anew.

Reflection:

"Nothing is worth more than this day. "

Goethe

How Choestoe Got Its Name
by
Sylvia Dyer Turnage

Maybe you have traveled south from Blairsville, Georgia, along U.S. Highway 19/129 or State Highway 180 East toward Brasstown Bald Mountain and noticed signs along the roads that include the word "Choestoe." It is not a word you're apt to see anywhere else, so strangers often wonder how they should pronounce it. If you're a native, you can't help smothering your laughter at their attempts to say it—"Choe's Toe" or "Koe Sto" or "Cho Sto."

The pronunciation is actually very melodic, with every vowel having a long sound: Cho-e-sto-e. It is the name given to this area by the Cherokee Indians, and it means "Place of the dancing rabbits."

The Cherokee named all of the different areas of their land according to what they saw in each place. Some examples of this naming practice are readily evident in our area, including "Walasi-yi" which means "Place of the big frog." Neel's Gap, where the Appalachian Trail crosses Highway 19/129, was previously known as Frogtown Gap. "Arkaquah" means "Crooked creek," no doubt because of the long, winding creek that flows through the community. "Tesnatee" means "painted rock," and when you travel the Richard B. Russell Scenic Highway through Tesnatee Gap it is not difficult to understand why the Cherokee chose that name.

So, do the rabbits really dance in Choestoe? In addition to the Cherokee stories, there have been many other people down through the years that say, indeed, they have seen the rabbits dancing here. Only recently, a woman was telling me that she and her husband had visitors at their home in Choestoe, when suddenly they noticed two rabbits at the edge of the yard dancing together. She said one would stand on its hind legs and hop back and forth, swaying rhythmically toward the other one.

Then, it would sit and the other would dance the same steps toward it. She said this continued for quite some time with the rabbits alternating the enchanted dance. She said, "I was glad we had another witness to the unique show, especially since it was our pastor, because a story such as this might otherwise not have been believed!"

When you see the full moon rise over Horse Trough Mountain and hear the wind whispering in the pines, it is easy to believe the rabbits could begin their dance at any moment. Maybe you can see them in your mind's eye as you read this poem.

The Choestoe Story
by
Sylvia Dyer Turnage

The Choestoe story is burning in my heart,
The Choestoe story to you I now impart.
The Indian legend tell us that on a moonlit night
The rabbits get together and dance with all their might.

They hop into the valley and round and round they go,
You really ought to see them; they put on such a show!
They seem to smile as they frolic there; it makes my heart feel
glad
To see these happy creatures, not one of them is sad.

Oh, see the rabbits dancing, and let your own heart sing.
Blend your smile with theirs now, and join into their ring.
You'll feel your foot begin to tap to the music of their feet;
Your cares will flee your spirits soar while you're swaying to the
beat.

Oh, come to Choestoe, the place where rabbits dance.
It's such a lovely place to be, I'm sure it's not by chance
That the rabbits made it their place of joy to let their freedom
ring.
They welcome you to join them there and let your own heart
sing.

Pine Top, The Little One-Room School
by
Sylvia Dyer Turnage

Soon after Union County was officially established in 1832 from Cherokee land, the State Legislature approved the founding of a school and appropriated funds to build the Blairsville Academy, an indication that the settlers already had been exposed to formal education and realized its importance to the success of their new community. The Academy was built just off the Square in Blairsville, approximately where Antoinetta's Restaurant is now located on Blue Ridge Street. The building had two stories and a chimney at each end for heating purposes. The Academy operated until the Civil War when all schools were suspended. After the War, the building was torn down and a school was never again located at that exact site; however, other schools did function in nearby locations within the town.

The Academy played a vital role in educating students, but it was the numerous little one-room schools scattered across the county that played an important part in the early history of this area. One-room schools existed here considerably longer than in other parts of the United States and the last of them were still functioning into the early 1950s. In some of the more heavily populated communities, the schools might have two or three rooms with seven grades divided among teachers. However, the most common arrangement was a small, one-room building in which one teacher taught all seven grades. Many of the buildings also doubled as church houses.

I have first-hand knowledge of one of these little one-room schools, Pine Top School, where I attended grades three through six. The school was located about three-quarters of a mile from my home, and my brother, sister and I walked (really most often we ran) to and from the school in all kinds of weather. There were fewer than twenty-five students during the years I attended. The little building was heated with a pot-bellied wood stove, and the neighbors brought the wood and stacked it outside for use in the winter. There was no water fountain in this building—we drank from a bucket of spring water that sat on a little table in back of the room.

We must have had pretty good concentration, for we would read, write and do arithmetic at our grade level while the other grades were reciting aloud for the teacher. We didn't have enough members for any organized sports, but we played many games outside during lunch and recess.

My fond memories of old Pine Top School are summed up in a poem I wrote. Join me in a sentimental journey as I go back there now.

Pine Top School was a very tiny school,
Sitting on a mountain side.
One teacher taught all seven grades
With considerable skill and pride.
The heat came from a little pot-bellied stove
Fed with wood that the neighbors brought
So we all kept warm as we tried to learn
The lessons that the teacher taught.

A is for apple, B is for boy,
We learned how to read and write.
1 plus 2 equals 3, you see,
So we learned how to cipher just right.
Brush your teeth, wash your face,
She taught us to guard our health.
"Learn your lessons so you'll all grow up
To have wisdom and plenty of wealth."

There was no lunchroom for this little group,
We ate what our Moms sent each day—
Biscuit and pork, maybe pinto beans,
Cornbread or whatever you may.
Lunch soon finished, we started to play
Our games among the tall trees.
Softball, dodge ball, hopscotch and tag
"Mother, may I, please."

The teacher rang a little brass bell
To tell us the time had come
To stop our play and go back to our books
'Til the evening bell was rung.
We learned of the continents, oceans and seas,
Of battles fought long ago
That we might have peace and enjoy our life
With liberty from all our foes.

We pledged to the flag with our heads held high
Our right hand across our heart.
We read from the Word and lifted our prayers
That from godliness we'd not depart.
"Please," "Yes, Ma'am," and "Thank you"
Were practiced by one and all.
No talking back to the teacher,
We knew this no matter how small.

Oh, that we might once again get to see
The simplicity of teaching this way,
With God and country held in highest esteem
By teachers and students each day.
With respect shown for others and loving care, too
No matter what level they be
Helping them reach their best in all ways,
And keeping the unity.

Autumn in The North Georgia Mountains
by
Jean A. Nethery

Shorter days mean that no more katydids are singing us to sleep and acorns drop like rain from stately oaks. We are reminded that fall is here. Bears, squirrels and wild boar come at night to fill their hungry tummies with fallen acorns.

The sourwood and dogwood trees are the first to change their costume to deep red; tulip poplars and hickories decide to convert to sunny shades of yellow. Migrating birds chase the Carolina wrens and nuthatches away from the feeder as if to say "You've had enough!" Wild turkeys flock together and appear to feel safer in numbers. White-tailed deer cross our path---their light brown coats changing to coarse grey-brown in preparation for the cold ahead.

Autumn festivals are in full swing, attracting local residents and long distance travelers. Many will sample tasty peach and apple butters, homemade pies and flaky biscuits dripping with sourwood honey or sorghum. An old, bearded mountain man sits in a rocking chair and strums his guitar, singing 'I'll Fly Away', as folks pass by, licking their fingers of fried green tomatoes and apple dumplings. Cloggers in short, full skirts, tap and spin to Bluegrass music and Gospel singers from the local Baptist church stand waiting for their chance to belt out 'Amazing Grace'.

Thanksgiving is only weeks away and we give thanks for the change in seasons and the splendor of the mountains. Summer has passed and we relish the chance to put on our sweatshirts and hiking boots and enjoy the crispness of the season. Pumpkins ripen in fields while red and green apples hang heavy from branches. Goldenrod and asters start to bend their heads like shy dancers, relieved that their performance is almost over.

The panorama of colors on the mountain sides makes us think of a kaleidoscope. Soon the winds and rain will come so leaves will whirl and fall to the ground. The scene will rapidly change to shades of gray and beige. Autumn is here and it's time to stand still, take a deep breath and enjoy every minute.

Summer Solstice
by
Nadine Justice

What really is this sister girlfriend thing all about anyway? Female bonding rituals have been around since before our grandmothers were gathering to make quilts. Empty nesters take up hobbies that require a group setting, and contemporary women get together to drink wine and invest money. No matter the life style or age, it's a thing only women get. Most men are clueless about it but we were born with an innate understanding that our parents will die and our children will leave us, but our friends are around for the long haul.

I've been told that if you had a good relationship with your mother then you would be able to develop good close and trusting girlfriend relationships. Well, that isn't necessarily true; at least not in my case. I did not have a good relationship with my mother but I do have great friendships, some going back to my childhood as early as eight-years-old. Just last week as I was leaving Lena's house I told her that some of my other friends thought it was really neat that she and I had been friends since we were little girls. As I was pulling away from her driveway I heard her say "we still are little girls". The sound of her laughter lingered with me, keeping me company on my drive home. When I recently found myself at the airport with no ride home, because my flight was late, I called Lena. Without hesitation she said "I can do that" and in record time she was there with a bottle of water and a snack to tide me over until we got out of the city and found a favorite restaurant. When I thanked her, and told her I would make it up to her, she responded with "you already have, many times". I do hope that is true.

When I was younger and better looking I probably, at least subconsciously, thought men were dispensable but I have never had that attitude about my girlfriends. I knew if my child was sick, or a man had broken my heart, that my friends would always be there with a few kind words, open arms, or a glass of wine, (sometimes both), ready to listen and offer help with whatever I needed.

One of my richest blessings is the diverse group of friends I have. Some of them seem to have nothing in common. At least one readily comes to mind; she could irritate a statue but I love her and, looking at the big picture, am thankful that her kind heart outweighs the annoying habits. How comforting it is to know that my friends will put up with me and my flaws if I am faithful and accepting of them.

Recently, my six-year-old twin grandchildren's dog died. It was quite traumatic because ole Bob had been around since before the kids were born and the whole family, especially Chase and Chloe were devastated. I called the next day to see how they were doing and Chloe, in her sweet, quiet, little voice said "Nana, did mom tell you about Bob? Well, he died". I said "Yes, I know, honey, and I'm so very sorry". She answered "that's okay, Nana, everybody has to do it and you'll probably be next". I then went to great lengths to explain that, in people years, Bob was about ninety-five years old and that my friend Tweetie was ninety-five and still healthy. I assured her that I planned on being like Tweetie, which means that I have at least another thirty years. I belabored the subject further but she remained clearly unconvinced.

I do hope Chloe is wrong about my being next and that I can continue to, as they say in Girl Scouts, "make new friends and keep the old. One is silver and the other is gold".

When this life is all said and done we will find ourselves at the end realizing that the sum total of all we are lies within whom we have helped and loved and the people who loved us. The older I get the more I value and appreciate these friendships.

I am truly thankful that I have been invited to the Summer Solstice celebration. I plan to be back with you again next year with bells on and, of course, my favorite hat! Tweetie asked if she may join us and is currently looking for a new hat.

Postscript: My dear friend, Tweetie, died last month. She was ninety-eight and still living alone in her own home. Yep, I plan on being just like Tweetie.

Reflection:
Teach us to number our days that we may gain a heart of wisdom. "   Psalm. 90

Summertime in The Mountains of Georgia
by
Eleanore C. McDade

The passage of Spring has occurred with all its glorious birth of new life after the cold days of Winter. Flowers are in full bloom with an array of colors equal to a pallets dream. Showers have filled the brooks and streams to the joy of fish and frogs.

I saw a firefly last night, no, not one...but many. They glow as they dance higher and higher into the woods and surrounding trees. City folks rarely experience this happening. Oh, and the bats are out! I'm glad to see them, for they help keep the mosquito population down.

I sat on the porch the other night with my neighbors. We enjoyed the quiet serenity of nightfall together and remarked at the fact that there were no mosquitoes... yet. Oh, I know they'll come, but most do not cross the Florida-line.

Early morning is solemn and peaceful, a time to reflect on the joys of being in the mountains or for that matter, just being. I gaze out my window to the stately beauty of these gorgeous hazy Blue Mountains that surround us here at the beginning ridges of Appalachia.

The birds are all chirping with their new families. I listen to their sounds, all different. They talk to each other in an array of music. Their chirps and twitters convey a message to each other. The day has begun. Other than the music of the birds, there is quietness in the air. Even the wind is gentle.

Yes, the tourists and Summer residents will come to enjoy these subtle beauties, but will they take the time to see and hear them? I hope so, for in this world where we live there is much to distract us from the quiet, peaceful beauty that surrounds us, here in the mountains on a Summer night or in the early hours of morn with the awakening of life to a new and glorious dawn of Summer in the mountains.

Some Memories of Ivy Log Creek
by
Charles H. Souther

The spring heads of Ivy Log Creek are nestled in the mountains of the southern extremities of Gum Log District, up in the direction of Juber Knob, the Hullander Knobs, Walnut Knob, and Ivy Log Gap. The creek meanders down through Gum Log and Ivy Log, on it's way to Nottely River.

The pioneering engineers (of two or three generations before the time of this writer) had harnessed the waters of Ivy Log Creek to provide the power to operate a corn grist mill. The mill was known as "The Swanson Mill." It was named for my great grandfather, Bartlett Swanson, whose family operated the mill for several years.

As the family boys grew up, and the older ones migrated to Oklahoma and the younger two moved away, operation of the mill became more difficult for their aging father. Some time after the Swanson boys had left home the mill was sold to another of my great grandfathers, Joe Townsend.

After my great grandfather had come into ownership of the mill he was in a dilemma as to who would operate it. His main residence was in Choestoe District where most of his land holdings were located. None of his close relatives lived in Gum Log near the mill, except my father and his family. So my great grandfather prevailed on my father to operate the mill for him.

As a result of this arrangement we moved the two miles from the old house where we had lived a few years to the old house on the mill property. The house we moved into was just across the road from the mill house and mill pond. The front of the house rested on a huge rock that extended into the front yard. The rock was so large that it covered at least half of the front yard.

Many of my memories of Ivy Log Creek occurred during the two years we lived at the mill.

On one occasion I was fishing at the fishing hole under the bridge below the mill dam. I sat on the bank next to the bridge with my line in the water. The cane pole was under my arm with the butt end extending about eighteen feet behind me. As the pole jiggled several times I thought I was getting a bite each time. However, I found out a little later that Charlie Smith had slipped up behind me and was jiggling my pole. But before I found out about this trick I got a real bite and landed a ten inch hog sucker. This became a big story that Charlie Smith liked to tell.

He said when I caught the hog sucker I said, "Oh my God what a fish."

Another time my mother had gone to visit my grandparents. My dad was home and had caught up with most of the urgent farm and mill work on that particular day. As my dad and I sat on the porch, we observed Charlie Smith and his dad, Will, emerge from the vegetation along the creek bank. They were carrying their fishing poles and a string of fish. They had come down the creek bank from the upstream cabin in which the two of them lived.

Will's wife had passed away a few years earlier and Charlie, a World War I veteran, had never married. When Will found out my mother was not home he suggested to my dad that we have a fish fry. My dad agreed but told Will that we would have to cook some corn bread to go with the fish since there was no bread in the house. Will readily agreed to cook the corn bread. He was accustomed to doing his own cooking anyway. I was given the assignment to bring in some stove wood and build a fire in the cookstove.

Will and Charlie proceeded to clean the fish, which consisted mostly of a horny head with one or two hog suckers in the bunch. The horny head was a native of Ivy Log Creek and got it's name from the pin-sized horns on it's head. It was probably the most bony fish in the world. After the fish were cleaned and cooked in some hog lard that my mother had in the kitchen, and the corn bread had been baked in the oven of the wood stove, we were ready to eat. As we began to eat Will advised that we should eat plenty of bread with the horny head fish. There may still be some bones in the meat which could get caught in our throat. I took this advice serious and almost choked myself with excessive bites of corn bread along with tiny bites of fish. My dad and the Smiths seemed to get a kick out of my seriousness.

Some of the fishing holes in Ivy Log Creek were deep enough to be used as swimming holes by the boys of the settlement. The boys that went swimming in Ivy Log Creek didn't have store bought swimming suits but they found that their birthday suits were quite adequate. There was not much risk of the boys being accused of indecent exposure since most of the swimming holes in Ivy Log Creek had natural privacy fences, consisting of the small variety of bamboo cane, blackberry briars, weeds, grass, and other vegetation. One of the boys had a standing joke that he would repeat every time he got out of the swimming hole.

He would say, "Boys put your cap on as soon as you get out of the water so if any women come around they can't see your private parts." Only, he didn't say "private parts."

On many occasions Ivy Log Creek has been utilized for a religious purpose. The converts, resulting from a protracted meeting which, at times would go on for three or four weeks, were usually baptized in Ivy Log Creek. The creek would be dammed up at the Hemphill bridge and the Henson bridge, and in earlier years below the Swanson mill to create a pond deep enough for the purpose. The baptizing would usually be held on a warm Sunday afternoon After a prayer on the bank, the candidates for baptism would start single file into the water while a group from the church would sing *Shall we Gather at the River,* or some other appropriate song.

When the preacher was ready to baptize the singing would cease and the converts were immersed one by one.

The preacher raised his hand and said something like the following: "Upon the profession of your faith in the Lord Jesus Christ, my brother (sister) I baptize you in the name of the Father, the Son, and the Holy Ghost."

After all the converts had been immersed and as they filed out of the water, the church members on the bank would continue singing. A dismissal prayer would be said and the converts would go to a covered pickup truck, a van, or nearby building if available to change out of their wet clothes. In earlier years covered wagons may have been used for this purpose.

During the time we lived at the mill, I attended a one-room school about one and one-half miles "up the creek" from where we lived. The unofficial name of the school was "Stump Toe" It is said it got it's name from the fact that there was a toe nail under every rock in the school yard from the bare footed students stumping their toes while playing during recess.

One of the most pleasant memories of living at the mill was the sound of the rustling waters pouring over the mill dam and splashing against the rocks to help put a tired boy into a peaceful sleep after a hard day of work.

Valley of The Light
by
C.G. Williamson

Note: This story was taken from C.G. Williamson's book "A Place In Time," published in 2006, relating family history and events in his life.

In 1943 when I was eight years old, the family moved to the farm that I now live on. I went to school nearby in a one room schoolhouse with seven grades. It was part of the Ebenezer community.

There was no electricity in the area so it made living conditions somewhat crude. The school in its long history never had an outhouse. The teacher Mr. Ross, believed in discipline. One day when I was in the forth grade, Mr. Ross was teaching the sixth grade about dental and bathroom hygiene. No one that I knew had a toothbrush or a bathroom. It all sounded like science fiction to me. I started laughing and the other kids started laughing too. Mr. Ross didn't laugh. He sent me to the woods to cut a hickory switch. He was going to smoke the seat of my pants. I had to think fast. He didn't tell me what length to cut the switch so I cut one ten feet long. When I handed it to Mr. Ross, it touched the ceiling. Mr. Ross laughed until tears rolled down his cheeks.

I loved that school. I learned to read and life became an adventure.

The way we lived was in accordance with nature. Our night vision was very sharp and any sound or movement that didn't correspond with the order of nature, as I knew it, immediately came into question.

Most everyone walked wherever they went locally. The only vehicle in the community was a log truck. Our house was on a road that ran north across a creek, then east along a ridge running with the valley.

One night when I was about eleven years old, my brother James and I were walking home from a summer revival at church. We looked across the valley to the barn about four hundred yards away and saw a ball of light. The light was about the size of a headlight on an old car. It seemed to be about fifteen feet over the barn and was stationery. We decided to sit and watch it for awhile. Ten minutes later, the light moved about three-hundred and fifty yards in a straight line to a point over a branch. There it remained ten minutes and then returned over the barn. As it proceeded to follow this pattern of movement, I was amazed at its precision in terms of height, direction and time. When it stopped at the branch, it appeared to be about ten feet from the ground, always at the same place. My brother and I watched it for about an hour. The light never changed its pattern.

The following night we went back to the church with some of the neighbors. When we returned to the point overlooking the valley, there was the light, following the same lonely path. I was very curious, mainly because the light was something which I could not identify.

Summer passed into fall and you would think I would have waited in the barn for a close view of the light. I thought it would sense my presence and not return. So I more or less forgot about it.

But not for long.

One night I woke up in the wee hours of the morning feeling very thirsty. I went to the kitchen for a glass of water. As I looked out the window, I saw the ball of light over the barn. It was unusually bright even with the full moon shinning. I wanted to see the light up close so I didn't take the time to put any clothes on. I eased out the back door, and ran towards the light. When I got near the barn, it seemed as though it saw me and moved very rapidly on it's aerial path to the branch. I was shivering and my butt was cold. I quickly ran back to the house. As far as I know, the light didn't come back that night.

Years later I came back home for awhile. My Paw and Mom and I built a house where the old barn once stood. It even had electricity. My maw and Paw lived in this house for many years.

During this time, I asked Paw if he ever saw the light again. He said he saw it on the face of Rogers Mountain at the end of the valley. He watched it using binoculars for about an hour. Paw said it never changed its pattern of movement.

I asked Paw what he thought it was.

"I think it was a mineral light son."

"What is a mineral light?"

"It's some type of gas that seeps up through the ground that glows like foxfire."

"Why did the light follow a certain pattern of height, time and direction?"

"I think the gas becomes negatively charged as it comes through the ground and follows a positive charge iron ore vein that runs to the barn. It then reverses its polarity and goes back to the branch."

"That won't hold water Paw."

"Have you got a better Idea?"

"The light was probably in Atlanta and due to a certain atmospheric condition it created an atmospheric lens and transferred the light image to the barn."

"That won't hold water son."

"Why?"

"It happened more than once at the same barn."

"Suppose it's an intelligent life form and if we learn something about it maybe we can increase our knowledge of who or what we are."

It hasn't done anything for your knowledge so far, although it sounds better than that artic lens stuff."

"That's an atmospheric lens, Paw."

"Whatever."

Due to the changes in the way we lived and traveled, I never thought I would see that light again.

One night a few years later, my girlfriend and I were sitting in a car on a side road off Richard Russell highway, enjoying the moonlight and the view. Suddenly, here came the light at about a twenty-five degree angle. As it passed my car, it slowed and stopped about forty feet beyond. It then moved slow and cautiously back to the side of the car, staying about two feet off the ground on the road bank about seven feet from the car. I felt it was looking at me; it came to the side of the car I was on. As we sat there and stared a number of questions came to my mind.

Did it remember me from long ago? How did it find me miles from home? What was its purpose?

In a few minutes, I had this really brilliant theory that it was a space probe and I would get my rifle out of the trunk and bounce a bullet off the light to see if it was metal.

(Was this stupid or what?)

As I slowly opened my car door to get my rifle, the light disappeared. It appeared to have the power to be larger or smaller. It certainly had the power to vanish.

Later, I mentioned to my brother Richard that I had seen the light that James and I saw when we were kids. My brother told me the light wasn't solid, like metal. He said that when he was a teenager he and a friend were walking one night near Antioch Church on, Old Gumlog Road. He looked back and a ball of light was following them, It was about the size of a basketball and about five feet from the ground in the center of the road. He remembered the light always followed a certain pattern when it was in this particular mode of movement. So my brother and his friend hid behind some bushes on the bank of the road to watch it.

It stopped near where they were hiding, stayed about ten minutes, and then went back to the point where it began. It stayed ten minutes, and then came back. In the moonlight my brother determined the position the light stopped each time in the road. As it moved away from them, my brother positioned himself in the road where the light would stop when it returned. When the light reached that position, it stopped. Three feet from his face.

POSTSCRIPT

When the light is in this particular mode of movement, it is always during a full moon.

It is always larger and brighter. Is it drawing energy from the moon?

When it is not in a particular pattern of movement it becomes smaller.

WHY?

Personalities

Some of Our Published Authors

Winslow King and TC
Mountain Legend and Last of a Breed
by
Sonny Boyer

I became acquainted with Winslow my very first trip to the mountains about forty-three years ago. Things were so different then. We rented a two bedroom cabin for ten dollars a night and the seventh night was free. We knew we had found a paradise.
We didn't have much money and what extra we had was going to be spent in South Carolina for fireworks on the way back. My wife was just as bad as the two boys about loving fireworks, so I was out voted. We found things to do and places to see, we couldn't find in Miami. Our cabin was in Hiawassee and we used it for breakfast and sometimes supper, and a place to sleep at night. The rest of the time we roamed all over these mountains. We explored every waterfall we could hear, or see from the car; explored the mountain roads and just reveled at the beauty we were seeing.

On one of our roams west on highway 76, my wife noticed a small building with a sign above it saying "GUNS." She pointed it out for me because she knew that I had been hunting for an Ansley Fox, double barrel, shotgun, ever since we had been married. I pulled into the parking area and went in to find an elderly, small man with a little felt hat, squatted down on his haunches. He was behind the counter, checkering the stock on one of the finest Parker shotguns I had ever seen. He greeted me with a hearty "Howdy neighbor" and we started talking like we had known each other for years. Little did I realize this man would have a profound effect on how I looked at life.

I soon found that Winslow did a lot of his work, squatted down on his haunches. He got the habit honestly because his two brothers Thee, A.L. and his father Tom, all could squat like that for hours. Sometime I would join in, but my limit was about ten minutes, and then my legs would start to ache. I would have to stand or sit all the way down on the floor.

Anyone who went to the Hiawassee Georgia Mountain Fair and saw the mountain man running the still, will have Winslow's brother Thee, etched into their minds. Winslow told me, Thee had been let out of jail, several times, for making moonshine, so he could be available to demonstrate the still when it became fair time. Thee wore a tall pointed felt hat with a small brim, and had a grey beard, pointed also, that hung down as much as the hat went up. His striking feature was his crossed eyes and the fact that he too squatted by the still.

I never met their mother but Tom the father, Bonnie (the sister), Thee, A.L. and Winslow were raised in King Cove, near the Brasstown of Towns County. Tom was known for making moonshine but his real talent was making what he called a, "Turnip Still." They were made out of sheet copper and Tom was an artist at forming copper into a shape that resembled a turnip. When I met Tom he was retired and enjoying life. He obviously had a small income and spent a lot of his time and what little money he had, being generous to several widows that were his friends. He lived by himself, with a couple of dogs, in a small frame house next to his son A.L.

A.L. drove a school bus for years and like most old time mountain families, did what he could to provide for his family. He, as well as Tom, and all the boys were excellent traders. I knew that I was accepted when A.L. took me in the woods and showed me his ginseng patch. He had an eagle eye at spotting ginseng and made good income gathering it in the summer. A.L. told me that if he pulled all the plants in the patch and dried them, the value of the dried ginseng would be around $40,000 dollars. He cracked black walnuts in the fall and did small jobs to supplement his income. Isadore, his wife, worked in the kitchen at Young Harris College.

Thee lived in Boone, North Carolina and used his looks and mannerisms to try and obtain fame for himself. I heard him complain several times about Junior Sample being on Hee-Haw. He stated he would have handled the job better than Junior. Thee and Governor Zell Miller were good friends, and people tell me that Thee had walk-in privileges at the governor's office. I never was around Thee that much and I knew Bonnie even less, but her husband and I hunted together several times. Bonnie is the one who came back to the mountains and re-purchased some of the old family land.

After that first trip, my family came every year until 1978, when we decided to sell out and move here. By that time, Winslow and I had become pretty good friends. He helped me find and purchase my first property here in the mountains.

Laurie, my wife, and my youngest son moved to the mountains ahead of me. I stayed in Florida closing out my business and spending a month at a time in Blairsville, building a shop and apartment for us to live in. After we moved to Georgia, I found some work doing carpentry and helped build a few houses, but I spent more time at Winslow's. Winslow's first love was music. He loved the violin and by the time we moved to the mountains he had decided to stop buying, repairing, and selling guns and concentrate on repairing violins. For him it was a good choice, because he was a genius at what he started doing. He took all of the guns he had, went to a dealer he knew, and traded them for a single gun. It was a double-barrel shotgun that had rosette engraving with silver and gold inlays. It had been made for Heinrich Himmler before World War II. Without a doubt, it was the most beautiful shotgun I had ever seen.

Winslow didn't have a regular machine shop, so he used a case knife about 6 inches long. He could do anything with that knife. He would take the top off of any violin just by prying with that case knife, without any concern for what might could happen. It didn't matter about the value of the instrument.

He said, "the value of a violin was not the cost or the beauty, it was the sound that made it beautiful and valuable to him."

He used the knife for scraping the old finish off the instruments, or carving replacement pieces. It was always as sharp as a razor. The only power tool he really depended on was a small band saw. He also had several small C-clamps. That is about all he needed, other than a box of assorted rubber bands that he used for clamping things together.

Winslow's specialty was reworking old violins and improving the sound that came from them. He cherished finding one of the old violins that were sold by Sears and Roebuck during the depression. They sold by mail-order for around $10.00. Winslow knew that the wood had aged in all these years, and he could fine tune it by thinning and scraping the violin from the inside. He also would remove the sound board stiffener and replace it with one he had hand carved. Every instrument that came into his shop, he treated differently. He would hold it to his ear and tap on it with his finger, all over both sides, listening intently to the sound. He catalogued it all in his mind and when he finally decided to open it up, he methodically removed and thinned the wood until only he knew it was just right. From the time it came in, until he was satisfied he had done all he could, would usually take about a week. When he reassembled the violin and installed the strings and sound post, he would still scrape here and there as, he tuned it up. He believed a violin had to be "woke up" and the more it was played, the better it sounded.

Winslow had a small dog named TC that lay right beside him at all times. Winslow would say, "When I get this just right, TC will let me know by her howling." I suspect the dog was just reacting to a note that Winslow hit, but when she heard it, she would howl for him. Winslow would say, "That's it, TC knows when its right."

A customer once brought in a violin in a box that had been stepped on in the attic. He asked Winslow if it could be fixed and Winslow said, "Maybe, but it would cost you more than its worth. I could give you $25.00 for it and use it for parts. Better yet, sell it to Sonny. It would be a good project for him to work on at home." I bought it from him and when I got home, I counted the pieces and there were one-hundred twenty-five of them. Off and on, I messed with it for a year and finally got it back together.

Winslow started having eye problems and he needed help seeing the details of his work. I knew nothing about music, but I have always been handy as a craftsman so I began helping him. It was a real gratifying time in my life. Winslow became well known for producing very fine sounding fiddles, as he called them. He attracted fiddlers from everywhere. They would come and play everything he had for sale. Most liked to sit under a tree while they were trying to decide which violin they thought played the best. I had a cheap recording machine, and I would leave it on under their chair. I really treasure those recordings, because they are played by artists who were under no pressure and were playing music strictly for their own pleasure.

As I was still traveling back and forth to Miami, I would check out the pawn shops. I found him several fiddles that were just what he liked. Winslow was fascinated with Florida and really wanted to go with me on one of my trips back and forth, but he never made it.

Once after I had gone fishing to Sanibel Island, I took a lot of pictures by to show him. I just gave him the stack and let him sort through them. I was sitting next to him so I could explain each shot. One picture I took was of a pelican on a fishing pier post. In reality the bird was about seventy-five feet from me, but I zoomed in on it and all you could see in the picture was the pelican's bill, neck and head. They sit with their long bill lying back against their neck, and their eyes look exaggerated. I knew what it was, but I never thought how strange it must have looked to Winslow when he got to that shot. He stopped sorting, took a long look at it and even turned the photo sideways. I didn't say a word. I could see the puzzlement in his expression. He finally took his eyes away from the photograph and looked at me and said, "Sonny, what kind of a critter is that?"

Some violin makers here in the mountains accused him of ruining perfectly good violins with his crude methods; but I say the proof is in the pudding!

One year I was back stage with him as he was listening to the various artists jamming before their performance in the fiddling contest at the Georgia Mountain Fair. Just as a matter of curiosity, I asked each of the men where they got their violins. All but one of the twelve had one of Winslow's fiddles.

It wasn't just fiddling they were good for. My wife bought me one of Winslow's violins for Christmas. I took it back to Florida with me, thinking this would be a good time to learn how to play one. I found an old man who had played in the Boston Symphony Orchestra and he gave lessons. I spent thirty minutes a week for three weeks while he taught me the basics of reading music, before he would let me bring in my violin. He told me, "bring in your instrument next week and I will tune it and teach you how to bow it". When I brought it in, he picked it out of the case and remarked "very beautiful." He tuned it to his satisfaction, picked up my bow and drew it slowly across the strings, fingering the board through the various notes. He closed his eyes and went into an almost trance like state, as he started playing what I call classical music. After thirty minutes, he turned to me, with tears in his eyes and said, "You have ruined my day." He walked over and pulled a violin out of a case, and laid it down beside mine, and said, "I bought this violin during the Depression, and paid $3,300.00 for it. Up until today I thought I had a very good violin. I would trade it right now for yours. Yours has the most beautiful tone I have ever heard."

I was proud of Winslow as I left. I couldn't tell the old man that my violin, new, had first been sold for only 10 dollars from Sears and Roebuck. It didn't take me long to discover I just wasn't picked by God to learn how to play a violin.

The Saint Francis of Assisi Catholic Church owned the land adjacent to Winslow's. They wanted to expand and offered a fair price to buy Winslow's place. He wanted to get off the highway; and his sister offered him space on the old home place, so he agreed. Winslow, his son Harry, and I built Winslow a new home up the mountain, behind A.L.'s home in King Cove. Where we put the well in the branch there was some ruins, where you could tell someone had constructed something. I asked Winslow what he thought had been there?

He answered matter of fact, "Why that's where Daddy's old still was."

I knew nothing about Winslow's finances and just before we finished the house, he told me he had sold his double barrel to finish the house. I understood, until he told me he only got three thousand for it. I was shocked! He said he was embarrassed to tell me he had to sell it. I didn't dwell on it, but I know that gun with his documentation would have gone for at least $10,000 and maybe more at any gun show.

Working there, I became better acquainted with his father Tom and brother A.L. A small anvil sat in the corner of Tom's living room and a strange implement was lying on the hearth. It was a solid iron casting that was round, about the size of a large cantaloupe, and had a square peg that probably fit into the hole in the anvil. I looked at that thing every time I went to his house and I finally couldn't stand it any more and asked, "Tom, what is that thing used for?" Tom grinned and said. "I carved that shape out of poplar first; then I rode my old mule all the way to Chattanooga, to the foundry, and had them cast me one out of iron. That thing is the secret of how I shape the bottom of my stills."

Winslow told me later that his daddy got good money for his stills.

Winslow said, "It ain't as dangerous as making whiskey. He got into trouble making whisky, and was warned to not get caught again. He's not even supposed to make the stills, but a feller has to make money somehow."

When Tom died, I went to the viewing and had intentions of going to the funeral. I dressed up, and even had a tie on; but when I got to Winslow's house, the family asked that I stay there and keep Winslow company. Winslow said, "The only funeral I will ever go to will be my own."

The family had brought Tom's two dogs to Winslow's house, and he and Sally (Winslow's wife) were going to take care of them. I fixed us some coffee, and we were sitting around small-talking, as we tried to keep our minds off the funeral. At exactly 2:00p.m., the exact time of the funeral, his two dogs sat up suddenly, pointed their noses to the ceiling, and started howling. I don't know about Winslow, but the hair on the back of my neck was crawling.

The next day when I arrived, Winslow said, "Come on, we have to go down to my dad's house, I have to get something!" Winslow told me to stay in the pickup he would be right back. I could hear voices coming from the front of the house, and they were talking rather loud. It took Winslow two trips; but, he loaded a complete, brand new, copper still in the back of my pick up. Grinning, he said, "They are all in the living room fighting over who gets what, and this is all I want! I don't think they even noticed me going out the back door."

As a family they are strong in their convictions, as they proved when they paid a questionable bill that was sent to them. A merchant had sent a bill for several hundred dollars, claiming Tom had run it up. No one knew anything about it, Tom had signed nothing; yet the family divided the bill up and paid it, because they did not want gossip started about their father.

Winslow was an excellent shot in his younger days and when he ended up in the army during World War II, they discovered his talent and assigned him to the rifle range teaching new recruits. He told me the most exciting thing that happened to him during the war was meeting and talking to Clark Gable.

I saw people bring in a violin with a crack in it and they just wanted it fixed. Winslow would sometimes rework the whole violin, along with fixing the crack; only charging for fixing the crack. The customer would be amazed how much better it sounded, from just fixing a crack. Winslow just thought that all violins should sound beautiful. I discovered that Winslow could actually play a violin rather well, but he always claimed he could not. I think he would forget I was there, and unconsciously play something beautiful.

Although his education was limited, he managed to stay current on politics. It was a pleasure to listen to his simple solutions to political problems.

Winslow was a very gentle person that saw good in everybody. I ended up being his driver, as he tried to get help for his failing eyesight. He thought he had arrived in heaven, when I took him into a large cafeteria where he could eat all he wanted. He really loved his mountain heritage and ate some food that might seem strange. I came over one day and he was just starting on a plateful of pig ears. He wanted me to try them. I just couldn't. I believe his favorite food at home was a big plate of squirrels and gravy. His son-in-law, Jimmy, would occasionally provide him with a supply to satisfy his yearning.

Winslow told me stories about his Mama and the kids leaving their home on Saturday morning and walking over the mountain to the Winchester's, his mother's people. They would spend the night and attend Many Forks Baptist Church, then hike back for dinner at Grandma's, and on back to King Cove before night fall, if they could make it. Once they were caught in a snow storm making one of these treks.

Winslow told me that the Winchesters raised twelve or fourteen children up on that mountain. I never thought about it, until I actually found the foundation, while hunting for ginseng myself. I didn't realize it at the time, but I told Winslow about the foundation and fallen-over chimney and Winslow knew right away that it was where the Winchester home was located. When I told him there was an old apple tree in the yard he said, "Yep that's it." I questioned the family size, because I couldn't imagine raising that many kids in a building less than fifteen feet on either side or less than two-hundred fifty square feet. Winslow told me, "All the kids slept in the loft, only Grandma and Grandpa slept on the main floor. They had a food safe in the corner, with a place to hang their few clothes, a home- made bed, and a crude table. All the chairs were hung on the wall when they weren't eating, and Grandma did all the cooking in the fire place."

He said, "Any bigger and it would have only been more area to heat and chop wood for."

What impressed me was them walking uphill all the way to the Winchesters, and then down hill to Many Forks, back uphill to the Winchesters for dinner, and on downhill to home. I'm talking miles here! No wonder the old timers were in such good shape and most of them skinny.

Winslow said, "Daddy raised a bunch of turkeys one year, and we walked them all the way to Gainesville to the market to sell them. Daddy forgot one thing about the turkeys, he had planned to walk straight through, but when it started to get dark, those turkeys started flying up in the trees to roost, and we couldn't stop them. We spent one cold night sleeping on the ground waiting for them birds to fly down in the morning."

Winslow's great-grand-niece, Katie, was born in A.L.'s house, and she was a shy child. John Dills, her father, played a banjo as well as or better than anyone in the mountains. As a small child, John taught her to play base guitar, so she could take part in the jamming that constantly went on in King Cove. It was obvious she had talent, for she picked it up easily. She wouldn't go away from the house and play for a long time, until she discovered people would pay to hear her. One of the musicians saw her talent and started her playing a violin. In just a short time, she was almost professional sounding. When she sang, her voice impressed me. I heard her sing that song "Blue" when it came out, and it was absolutely beautiful. She had no idea who Patsy Kline was, but a friend after hearing Katie sing had her sing Patsy Kline's, "Crazy." If you didn't know, you would swear it was Patsy. Her dad only wanted her to sing bluegrass, and she wanted to please her father, so that's what she sang. Winslow was proud as a peacock when she played and sang where he could hear it.

Winslow started having health problems and he was almost blind, but he never lost his love of music and the fiddle. One Saturday afternoon Sally called me to say Winslow had an accident at the house, and they had to put him in the hospital in Blairsville. When I got in the hall I could hear a violin playing, one of those special tunes you only hear in the mountains. I looked in the room and there was Katie standing at the foot of Winslow's bed playing the violin. Winslow was as happy as a lark, propped as high as the bed would go, grinning from ear to ear and clapping his hands in time with the music. I think everyone who could walk, was in the hall or near enough to hear and enjoy the music. After Katie and her family left, I talked with Winslow for a while, and we talked the good times.

A minister Winslow knew, came in and prayed with us, and asked him, "Do you want to get right with the Lord?" I think it kind of hurt Winslow's feelings, because he immediately answered, "No need John, me and the Lord got that all worked out years ago."

When I got up to leave I said, "I will come by Monday and visit with you." Winslow replied, "Oh no, I'll be dead by then!"

I was sure he was kidding with me, because he didn't seem to be in any kind of pain. I came back with, "You better be here. Who would I have to buddy around with?" He said, "Sonny it's time for me to go. Why I'm eighty year old, and I have been on this earth long enough."

I gave him a hug, shook his hand and said, "Don't talk like that, I'll see you Monday," as I walked out the door.

I got a call either that Sunday, or early Monday morning, from his daughter. Betty was in tears telling me he was gone. I really miss him. The mountains miss him.

Reflection:

Friendship isn't about who you have known the longest – it's about those who came and never left!

Author Unknown

Jethro's Story
by
Sonny Boyer

Jethro hated bears and to him he had good reason. You see, Jethro kept bee hives and he always had a problem with the bears destroying his hives. However, Jethro was not having problems with the hives that he maintained on the edge of the woods on the experimental property grounds. He had seen a female and cubs near his hives. He made up a story and told the DNR that the bears had been in his hives. He applied to the DNR for a permit to move the bears. They responded with a trap and caught a large momma bear and two yearling cubs. Jethro, after quite a bit of sipping from the contents of a canning jar, had to be on hand to witness the capture. Seeing them in the culvert pipe he decided to take out his frustrations by agitating them. He would jab at them with a stick. The bears would respond by tearing at the end of the trap, reaching and trying to grab him. They were growling and screaming with both revenge and fear in their actions.

The DNR man, Jim, finally put a stop to the taunting saying "Jethro, you better stop, before you or the bears get hurt."

Jethro would move toward the culvert and stamp his foot, trying to agitate them. He was real brave letting them know who was boss with them in the cage and him safely outside. Jim was hooking his truck to the cage and the commotion was more than he wanted.

He finally said "Jethro! You have two choices, stop, get in your truck and leave, or I am going to take you and put you in a cage".

Jethro responded, under his breath with some sort of unintelligible grumbling, as he slowly moved toward his truck. Jim didn't care for Jethro very much and had his suspicions about him hunting out of season with a crossbow. To this point it was only suspicion, for Jethro was one of those crafty mountain men that believed the mountains were put here for him, and all the game were his to harvest any time he wanted. Jim finally got his trap-trailer connected and left the bee hive spot with his captives. By this time, being a compassionate man,

40

he was showing more sympathy for the bears than Jethro and his hives.

As he pulled out on the highway and headed south toward Neil's Gap and to the other side of the mountain, he thought to himself, "If I take these bears miles away from here, they are going to have a tough time trying to find food in a new area. They haven't given any trouble to anyone but Jethro and I really think most of Jethro's problems are imaginary. The employees around the experiment station have told me how they can almost hand feed the bears, so why should they be punished because Jethro doesn't like bears? I'll just turn east here on 180 and find a side road, and they won't be far out of their feeding range"

It wasn't too many days until the bears were back looking for handouts from the employees at the station. They all were abuzz about how fast the bears found their way back from the other side of the mountain. It didn't take Jethro long to discover they were back either.

Jethro had a piece of plywood nailed in an oak tree, alongside of an abandoned corn field near the station where he would take his crossbow and kill a deer when his supply ran low. On the way to the stand he saw the fresh tracks where the bears had been gleaning for leftover corn. Jethro was infuriated.

He thought, "Well, I'll just take care of this myself."

He went back to his cabin, to his beekeeping shed, and started to assemble his plan. He had a five gallon thin plastic jug that he had salvaged from the garbage can behind a restaurant, the kind that fry grease comes in. Over the years he had poured dirty honey into it, and he had accumulated several gallons in it. He couldn't sell the leftover from the extractor with particles of trash floating in it, so he figured this would be good bait for the bears. Jethro went back to the field with the jug tied on his back. When he arrived in front of the oak tree where he wanted to spread the honey on the ground, he leaned his crossbow on a bush and proceeded to try and remove the bottle from his back. Jethro hadn't noticed but the old plastic bottle had already started to split. He had to lift it over his head to set it down, from the awkward way he had tied it on his back. Just as he got it over his head the whole bottle burst, spilling all the honey all over him. He was in shock! He was a mess! He picked up a stick and tried scraping it off on to the ground, but it only made it a bigger mess. Jethro's dilemma was, this was all the bad honey he had, and he had to go through with the hunt. He knew bears feed mostly at night, and it was getting later and later. He decided to continue his hunt, (no matter how messy he was), so he got on up in the tree. He had tied his flashlight on his bow, so he could see to shoot when the bears came. He hadn't been there long when he heard some rustling on the ground. He stood up, without making a sound, and eased out on the plywood for a better shot. He could see the bears, fairly well, for it was a bright night. He didn't turn on the light. Just as he was about to fire, his feet (slick from the honey) went out from under him, and down he went. He lit flat on his back where his head struck a root, knocking him unconscious. Momma bear heard the commotion, but when she sniffed into the air, all she could smell was a big gob of honey, and she led her cubs to the site. The bears worked on Jethro until they had stripped all of his clothes off, as they chewed all the goodness from the tatters.

Jethro was not seriously hurt from the fall; but the bears had managed to scratch him up pretty good, flipping him over and over like a pancake, trying to get at the honey. Just about the time the bears were finished cleaning up the honey, Jethro woke up and realized what was happening to him. He groaned and tried to rise up. Momma bear put her big paw in the center of his back and easily pinned him down. He became more frightened and let out a bloodcurdling scream! It was hard to tell who was frightened the most, Jethro or the bears. They both took off in different directions, with Jethro ending up at the experiment station, waiting for the first employee to arrive and get him some help.

Jethro's dilemma was how would he explain this? Here he was buck naked. He was hunting out of season, on government property, at night, with a light, and with bait. Wow! Was he in trouble? This was one time the truth wouldn't work.

Note: This tale was an assignment for a club meeting. A man was truly found on the experiment station grounds and there was never an explanation in The North Georgia News as to what happened. This is my wild imagination at work.

A Pioneer Aviator's Long Wait for Honor
by
Sylvia Turnage

You shouldn't discount the truth of old legends passed down to you through several generations. As I discovered a few years back, evidence to support a folk tale can sometimes pop up at a time and place you'd least expect. Here's the way it happened with a legend in my family.

Upon retiring, I moved back to Blairsville, Georgia to live on the old home place where I was born in the Choestoe District of Union County. Here the mountains rise tall and the crystal clear creeks sing peaceful melodies as they wind their way toward the sea. The property is isolated from the rest of the community, and the only manmade sounds come from the occasional whir of an airplane as it travels across the sky or the rumble of a visitor's auto coming up the road that ends at my house. It is the kind of place that welcomes you to dream impossible dreams. And certainly the legend that came down through my ancestors about a dream that filled the mind of my great-great grandfather, Micajah Clark Dyer, seemed at that time to be impossible.

He lived in this little hidden valley between Rattlesnake and Cedar Mountains where I now live. The legend said he was a uniquely intelligent man and built a gristmill on the creek that runs through the place where he ground his and the neighbors' corn. He hollowed out logs and piped water into his house, giving him the distinction of being the only resident in the county to have running water. He was always working on some new technique or invention in the shop in back of his house. Some of his neighbors thought he was a kook to spend so much time tinkering on gadgets that didn't seem to them to be worth anything. Their unkind remarks caused him to become very secretive about his creations, and he kept his shop locked, shielding his work from their prying eyes.

His impossible dream began in the mid-1800s when he was just a young man in his twenties with a growing family to support. As he watched the birds flying over his farm he wondered, why can't a man fly? His education had not advanced beyond the little one-room school in his community. He was a poor farmer, with only primitive tools for building things. Yet, we all knew from the story that had been handed down for more than a hundred years that he designed, built and flew a crude airplane right off the side of Rattlesnake Mountain.

According to legend, the family and neighbors actually saw him navigate the craft over his fields. He reportedly applied for a patent for the machine, and it was believed that after his death in 1891 his widow sold both the contraption and the plans to some brothers named Redwine from Atlanta. The family still firmly believes that those items eventually wound up in the hands of the Wright brothers, who were credited with making the first manned flight in 1903.

In 1980, Kenneth Akins, great-great-great grandson of Clark Dyer and a teacher at Union County High School, became very interested in knowing whether the family legend could be verified. He teamed up with another historian, Robert Davis, and they searched records, interviewed all of the elderly residents of Choestoe, and tried to find as many facts as possible about the flying machine. They wound up with many verbal testimonies from credible people, and they were convinced that the story was true, but they could not find a patent or any contemporaneously written report about the remarkable invention. Cameras were not available in the mountain area at that time, so there were no pictures made of the airplane. *The Times*, a Gainesville, Georgia newspaper, published a story about the findings of Akins and Davis on March 16, 1980, with the headline "Not everyone believes Wright brothers first."

It began to look as if the legend was going to fade from memory and be lost to future generations. Wanting to keep it alive and believing the story was really true, in 1994 I wrote and published *The Legend of Clark Dyer's Remarkable Flying Machine*. I included in the book everything we knew about the invention and what we had heard about its outcome. By the time I finished the book, I had reconciled myself to the sad reality that my family and I would never have any documentary proof that my great-great grandfather built and flew an airplane here in the North Georgia Mountains almost thirty years before the Wright Brothers flew theirs.

Then, in late 2004, a relative whispered to me in church something about finding Micajah Clark Dyer's patent. I thought he was asking if we had ever found it. I shook my head and whispered back that we were never able to find it. He said excitedly, "No, no. I'm telling you that someone has found his patent!"

He said a young man named Steven Dyer, one of Clark Dyer's descendants, had typed in "Micajah Clark Dyer patent" on Google, followed the links, and succeeded in accessing the patent in the U. S. Patent Office files.

Sure enough, when I got home I was able to perform the same search and get to the Patent Office where, for the first time, I was able to see Patent No. 154,654 issued to Micajah Clark Dyer of Blairsville, GA on September 1, 1874, for an "Apparatus for Navigating the Air." The drawings and specifications looked like something an engineering PhD. had drawn up! The aeronautical principles he had addressed were far ahead of anything that others trying to invent a flying machine had yet envisioned.

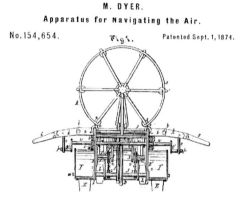

M. DYER.
Apparatus for Navigating the Air.
No. 154,654.   Fig¹.   Patented Sept. 1, 1874.

Here was proof that the legend was fact; Clark Dyer really was a genius who had designed a craft that included new and innovative methods for navigating the air. He had done this despite living in the remote mountains of North Georgia, without any formal education, without any sophisticated tools, and with only basic building materials.

Shortly afterwards we found two 1895 newspaper stories that told about the invention, one in the *The Eagle*, a Gainesville, Georgia publication, and the other in the *St. Louis Globe-Democrat*, a St. Louis, Missouri publication. Much later we found a third 1875 article about the invention in the *Macon Telegraph & Messenger*, a Macon, Georgia newspaper. The most recently discovered article is in the 1874 Official Gazette of the United States Patent Office, an annual publication with a synopsis of each patent filed that year, reporting that Clark filed his patent on June 10, 1874. Of particular interest to the developing story of Clark's invention, the description listed in the Gazette gives expanded details about how the parts of the apparatus fit together to operate.

Obviously, there has not been enough publicity to get Clark Dyer included in the history books, but he should have public recognition for his accomplishments because he is very deserving of honor for his work. Even though it is long past due, I have made it my goal to do whatever I can to see that he finally gets credit.

In 2005, I decided to write our State Representative, Charles Jenkins, and ask him if he would introduce legislation to name State Highway 180 the "Micajah Clark Dyer Parkway" from the junction of U.S. Highway 19/129 to the Brasstown Bald Mountain Spur. Mr. Jenkins responded favorably and enthusiastically, saying he agreed that the evidence I sent him fully supported giving Clark Dyer this honor. He introduced the resolution during the next legislative session of the Georgia General Assembly. In due time, the House and Senate passed it unanimously and it was signed by the Governor on April 28, 2006.

On July 15, 2006, the road sign was unveiled at a well-attended ceremony, and now everyone who drives along this popular road gets the opportunity to recognize a pioneer aviator who had to wait 132 years for recognition to come.

Clark has been honored in several other ways since the discovery of his patent. A U.S. Postage stamp was printed and a framed copy of a sheet of the stamps now hangs in the Union County Courthouse. An exhibit of Clark's patent, a model of his airplane and pictures of his homeplace are now on display in the Old Historical Courthouse on the square in Blairsville. Windstream's cable station produced a video for its *Mountain*

Trails series and has broadcast it numerous times to a wide audience. The story also has been presented to many civic and church groups throughout the mountain area, with many more still in the planning stage.

The little hand-carved, soapstone marker in the Old Choestoe Baptist Church cemetery placed at Clark's grave following his death in 1891 has been replaced by a monument honoring him for his invention. The new monument was placed in July 2010 and has the original tombstones that marked Clark's and Morena's graves embedded in it, along with pictures of the drawings from his 1874 patent. Since he died unknown and unrecognized for his important work, it is very exciting to see this beginning to change.

Grandma Jessie's Front Porch
by
Juanita J. Schneider

Basketball season over, thoughts moved to summer vacation at Grandma Jessie's. We sat on her front porch hearing her exciting stories. We were waving and talking to neighbors walking down the road. My favorite person, Grandma Jessie, was a happy and loving lady, short and plump, of true American pioneer stock. Hugging her was like being caught up into a huge, puffy white cloud, her softness was wonderful. She smelled of sweetness, a dab of vanilla extract she placed at the base of her throat.

During a normal day Grandma wore a cotton dress, covered with a full apron, the length going down to the top of her sturdy laced shoes with its thick inch and a half heels. In the evening, if we went to a movie show or a traveling revival, she wore her dark navy crepe dress with printed small creamy flowers.

Grandma loved to reminisce about her childhood and share her love of family, country and history and her grandfather's life with her granddaughter. She was my channel through history, between the 1860's and the 1940's.

Neighbors passed by our porch, on their way to daily errands, maybe picking up food at the small 'Red and White' Market, a 20 minute walk across the bridge and railroad tracks.

Hearing the loud whistle of an oncoming train, we kids ran to the top of the bridge and looked down as the steam engine passed under the bridge. The dark sooty smoke billowed up into our faces, leaving bits of ash and soot embedded into our hair and clothes. We danced with gleeful excitement as we ran to the other side of the bridge and watched the train speeding toward the West and Kansas City, less than 10 miles away.

Our friendly neighbors, passing by, sometimes went in the opposite direction, walking along the tree-lined shaded thoroughfare, to the local drug store down on Hwy 24 in the middle of Fairmount, close to the Byrum movie show.

Before we could relax on the front porch, daily chores had to be finished. Grandma Jessie made it clearly known the kitchen needed cleaning, including sweeping and mopping the floors.

Outdoors, weeding was my chore, keeping pesky weeds away from the lush garden crops. Grandma picked fresh new leaves of lettuce that she later wilted in hot bacon fat and vinegar for lunch, to go along with her home-made biscuits and steaming hot white pan gravy with specks of dark black pepper.

On special days we picked cherries from the large tree overpowering the outhouse. "We will have some nice cherry pies for dinner, if we pick enough," Grandma said as she filled her apron, pulled up to make her own ready-made basket.

Settling down on the porch after chores and lunch enjoyed, Grandma settled in her favorite large wooden rocker and I got comfortable on the long metal glider, filled with brightly colored plump pillows. "Tell me more about your Grandpa Jackson Waddell."

Grandma started rocking in her chair as her thoughts traveled back through time. "Grandpa lifted me up on his knees and told me stories about when he was a young man in the 1860s and the trouble our country was going through during the war of the rebellion. Jackson and his brother Harrison volunteered back in 1864, joining the 134th Infantry, out of Indiana where they lived. Our troops walked from Indiana down through Kentucky and into middle Tennessee. We had no idea of our fate during that horrible war, but duty called. It was early spring, the weather good, 'ceptin' all the rain pouring out of the blackened sky in Tennessee. It was messy walking through the muddy land. Walking all the way, absolutely, all the way down to mid-Tennessee, Alabama and down close to Atlanta. We joined other regiments there and were assigned to railroad guard duty, reinforcing the Army of the Cumberland. Within a few days we were in our first skirmish with the Rebs. They came up out of the southeast. Fighting got fierce. They finally ran off into the hills after giving back some of their own fire. After the first couple of weeks it was pretty calm down there. Our Company D guarded the trains going into Atlanta, where the tough fighting was going on. All in all, we had it pretty easy for being war time."

"But Grandma, wasn't that scary for Grandpa having them rebs shootin' bullets at him?" "Oh yes, my sweet Jessie Ellen Mae. It was a scary time for us. You gotta know, even a 10-year-old little girl like you, have a responsibility to stand up for what's right. America is a good country; we need to keep it that way."

Grandpa Jackson told Jessie that during the Civil War, their new home, now in the state of Missouri, was called a 'mug-wamp' State.

"What's a mug-wamp, Grandma Jessie?" I asked. "Well, as my Grandpa explained to me, a mug-wamp is a bird". "A bird? I've never heard of that kind of bird."

Grandma Jessie, pulling out her hanky, hidden between her bosoms, wiped the summer perspiration from her forehead, laughed loudly, her large bosoms heaving with each laugh, "Sure! A mug-wamp is a bird. It's a bird sittin' on a fence, its mug on one side and its wamp on the other."

Grandma Jessie laughed again, remembering the day so long ago, when she had her own conversation with her grandpa, re-telling the story now, so many years later to her own ten year-old granddaughter.

Grandma's family traveled from Indiana to Missouri in a covered wagon, stopping along the way to cook supper on an open-fire. "We always seemed to stop close to a lake or running brook for our drinking water and bathing."

Her eyes welled slightly with tears when she talked about one of her childhood experiences. Grandma was six years old in 1892, when her parents along with other family members, decided to move further west to Oregon.

They met in Nebraska, where the wagon master checked each of them for the long journey. Those with fair skin were allowed to join; those with darker skin were not, as they looked too much like an Indian.

My Grandma Jessie and her family had dark complexions naturally, but tanned darker from living their outdoor life. Grandma's favorite cousin, along with her family, did make the trip westward. Grandma often said she never again saw those relatives.

I love you, Grandma Jessie, thank you for those memories.

A Journey Into Grief
by
Ellie Dobson

I talked to God all the way to the hospital, please, please, I prayed; help us to be strong for Jenny.

The phone call came in the middle of the night, the one all parents fear. The voice at the other end of the line said, "I am looking for Eleanor Dobson. The mother of Jennifer Vickers. When I confirmed that was me, the voice continued saying, "your daughter has been in an accident, she is in grave condition, bring someone with you."

All the way to the hospital my mind was locked into one thought, we are going in to assess the situation, nurse her back to health, and then bring her home when she is ready. My mind would not allow me to think any other way.

That was not the case; the worst awaited us as we entered the emergency room. After the formalities, we were ushered into a private little room. A nurse came in, sat down and began to explain how, when, and where the accident had happened. The nurse went on to explain that Jenny's fiancé, Tim was being treated at another hospital. The look on the nurse's face gave it away before she ever said the words, "Your daughter did not make it."

The pain was as if someone had taken a knife, and plunged it into my heart so deep it should have killed me. Instead it produced shock, a shock that helped to stabilize me so that I could get through the next few days.

After a period of time of uncontrollable crying, my husband, my oldest daughter and myself, my Mother's instinct kicked in. No matter what the circumstances or how old our children get, a Mother's instinct is always to take care of her children. I had to see Jenny. I had to be sure that my daughter would be taken care of in every way, the right way, and the way she would want to be taken care of.

The nurse led us into another room. My oldest daughter stayed behind, and began to make the necessary phone calls. Jenny had been dead for probably around four to five hours. Jenny looked as if she was asleep, but the bandaged head and swollen body confirmed what we had been told. A blanket had been pulled up to her chin, I found her hand, held it, and I began to talk to her. Jenny, as a little girl was afraid of the dark, she always wanted a light on in her room. Only a month before, we had seen the movie <u>Ghost</u> together. As we were leaving the theater, I remember her saying to me "how scary the dark figures were, the ones that came up out of the ground and took the bad guys away." I hugged her and said, "You my child will never have to worry about that for you have God on your side and he will take you only where the light is."

So, as I held Jenny's hand, I told her over and over not to be afraid of the dark to look towards the light, and to reach for the light. I know I must have sounded like the ravings of bereaved mother, but I had a definite purpose in what I was doing. I have a deep faith in God, and I was calling out to Him also, to take my child into His loving embrace. I continued for quite a while to try and assure her spirit, that she would be ok and that she should be in the arms of the angels by now.

I don't know how long we stayed there, but finally we moved away from her body. As we were trying to leave, a nurse rushed up to us, with lots of paperwork to sign. Information and instructions were given to us and then they handed us her personal effects. The nurse gave us jewelry she had been wearing; it was placed in my hands. I held the jewelry for the next two days, and finally placed it back on her as she lay in her coffin.

As we left the hospital, I wanted to run back in and stay with her. Things like this happen to your irrational way of thinking, this is why it is so important to have people around you at a time like this. People help keep you centered.

As the arrangements were made, and I saw her injured fiancé after talking with him bits and pieces of information began to come to me concerning the accident. I felt myself coming out of the shock stage and pure terror began to hit me. I moved from shock to full blown grief the way you might enter from one room into another.

There was information about how Jenny actually died, things you don't want to know, but things you feel drawn to know. Moments of knowledge would open up; allowing me glimpses of that horrible moment of impact, then the moments would close as quickly as they came. These image's brought so much pain, I had panic attacks one right after the other. I felt like I was standing at the edge of a cliff, fixing to fall off at any moment. This sort of knowledge drains the blood from your body, leaves you weak at the knees, drains the air out of your lungs until you feel like you can not breath, and it continues to hit you again and again, especially when you least expect it.

I found myself burying my head in my arms often, hoping this would block out the reality of all that was going on around me. I needed these moments as a place to go to, to re-group and catch my breath literally.

I kept wishing I would wake up, and find this had been a bad dream, or that someone would come and tell me this had all been a big mistake. Erratic thought of grief.

It is really strange how normal you can appear to be, when seeing people during this ordeal. I remember the looks on people's faces, their faces were full of apprehension, as if expecting me to breakdown in front of them and then what would they do. I stayed strong for everyone else, while I was dying inside myself.

I found the strength to make all the arrangements that included picking out the casket that my child's body would lay in for eternity, picking a time and place for the funeral, picking out her dress, and writing up the article for the newspaper announcement. So many important decisions to make and make quickly. As her mother I wanted everything to meet with my Jenny's approval. Jenny was only twenty-seven years old, and had a strong and vibrant personality. I wanted her funeral to reflect this.

It did, hundred's of people attended her funeral. Jenny was surrounded by all of her family, all her friends and co-workers. The company she worked for let a bus load of employees off work long enough to attend her funeral. Jenny had made a lot of friends in her short life span. In the midst of death, love abounds.

Jenny's spirit stayed around her family as we all stayed together at my home for the next week. Jenny's two sisters, her brother, my husband and I felt her presence. When everyone had to leave and return to their jobs and life, Jenny's spirit lingered with me a few more days. I knew the day her spirit left.

We continue to see and feel her beauty everywhere. I talk to her often, as if she were still here. At every family outing we talk about Jenny as if she is still with us. I have a grandson, who was not even born when Jenny died, and he talks about his aunt Jenny as if he knew her. I have no doubt that he does.

After about three years the pain eased a little, but grief is always with me, I walk with it daily. Sometimes it hits so hard and when I least expect it, kind of like a wave slapping me in the face. I cry myself out of it, and go on with life. Life does go on, but it is changed forever. I still believe in God and God is good. He gave us this beautiful child to love, and left us with beautiful memories of her.

I continue to take care of Jenny, even 21 years after her death. I visit her grave site often, keeping it clean, and putting out seasonal flowers. The need to take care of your child never leaves a mother, even after death has invaded life.

Jenny's Mom -- Ellie Dobson

Reflection:

Do not stand at my grave and weep,
I am not there, I do not sleep.
I am a thousand winds that blow.
I am the diamond glints on the snow.
I am the sunlight on ripened grain.
I am the gentle autumn's rain!
I am the soft stars that shine at night.
Do not stand at my grave and cry.
I am not there.
I did not die.

Author Unknown

The Confession of Freddie Wright
by
James Goode

[Freddie Wright, (NRN) *not real name.* The name is changed to protect the story teller from frivolous law suits from present or future family members.]

Police officers have many times stated that criminals are not intelligent, sometimes clever, but most often, no match when confronting a shrewd interrogator.

Many had tried and many had failed. The probable cause for an arrest was present. Reliable informers had pointed out Freddie as a seller of illegal lottery tickets. Many buyers were seen giving Freddie money. Freddie was seen removing a pencil from his shirt pocket and appearing to write something down. With each arrest Freddie had to be released. The vital evidence, a record of his bets could not be found.

A newly assigned officer at the police academy knowing of the Freddie Wright failures decided that he would try his hand with the arrest of Freddie.

Faced with the same failure to find any records of bets on Freddie, the officer decided he would bring his "Subject" (or in FBI terms, "a person of interest") to the Vice-Squad which was located at the Police Academy.

I will recall a brief but accurate conservation that took place in the Academy/Vice Squad office.

Vice Officer to Officer Faurot--"Did you advise Freddie of his Miranda rights after his arrest?"

Officer Faurot—"Yes I did, and he said he didn't need a lawyer. I checked him for a weapon and he is clean but he has his pockets full of money, and his pencil in his shirt pocket. "

Vice Officer—"Remove and count the money as evidence. Use gloves to remove the pencil and seal it in an evidence bag."

Vice Officer to Officer Faurot—"Additional information for Freddie's benefit."

"Gary take the pencil into the back room where we have the new 'Carbon multiplier' set up. Tell Sergeant Branch to run the pencil on the machine and send me the total amount of money that the pencil has written. We will use that amount to set a bond and I am sure it will be high enough for a felony violation."

As Gary started for the door, this statement came from Freddie; "Now there ain't a bit of need for you to run my pencil on the machine, 'cause we both know it's done wrote thousands of dollars worth."

The threat of the information laden pencil prompted Freddie to reveal his method of recording his bets on his hand. With a handful of bets he would go into the store of a friend and transfer the bets to a common type of lottery pad.

As with many of the sellers, Freddie was turned into an informer and it was Freddie's tip that let us follow a "Pickup" man to a "Check up" House.

About the "carbon multiplier," we never could get that darn thing to work.

Reflection:

Oh I have slipped the surly bonds on earth;
and danced the skies on laughter silvered wings; put out my
hand and touched the face of God.

Author Unknown

Granddaddy Joe
by
W. Franklin Boulineau

He was a small man. With a height of five feet two inches and a weight of one-hundred fourteen pounds, Granddaddy Joe Boulineau was dwarfed by people around him. The people in Jefferson County, Georgia called him Joe. More often I heard him called Daddy by his children ... my uncles and aunts... or, Granddaddy by my cousins and my sisters and me. "Granddaddy" was fun to hear, to speak. Images of Granddaddy Joe were a pleasure to have, well, for the most part. Careful thinking recalls a few times when he was devilish! I enjoy my thoughts of him. Unexpectedly, thoughts of what I experienced of him are triggered some days by something that happens. This story of Granddaddy Joe is a collection of several of those memories that I have of him.

Granddaddy was a cotton-picking-man. At my young ages of pre-teen I got aggravated with myself for not being able to keep up with him even though I gave it all I had in sweat and aches and pains on my knees on a cotton row next to his. That old, small man rarely complained of his own hurts. I would glance at him ahead on his row with back bent and hands a-moving. The cotton sack that was increasing in weight from the added cotton was tugging at his left shoulder. A look at that sack caused me to think of the way he taught me to make a cotton picking sack from materials readily available. Needed: a creek-stream, washed-out guano, cloth sack to place the cotton picked, a two-feet length, two-inches wide piece of leather or strong cloth to serve as the shoulder strap, two six-inch long pieces of baling twine and two playing marbles (or, two small rocks would do). The twine pieces connected the sack to the two ends of the strap by tying one end of the twine to the strap and looping the other end around the marbles embedded in the top edge of the sack. Granddaddy was expert at making his picking sack. Every year he had to help me adjust mine to best comfort over the left shoulder and to make sure that, as the cotton weight in the sack increased, the bottom of the sack would just drag the ground. Having that sack right allowed one to expend less energy keeping it on to the end of the row.

Granddaddy did get pretty much ahead of me in that hot cotton field. It was a sure thing that before he got very far ahead, he would quietly reach over on my cotton row and clean-pick a sizeable length for me. This he did while keeping his row picked at the same time. When I got to the place on my row where he started helping me, I would trot up to where he was.

He would smile and ask: "Where have you been Brother?" Grateful, I was, but, it was not long that I was behind again. He called me Brother because this is how my sisters and parents called me.

Weigh-up time! At the end of the day, the farm tractor pulled a large trailer at the ends of the rows. There, a cotton sheet for each picker in the field was weighed and the pounds picked were recorded in my daddy's record book. Granddaddy's number by his name was close to twice as much as my pounds. Friday was the last day of the week to pick, so each of the week-day's amounts were added together. At that time, my daddy would reach into the cigar box for the cash to pay each cotton hand. One cent per pound was the promised pay. Granddaddy got close to $8.60 in his hand most every week. If you know how to do halves, you know that my hand put close to $4.30 into my pocket. That's from my week's cotton contribution to the farm's trailer of only four-hundred thirty pounds.

I often wished that I could have helped Granddaddy get the cotton amount quicker that was needed to head that farm trailer to the cotton gin in town to make a bale of cotton!

The small town called Wrens, Georgia was three miles from the farm. It was on a dirt road and waiting for Granddaddy and me to place our feet, one after the other, side-by-side next to each other, fast-paced toward town each Saturday morning. After getting the Friday pay, he and I spoke of whether the movie calendar showed Gene Autry, Roy Rogers or someone perhaps like Lash LaRue, as being the western matinee feature the next day. We would make our plans to go to the movie and would mention some other things we needed to get in town. We were ready to spend our hard-earned money!

Senior people who grew up on farms are likely to be familiar with that durable working animal called mule. Granddaddy changed his mind about walking the dirt road to Wrens that Saturday morning and chose to hitch Ada & Maude, two mules who had proven good as a pair to peacefully pull a wagon. We rode on a wooden seat directly behind the two mules. Granddaddy knew just how to speak to his mules to get them to walk faster, and, at times, break into a trot. He knew when they needed their "Nature calls," breaks and would yell "Whoa" to stop them to allow for easier excretions. It was not very pleasant riding close enough to place your feet on the rump of a walking mule. I could tell Granddaddy anything, so I told him that I had rather walk to town rather than ride behind those stinking mules. He did not hitch them for Saturday trips ever again. It was fun walking to town with my granddaddy.

It is clear in my mind that I got educated on the road to and from town with Granddaddy Joe Boulineau. He would listen to things I easily told him and would respond with understandings and cautions and encouragements. My daddy was a good man, but was so busy running the demanding elements of the farm that he spent little quality time with me. I could fuss about things, ask about God, tell about my hope with girls, ask about what to do if I had a girl, tell him about my dreams and hope in life, and my granddaddy would be patient, concerned and caring for me. Getting sympathy and advice from him was easy for me. I liked it! I did not know it at the time, but I was growing up on it!

I spoke of Daddy. My daddy saw me as his only son of whom he had reasons to be proud. He was very good to me. He gave me lots of things. My Daddy is another story. I mention Daddy Jordan Boulineau to bring Granddaddy Joe's exciting trip with me in the very, very small 1946 Crosley Pick-up that Daddy gave me to use around the farm and to go to school in and have a ride home from ball practice. That little green pick-up was so little that I would find it propped on the school's flag pole when I came out of the football shower room. Ready I was to go home, but had to convince four of my teammates to get it down before I could head home to do farm chores.

Granddaddy Joe loved socializing whenever he could figure the chance. One Saturday morning when I was early at the tractor shed borrowing dad's good tractor tools, Granddaddy came by to see what I was doing. I told him that I hadn't had a first gear nor good brakes on my Crosley since I'd had it for three months traveling to and from school and felt that this was a good time to do something about it. Granddaddy said he would help. We soon found that we didn't have enough mechanical experience to come close to fixing a bad gear and bad brakes.

Those tools went back into the toolbox. As I usually did on a Saturday morning which did not follow Friday afternoon work in the fields where we would have already spoken Saturday plans, I asked Granddaddy if he wanted to go to the matinee. He said that instead he wished he could visit his son, my Uncle Hugh Roy Boulineau who lived in Swainsboro, Georgia. I said that my daddy was gone with Mama to see about Grandpa Jimmy Perdue, my mother's daddy, and, so, I could not ask Daddy if we could. But, then, all of a sudden, a great idea entered my mind! Surely, Daddy would certainly want me to help out his Poppa, as he called him, whenever I could. So, I told Granddaddy that we would travel the forty-five miles in my Crosley. After all, I had managed for months to start the Crosley a-rolling in second gear and to anticipate the place I wanted to stop by gradually slowing down way ahead. When the place to stop was evident, I would open my door and place my brogan-protected, left foot on the ground and drag to a stop.

Here was the golden opportunity to get praise from everybody for helping our quite popular Joe out and, at the same time, I would get to show off my own little vehicle to cousins Roy Joe Boulineau and Billy Hugh Boulineau. A bit of fright began to gnaw in my stomach because, at twelve years-old without a driver's license, I knew that a Georgia Highway Patrolman could stop me on that busy Number One Highway.

It was an easy decision to take the risk! Yet, this trip would not be like the short trips from farm to Wrens where the Wrens Town Police allowed underage, farm kids to drive in town.

Granddaddy helped me keep a sharp eye out for those Smokies, as the state patrol cars were called. He saw one coming toward us way down the road and said " Sit up tall, Brother, and do not look at him!"

After we passed, Granddaddy added "Don't look around boy, he might get suspicious!" Whew! The State Trooper did not turn around and come for me!

We had a good visit with Uncle Hugh Roy and Family. Only one thing went wrong on the way back home. About half way, Little Crosley's motor began to run too hot. Lucky I had put two glass gallon jugs of water in my truck. We stopped for a little while on a side road to someone's farm, let it cool a little,

60

carefully released the radiator cap and poured the cool water in. We made it home fine. Granddaddy gave me that special smile of his and told me to put his two dollars in my pocket. I proudly told him that I did not want his money that the fact-of-the-matter was, early that morning I had pulled Little Crosley up to the tractor gas tank and had pumped her full. Granddaddy agreed that we did not need to let Daddy know that I had taken the gas since it went for a good cause.

When Daddy got home that night, I let him know how I had been so good to Granddaddy and that it had made Granddaddy happy. Daddy said that I did a good thing, but I should always be careful with Granddaddy, especially when driving on the Number One Highway with all those Yankees speeding toward Florida in their big, long Cadillac's. Relieved that Granddaddy and I were not in trouble, I gave Daddy a loud "yes-siree!"

Another ride that Granddaddy liked a lot was in the rider's seat with his next to the youngest of his six sons. This was my Uncle Johnny Thomas Boulineau, known to us kin as Tommy, who had been drafted into the US Army to help fight the Japanese after they attached Peal Harbor. I can plainly remember when the *Augusta Chronicle* came out with very large, bold headlines **JAPAN SURRENDERS**. Everyone was happy! When I saw a distant figure a couple months later, that looked like a man in an army uniform coming fast paced toward our farm houses several weeks after the great war victory news, I ran across the road to Granddaddy's back porch. My hollering woke him up.

He asked: "What's the matter Brother; anyone hurt?"

"Granddaddy! Granddaddy!" I shouted, so out of breath I could hardly speak. "Granddaddy! I believe its Uncle Tommy coming home from the war!"

Granddaddy and I ran up the dirt road that he and I had many times before walked for the matinee fun trips. It was special to soon seethat it was Uncle Tommy. Uncle Tommy threw his duffle bag to the ground and picked Granddaddy off his feet. They were hugging, crying and laughing at the same time! I felt that I was a part of making Granddaddy extra happy again. Feeling good for him, I stayed to the side keeping myself busy trying to lift the duffle bag to my shoulder. We were soon seated on the back porch with Grandma and other kin.

Gradually, friends and neighbors started showing up. They were glad that Uncle Tommy was home safe from that terrible war.

Uncle Tommy, some several years later, bought a large 1951 light blue, new Ford car. This allowed Granddaddy a quicker trip to town to get those important items that he needed. Most important to him was to not run out of the little flat, red, tin can of Prince Albert Tobacco. He never did forget to ask for the book of cigarette papers that came with the tobacco purchase. This special paper allowed Granddaddy to show his skill of "rolling-his-own" and produced a more even smoke than ordinary paper. Sometimes my granddaddy would buy a plug of *Bull of the Woods* chewing tobacco. When sitting restfully on the bank of the creek watching the cork on the line from his fishing pole, it was a treat to be able to reach in the bib pocket of his overalls and, with pocket knife always kept sharp from earlier rubbings on a brick, cut a chew and put it into his mouth.

One of the Ford rides home was not so pleasant. Uncle Tommy lost control of the Ford and the car went into the ditch pressing the rider's door hard against the outer wall of the ditch. Granddaddy was limp when the car stopped. I couldn't help it. I cried when I thought that my granddaddy would not be able to be his old self again. His neck had cracked. Uncle Tommy and the rest of us were worried a lot!. Dr. J.J. Pilcher said Joe was lucky that the spinal chord did not break. A neck brace and lots of easy time healed Granddaddy pretty good.

When I mentioned Granddaddy sitting on the creek bank fishing, I referred to what most men in his day did with spare time. Actually, this was done for pleasure; however, there was at the same time serious hope that a good catch of fish would put meat on the table. Granddaddy taught me how to put a July Fly on the hook just right so as to keep the fish from getting it off without getting hooked. For good luck he showed me that it would not hurt to spit on the bait. I did it the best I could, but

Granddaddy always caught more fish than I did. I began to think that it was the Bull of the Woods that he spat that made the difference. Granddaddy heard loud and clear my protest that he had an unfair advantage. So, being the caring man that he was, he cut off a small chew, told me to put it in my mouth, slowly chew it, and regularly push it with tongue to a tight hold between upper lip and teeth. The important step that he said he told me, that he said I must not have heard, was not to swallow the juice. I chewed, pushed, attempted to spit, and most times missed my target. I quickly saw that learning to do this new thing was not going to be easy. Tobacco juice swallowed was ten times the juice I spat. It was not long before my head was spinning and my stomach was hurting.

Granddaddy laughed hard and said: "Brother, I believe that you should give up chewing tobacco." "Yes sir, believe you're right." was my quick answer. I felt his usual, quick pat on top of my head and was so tickled when he added: "Before you throw your bait in the water for the fish, let me spit on the grasshopper, cricket or worm just like I do mine."

Fishing trips often put needed meat on the table. Granddaddy did his share of killing other types of wildlife so that we never went hungry because of lack of fresh meat on our plates. Boulineaus' knew better than most how to raise chickens, guineas, hogs and cows for year round domestic meat to go with our farm vegetables.

Many times I heard Granddaddy say, during those first years after World War II, "We are 'po' and don't know it. We have always had plenty to eat."

When it came to shooting doves with a 410 shotgun over a brown top millet field, to using same, beginner's shotgun to shoot quail behind a pointer birddog trained from a pup by Daddy, a gifted trainer, to shaking squirrels from tree nests for sudden appearances up a tall tree in range of a 22 rifle, to building wooden rabbit trap boxes for morning checks in hopes a rabbit was tricked, and to following with lanterns at night the trailings and howlings of coon dogs hot on the tail of a raccoon, Granddaddy was as good as anyone. These fun times placed additional meat on the table. Wild meats were considered delicacies that most city folks could not take advantage of. My granddaddy taught me the fine points of these wildlife harvests, except the quail hunting. What I knew as "The whole world", at that time, that "World" knew that Jordan Boulineau was the quail pro. Granddaddy told me to be sure to thank God every night before going to bed for Mama and Daddy and the many other things God provided us that kept us from hunger.

Granddaddy said; "We are not rich with dollars, but God allows us the riches from His land and His creatures." Never have I forgotten what he told me. His example of humble living provided me with a spirit which is still important to me today.

Certain wildlife hunts were more successful when little Frank, Granddaddy's favorite dog, came along. Little is correct since, like Granddaddy, Frank was dwarfed when seen with others of his kind. He had a short tail on a black body that was accented with brown hair curving from his underbelly. His usual frisky and excited manner helped him outshine much bigger dogs. Frank was feisty, but performed in ways that got big results. When Frank went into the woods to hunt squirrels with us, his excitement resulted in quick scouting of the terrain. This caused squirrels on the ground to scurry up trees and well into our rifle sights. One night on a coon hunt we hurried to where the large hounds had stopped chasing but kept barking loudly. This allowed us to find that spot in the woods. The hounds were not barking up a tree, as we were expecting, but were barking around a large, old stump. One hound kept looking at a hole in the ground at the base of the stump but was too large to enter the hole. The hound acted as if it really did not want to go in that hole.

Granddaddy shouted: "Move back, hold the coon hounds back!"

After the large dogs were held back, Granddaddy showed Frank the hole. Little Frank did not hesitate. He eagerly dashed into the hole and seconds later backed out with the coon attached to his snout. Granddaddy was ready! He pulled the trigger of his "Pea shooter," his little single shot 22. The coon kicked a little, turned Frank loose and died.

Granddaddy picked Frank up with a loud "Good boy!"

He told Uncle Alex Boulineau, his oldest son, to bring his lantern, that he wanted to pour some kerosene from it onto Frank's bleeding face. Another time Frank was chasing a huge, corn-fattened rat in a deep ditch covered with blackberry briars. Uncle Billy Boulineau, Granddaddy's youngest son, told me to step back. He picked up a huge discarded chimney rock, held it steady over his head and soon slammed it down into the ditch.

Uncle Bill let out a frighten cry saying: "Doggone!! I hit Frank instead f the rat! Frank's not moving!"

He told me that since I was smaller, to wiggle between briars, get little Frank and hand Frank up to him. Crying the whole time, I did as I was told. Uncle Bill said that he dreaded telling his daddy what he did and continued to hold and shake Frank. We thought that he was a goner, but half way to the house Frank started wiggling so hard in Uncle Bill's arms that he fell to the ground and ran the rest of the way home. Uncle Bill and I changed our sobbing to wild laughter and ran toward Granddaddy.

My granddaddy said: "Don't worry. Worst things have not taken Frank away yet."

He told my Uncle Bill to hold Frank tight while he cut the little piece still holding the dangling left ear the rest of the way off. He told me to run to the hog feed barn and get the can of tar that would stop the bleeding. We were so happy that Granddaddy was not mad at us and that Little Frank was a tough little dog who would live to chase again.

Earlier I spoke of tobacco being an important need in Granddaddy's life. This was obvious. There were two other cravings that Granddaddy had that I definitely shared with him. First, the often as possible churning homemade ice cream. When I felt that there would be an excellent chance for approval of my request, I yelled from my house, across the road toward his house. This was a time when he was likely on his back porch within earshot: "GRANDDADDY! WANT TO MAKE SOME ICE CREAM TONIGHT?"

A reply would most always be something like this: "WE ARE LOW IN COW'S MILK, EGGS AND ICE CREAM SALT. BRING WHATCHA GOT. WE HAVE ENOUGH FLAVORING, SUGAR, AND ICE .... AND, THE HAND CHURN IS READY FOR YOU TO TAKE FIRST TURN AT IT!" Both of us did well with our yelling, near screaming, a method of communication for us. Our voices had obvious exciting, happy tones.

Once the churning was declared finished, recognized by a firm churn handle resistance, Granddaddy let me open the top and dip portions for many cups in anxious, outstretched hands. When I reached about one-third deep into the churn, I got to pull the dasher out, place it in a big bowl, put the cap on the churn and get my spoon rapidly moving from dasher to mouth.

When Granddaddy and I finished eating all that we could hold, we pressed our tight stomachs and said: "Mmm, Mmm Good! We're going to do this again real soon!"

Another craving that I shared with my granddaddy was sopping homemade sugar cane syrup. Pour lots of syrup on a plate. Mix in homemade butter. Tear off a piece of hot, buttermilk, homemade biscuit. Place the biscuit into the buttered syrup for a lingering, few seconds, just long enough for that sweet, heavenly liquid to soak deeply into the bread, then, place into mouth. Repeat until you feel that your stomach is about to pop.

Granddaddy could not outdo me with this craving either! Again a time for "Mmm, Mmm Good!"

I could go on and on with tales of happy relationships with Granddaddy mixed with some sad experiences. I have told enough to provide a clear picture of how I benefited from, respected and loved Granddaddy Joe Boulineau.

Granddaddy Joe Boulineau (1877-1954) was married to Ethel Avera Boulineau (1885-1962). While napping in his favorite chair one afternoon in the dining room in front of the fireplace, my granddaddy quietly died. Mama, Clara Mae Perdue Boulineau, called me that evening at my Emory-At-Oxford dormitory and told me that she knew that I would need to know right away what happened. I cried. I told Mama that I did not want to see Granddaddy at a funeral nor being lowered into a grave. She calmly told me that she understood and that she knew Granddaddy would understand. Mama added that Granddaddy was proud that I had left the sharecroppers, farm life and had gone to college. I already knew this, but it was soothing to hear Mama say it. Granddaddy would surely want me to stay, study some more, and do the best that I could on the important exams that were two days away.

With Granddaddy looking over my shoulder and patting me on my head, I did those things with all my heart. Even though Granddaddy had just died, he, the extraordinary little man with a giant personality, will live within me forever.

Reflection:

A cheerful memory brings joy to the heart, and good news gives health to the bones.

Author Unknown

Innocence Lost
by
Rhonda Kay Brigman

This story is fashioned as a continuing piece being readied for publication. The main characters will live on in a series for your reading entertainment. Herein, is a short excerpt of the actual first chapter. Be sure to continue to follow the story of Annie and Mitch to see how their lives intertwine...or do they? "Innocence Lost" will be available in 2012.

Chapter 1   Just Another Day

She decided; life *was* but a dream....even at her young age and relatively short time on this earth. Looking back now, she could almost see how everything could go so wrong. Though it had only been a short five years, it seemed like a lifetime ago.

Annabelle, known by all her family and friends as Annie, was a short, vivacious, beautiful young woman with iridescent blue eyes and a wide smile that welcomed you to get to know her.

She had grown up in a small, rural community and had been popular in her high school. Being brought up in a Judeo-Christian home, she had the Ten Commandments, John 3:16 and all the "Shall-Nots" drummed into her since she was a baby. Her home had always been a safe harbor, where she knew what was expected, and what she could push to the very limits set upon her. This had always been alright with her, until she began dreaming of all the tempting possibilities beyond her quite, day-to-day routine.

Magazines and television gave her glimpses of a world so different from what she had known. The freedom to go places and see all the high fashion, metropolitan areas and coastal resorts called to her imagination and desires. She wanted so much to get away from her small town America image and become the sophisticated woman she knew was trapped inside her. Though she was still a high school junior, she was frustrated to see most of her upper classmen living lives as young couples having babies and working right out of high school. There had to be more in her future and she decided only she could make it happen.

Planning her escape from her home and hometown was what she dreamed of daily now. She knew she was not going to live that typical lifestyle, if she could help it. Whatever it took, she'd relocate to somewhere that allowed her to grow and reach her full potential. Maybe she would be a Fashion Designer, or a big Department Store Buyer. Since she was too short to become a model, this would allow her to be an integral part of something exciting and glamorous. All she had to do was keep her focus on her goal and begin networking with any opportunities she could find.

She began applying for scholarships and intern programs that would relocate her to anywhere besides her small town. If only she could line something up that would save her from a dead-end future at home. Though she loved her parents and siblings, she knew if she stayed with them, she'd sacrifice her future development into the strong and successful woman she so desperately wanted to become.

Annie was fairly popular in school and had known all her classmates, ever since the Mothers kept them together in daycare, pre-school and parochial school. Though she was approached by many of her male classmates, she found them boring and uninteresting. She was allowed to date, however she just hadn't found anyone yet that she would rather spend her time with, instead of flipping through magazines and dreaming about her future. Anyway, why go through the motions of being interested in someone, when you knew you'd leave this small town in your rear-view mirror.

Days went by and time seemed to stand still. The months just dragged and nothing ever happened for Annie to get excited about. Oh, if only she could snap her fingers and be one-year-older and out of high school. Her only saving grace was dreaming of tomorrow, and where that would lead her. If only she had known what a twisted and bizarre path her life was about to take.

It all started when a new boy came into town with his parents and little sister. They had come from a large town, about 300 miles away. The rumors began almost immediately upon their arrival. It was said that the boy had been in a juvenile facility and his parents had bailed him out of trouble. Supposedly he had been with a group of boys that had been breaking into cars to steal change and anything that was of value. His parents had rescued him from a few scrapes with the law, but this last time he had spent a few weeks in juve and house arrest upon release. With that behind them now, his family had wanted a fresh start in a small town. They'd hoped getting him here would put him in an environment of a positive, lawful, and moral influence.

Annie remembers the first day Mitch came to school. He was tall, tan, and muscular, with the blackest eyes she had ever seen. He wore his black hair in a close-cut style that was so different than that of all the boys that she had ever known. He walked with a stride that let others know to steer clear and not to block his path. He seldom looked anyone directly in the eye, but when he did, it was as if he was looking through you. Annie had him in two of her classes. She actually sat directly behind him in her math class. Naturally, this gave her a chance to study him without his gaze or knowledge. She noticed he had broad shoulders and a small waist. His jeans and t-shirt were tight, and revealed an upper chest that appeared developed and strong. His hands were large and he held his arms mostly down by his side, with his hands always held in a fist. He rarely changed his expression from the cold, steady gaze he held on anyone near him.

As Annie studied him, she felt uneasy and tried to divert her focus back to the teacher. She was pages behind everyone due to her distraction. However, she wasn't worried; she was an excellent student and even tutored others in her class.

Finally, the class came to an end and she began to get up from her desk. As she grabbed her books and purse, she dropped her literature book. She immediately shifted the weight of her books and began to bend over to recover the lost book. All of a sudden, she and Mitch touched hands as they both reached down to pick up the book. While avoiding banging each other's head, they locked eyes and slowly rose up. Though Mitch said nothing, Annie began stumbling over her words as she attempted to thank him for his assistance. "Oh gosh, No!" "I'm so sorry... I didn't mean too... I mean...." "It's all my fault!" Mitch turned and walked away without response.

The days continued to come and go, without much difference from one day to the other. Annie continued to wallow in her day to day existence, with hopes that her future was on the horizon. Life was just so boring!

One Spring Saturday, when Annie could stand being shut in no longer, she decided to walk to the local park and see if any of her friends were around. After she got there, she was disappointed to realize her friends must have either come and gone, or just had something better to do than her. After a short time on the park bench, she saw Mitch sitting down by the park's lake. He was all alone and looked like he had been there for some time, as his soda cup was turned over and smashed into the ground. After much hemming and hawing, Annie decided she would take the risk and approach Mitch. As she walked up behind him, he jumped up so fast that she almost lost her balance. She realized he thought someone was sneaking up behind him and was ready to defend himself.

As per the pattern she'd set before, she began stumbling over her words as if they were suddenly a large bolus of vomit in her mouth. "Oh no, no … . I didn't mean to startle you, I promise." As they both had darted about so fast, they were further in distance than when she initially came up behind him. Mitch stared at her, once again without saying a word. Though his face was a little reddened, she could see him relaxing his gaze at her almost immediately.

She didn't know what else to do except pretend she was looking for her little brother, whom she was watching while he played in the park. With all the courage she could muster, she tried to smile and introduce herself in as calmly a manner as possible.

"Hi, my name is Annie. I sit behind you in Mrs. Connors' math class." Mitch nodded his head slightly in recognition to what she was saying.

"Have you seen my little seven-year-old brother?"

"His name is Larry and he was wearing a red checked shirt and blue jeans.

"He is such a brat... I told him to stay over by that park bench over there, but he wandered off!"

"You know about little bratty brothers, don't you?" "They never listen, or do what you tell them!"

Once again, Mitch was just staring at her; but, with a somewhat quizzical look on his face. Annie suddenly felt like a spotlight was shining on her and she could feel her face burning with the red color she knew it had. She always turned red when she got embarrassed and awkward. She wished she could just sink into the ground, disappearing as fast as she could feel herself uncontrollably blinking as she searched for what to say next. Her mind was so blank; she could barely remember what she had just said to Mitch. Oh why did she ever go over to him... then, make up that dumb story about her little brother.

All of a sudden, she noticed his face was softening as he broke out into the biggest laugh she had ever heard in her life! Annie's instinct was to run for cover, but she knew she'd *never* live that down. Instead she joined Mitch in his laughter and the whole atmosphere was once again at peace. What had made her join him in the laughter, she wasn't sure. However, that was the best move she had ever made, bar none!

Reflection:

"Out of clutter, find simplicity."
"From discord, find harmony."
"In the middle of difficulty lies opportunity."

Albert Einstein

Old Times

My Christmas Wish

by

Rhonda Kay Brigman

The time I'd been waiting for was finally getting closer. At least, the stores were beginning to put out "Christmas Trees for Sale" signs and our little town had the power company pulling out the big pole decorations. The town square would soon be decorated, and the Christmas Parade would follow.

It just didn't seem fair that it took a whole year for Christmas to come around; but then, Santa Claus was quite old and I guess it was still pretty quick considering he had to make toys and gifts for all the children in the world. At school, we learned that was thousands and thousands of people.

I left a note, about a whole month ago, for Mom and Dad to mail to Santa for me. With all that time, he should be able to make mine and my sister's present.

Weeks have now gone by and Mom tells me money is tight, so don't be disappointed if Santa can't bring the gift I wanted.

Well! Santa wouldn't do that to me because I've been a very good girl and so has my sister.

Every day I pray and only cry a very small amount at night, as I pray that Jesus will talk to Santa too. Finally, its Christmas Eve and me & my brothers and sister all go to bed as soon as we quickly eat our supper. I pray again... and now I reason that maybe Santa can only provide one special Christmas gift. As the "big sister," I decided to ask Jesus to let Santa know it's OK to bring only one special gift for my baby sister. I bargained with Jesus that if there is only one & it has my name on it, I'll still give it to my sister. Sleep finally comes and before daylight barely arrives, all us kids hit the floor at a dead run.

My first wide-eyed glimpse sees it right up under the Christmas tree. I only see one... a beautiful bridal doll in a little wooden baby crib.

My little eyes begin to water as I lead my sister over to the beautiful bridal doll and crib. I bravely smiled at her and told her to look at what Santa brought her. She looked at me with a strange look and frowned as she often did. Then she told me she wanted the dark haired doll, not the blond one. She pointed on the other side of the Christmas tree and there it was. Another bridal doll and wooden baby crib just for me!

Oh what true happiness that Christmas, as I knew Jesus did talk to Santa after all!

An Interview With the Past
by
Sonny Boyer

One of my sons had an assignment for a class in technical writing that required a detailed recipe. He knew I was friends with a person who was familiar with the art of converting a vegetable into a beverage. Here is the information obtained from that interview.

A kernel of corn contains four ingredients: starch, protein, oil, and fiber. Man has learned to use it in many ways. Here in the mountains for example: it furnishes our grits in the morning (or hominy if you are a Yankee), cornbread, oil to fry our food, feed for livestock, and batter and thickening for gravy. Nothing is better than fresh corn on the cob. These are just some uses. Even some people burn it for heat, and now it is used for fuel in our automobiles. The use that I am going to describe is the one the mountain people are most noted for; the fading art of making shine.

Money was hard to come by for mountain people, so anything they had to buy was reserved for their bare necessities. Originally shine was made just for family and friends. and around tax time ginseng and shine were two money makers for taxes. Buying sugar for making alcohol was not an option.

A kernel of fresh cut corn has a large sugar content and the minute you pick it, it starts to convert that sugar to starch. By the time it is completely dry, it has completely converted to starch. They needed to convert the starch in the kernel of corn back to sugar in order to make alcohol. According to my friend. here is how they did it.

Get a burlap bag tote or porous bag that will hold seven pounds of whole kernel corn. Make sure it is not seed corn, because seed corn has chemicals added that will poison you. Add the corn, soak the bag; and keep it wet and warm. The corn will start to sprout in four to five days. When it has started to sprout good, douse the bag and corn in hot water to stop the growth, and then cool it down. It's then called malt. The corn in this sprouted stage has started to convert back to sugar. Grind the corn sprouts and kernels through a hand grinder and add the malted corn to a five gallon container. Fill it to the four gallon level with clean water. The mixture will almost immediately taste sweet because the starch has transformed back to a simple sugar. Throughout the process this tasting is where you separate the men from the boys. Anybody can learn to make shine, but to make good shine, you have to have pride in what you are doing. Be clean, and have the gift of taste, like all the good cooks that I can recall.

This mixture will make alcohol. The old mountain people used this process, for it was all they had to work with. However the yield of salvaged alcohol was not very much! By adding sugar, honey, karo syrup, etcetera, you can increase the amount of alcohol that can be processed from a given amount of liquid.

Not having a hydrometer (to test the saturation level in the liquid for sugar content), they used an egg. If you float an egg in water, it will have a portion of the egg that is above the surface that is about the size of a quarter. If you add sugar to the mixture, the egg starts to settle lower in the liquid. Mix and dissolve the sugar until the portion of the egg (that is above water) is the size between a nickel and a dime, but not enough sugar to sink the egg. This method of testing originated in the Biblical days. Either way, the liquid should be at room temperature.

This is the point where you will add two packets of yeast, (the kind used for baking), stirring as you add. Cover the container good enough to keep the critters out; don't seal, and let it work (or ferment) at room temperature. Leave it for two to three days until the liquid is no longer sweet to the taste. It takes a lot of testing, and a good taster to get all the processes just right. Your ears even come into help, for you can hear it working if you listen carefully.

There are many types of stills, but the basic idea is the same. The liquid is drawn off the top of the fermented corn and sugar, being careful not to disturb the settlement in the bottom. Add this liquid to the cooker part of your still. It is important to have a thermometer to measure the heat of the liquid. Bring the heat up in the cooker until it reaches between 182 degrees and 200 degrees. Two-hundred degrees is ideal, but never let it boil, for you will end up with water. Your cooking pot is covered and sealed except for a pipe to vent the vapors and provide a place for the vapors to condense into alcohol. The pipe carries the vapor to a cooler place that condenses the vapor into alcohol.

Some use a container that is filled with cold water, for the condensing pipe to travel through. The most common was incorporating a small branch or creek to do the cooling and changing the vapor to liquid alcohol. You will be able to tell when the alcohol content is diminishing by tasting the finish product periodically. When it has stopped producing good high grade shine, it begins to taste more like wine. (See how important the tasting is?) When this change happens, stop bottling it as shine, but continue cooking for a while longer. Save this final liquid and add it to the next siphoned off liquid, and cook it again. Some stills use a second cooker that refines the finished liquid to a higher percentage of alcohol. This extra cooker is called a "Thumper." The thumper name comes from the pipe from the first cooker being run to the bottom of the second cooker. The fluid collecting above the pipe will start belching and make a distinctive noise that can be heard for quite a ways in the quiet woods. Not good when you are doing something illegal. Some people take this whiskey made with the single cooker and distill it again, to bring the alcohol content to a higher level. It's a matter of taste.

My friend said, "I got a real good reputation for making good whiskey, and found that just about anything that will ferment will make good alcohol. Good sweet pears, was my favorite and was most sought after".

The doctor from our town ordered for himself a charred wooden keg, and had me fill it with shine for him; and his socials became very popular. He came up with a community service that I joined in, and helped with. Having to look after all the people in the nursing home, the doctor decided to try and make life a little more pleasant for the patients. He took a container of my shine to the nurses, and gave them instructions to add a specific amount to the juice that the patients took after the supper meal. He told me he was amazed at what a change it made in their general well being, in a short time.

Everyone knew that if someone got their liquor from me, and if they misused it by getting mean drunk or causing trouble, that I wouldn't supply anymore. Consequently, I was generally left alone by the law.

I have to tell of two incidents that illustrate the social place and medicinal use shine has in the folklore of the area. On our road we made friends with an old gentleman and he furnished us with a potion for arthritis that was made with shine that was a smoky gray in color and was made by soaking it in yellow root, cherry bark, ginseng, and various other herbs. It may have been a mental thing with me, but a teaspoon at bedtime sure eased my back problems.

My wife moved here before me, and she met two men in their eighties who were building their own house. When I came up for one of my visits, she insisted I go over and meet these men, and see what a beautiful house they were building. We went after supper, and got a tour of the house. I was impressed. We settled at the dining room table, and were having a good exchange with the men, becoming good acquaintances.

One of the men made a special offer, and asked us holding his forefinger and thumb up as if measuring something small, "Would you like to have a little peach brandy?"

I knew we had a problem, but I could read Laurie's mind as she answered "I would love to!"

I knew she could picture a small crystal glass with a thick tasty sipping drink that was like a elegant ending for a close to a good evening. One of the men went in the back and returned shortly. He placed a quart fruit jar in front of her, she turned a flush red and her jaw dropped. Of course, it wasn't what she expected, but truthfully I did enjoy her squirming as she faked a sipping drink. I mused as we went home, "I believe our understanding and education about the mountain people's way is just beginning."

I had the general impression that this man is an artist of sorts, and he is not at all ashamed about his skills. In fact I can see that he is at peace with his Maker, so who are we to judge?

Reflection:

Every time history repeats itself, the price goes up!
Author Unknown

Milam Diary Lake
by
Sonny Boyer

It's a lake that you won't find on any map but it was my
buddy's and my play ground during World War II. I guess at the
time it belonged to the Government for it was created by
digging oolite and trucking it to build the runways for Miami
International Airport. Oolite is a base rock formed from coral
that when compacted and wet forms an excellent road. When it
dries it is like concrete. All of the removed material was hauled
away and there were no piles of rock left around. It is about ¼
of a mile long, and as I remember about 300 yards wide and it
was in the middle of Milam dairy. At the ends it was very deep
because we never found the bottom. The middle was only about
waist deep and the cattails had taken over. One small sandy
road led from the lake to Milam dairy road and back to
civilization where my home was located.

Flagler Street, the main road in Miami, had just been paved
(two lane) and our street was still a rock road. When asked
where I lived I used to say the eastern part of the Everglades, for
there were very few homes beyond us to the west. The lake was
about two or three miles from the house and to us it was
paradise. Bruce and I camped out there as much as we could
and rode our bicycles with our camping gear loaded to the hilt
on Friday after school and only returned Sunday evening. There
was one tree on the lake and it was on the far end. It was an
Australian Pine and was very large. Around large Australian
pines the saplings grow outwards for several yards and these
made for a perfect camping spot. We had a spot where we could
bend several of those saplings over and tie them together just at
head height. This made a great framework for our tarpaulin and
the roof of our sleeping spot. We used the pine needles for our
bedding. At first we just endured the mosquitoes with smudge
fires. We used packing blankets for sleeping bags and the food
we ate was always the challenge. We always managed to take a
couple of packets of Lipton chicken noodle soup for lunch.
Bacon and eggs for breakfast and a bag of grits and flour and
corn meal, along with bread and spices were our only brought
from home supplies. We didn't have any ice so supper was up
to us and you can be proud of our ingenuity with that meal. The

lake and the surrounding pasture was a treasure trove of supplies for two young boys with imagination.

The bacon grease was always saved for the supper meal. Fish were always our standby if we couldn't find anything else. This will probably shock you Sierra Club members, but our favorite meal was Meadow Larks. I know you have seen them; they have a yellow breast and what appears to be a black bow tie. They are about the size of a Quail and inhabit open fields and pasture land. One of us always took a single shot 22 rifle and we got very good at plinking the head off one of these birds while they were sitting on a fence post. We didn't skin them; we sat and pulled every feather like we had a chicken. We would split the carcass through the back and lay it out flat and salt and pepper and flour them till every possible spot was covered. Then we would place them in our bacon grease and brown them at a low heat with a lid covering them. All the while we had a pot of rice cooking away for the finished product. Sometimes we would have a swamp cabbage simmering along side the rice. When those birds were properly brown we would move the fry pan and lid to a cooler spot on the fire, add a little water and flour mixed and let it simmer as long as we could stand it or until they disappeared into that rich gravy. One of us would invariably say, "I wonder what the poor people in Miami are eating tonight," as we stuffed ourselves with tender larks and gravy.

Our diet was varied, for around that lake was plenty to harvest. Nighttime sometimes found us wading around in that lake after frogs that we would keep in a croker sack till the next night's meal. Occasionally we would be lucky enough to get a small gator and that was a real treat. Later when we were older, Bruce got a shot gun and we were able to wade in that lake and shoot one or two marsh hens for supper. These were even better than the larks.

One of the best lessons I learned about mankind was on that lake camping. We both knew that it wasn't according to Hoyle to be eating those larks but we did it anyway. One day as we were swimming in our favorite spot, a tanker truck pulled up downstream and started dumping something into the lake. We had to look. Lo' and behold, they were dumping bass into the lake by the thousands. They were all about 7 or 8 inches long. After the truck left we looked and they were all swimming around in one spot. Now at that time, bass were supposed to be 12 inches to keep, but this was too much of a temptation for two boys and these bass were hungry. We caught more than enough for supper and started fixing our meal early. Luckily, we had brought onion and tomatoes from home so we had the fixings for a good meal. I was glad, for Bruce thought a good dish was to mix a lot of strange stuff together, all in on pot. He wanted to open a can of Spam, and he could really contrive a mess when he cooked.

There were so many fish that I filleted each one and skinned them. I mixed half flour and yellow corn meal and battered each small piece until it was completely covered. I diced up that onion and mixed it with the left over flour mixture and made plenty of hush puppies. We even had brought a small jar of butter which we had placed in the lake to keep it fresh. I had made a good size pot of grits and they had been cooking on the side for about an hour, so they were as creamy as you can make them.

As we were cooking, I saw this man coming down the road toward us. He wasn't in a hurry, just seemed to be enjoying his walk. He had on a pair of bib overalls and we assumed he was from the dairy. He had a little dog with him that was friendly and was busy checking out my little dog. We talked all the time we were cooking those fish and he was really a nice man.

We asked him to join us with our supper and he said, "You know what boys, I'm just going to do that."

We had cooked almost a pound of bacon for breakfast and we had plenty of grease and I had it good and hot. I dropped those small pieces of fish in that grease and they settled to the bottom for a few seconds and as soon as they floated to the top I turned them over long enough to see if they were brown and then pulled them out and drained them on a towel. Those small fish with no bones and that meal was one of the better ones I ever ate and we all enjoyed every bite. There was even enough left over for both the little dogs. The man had introduced himself sometime during the meal and I promptly forgot it; however, I will never forget him as long as I live. After spending several hours swapping tales and food, he told us how much he enjoyed this meal and he had never eaten fish that tasted as good. He even helped us clean up the dishes. When he rose to leave, he pulled his wallet out of his pocket and we could both see the badge flashing in the firelight.

"Boys I'm the game warden for this area and I'm sure you didn't know, but the next time you catch any bass make sure they are 12 inches."

He tipped his hat to us and disappeared down the road in the darkness. I could feel the hair on the back of my neck crawling and I know my face turned beet red. Needless to say, that ended Bruce and my shooting the larks and catching small bass. His method of handling us was a lot more effective than if he had arrested us, and it was a lesson that has stayed with me my whole life.

Reflection:

Do not live to make a living, rather live to make a Life.
Author Unknown

Fish And Grits
by
Sonny Boyer

As you can see, my sister at three was already being taught the finer art of fishing, and by six years of age I was already a professional.

My dad was born in Sparta Georgia, early in the 20th century in 1906. He was one of six siblings all under eight, when his father was killed in a wagon accident leaving his mother in a terrible spot. They were tenement farming and had no money even though his father my great grandfather had accumulated a 7,000 acre plantation known as "Fairplay." It was lost during the Civil war. Her people and my dad's people helped where they could, by  doing the plowing and the things a woman just could not do. Having the privilege of knowing her, I know that those things that were done for her had to be few, for she was a proud and resourceful lady. She and the kids, three boys and three girls, struggled through life eking out a livelihood with the bare necessities.

As I grow older I realize the stories my dad told me of walking great distances to school and carrying a sweet potato, both for warmth and food for lunch, could not have been an exaggeration. There was no such thing as food stamps, or welfare. You had to get out there and scrape and struggle or you would starve.

At sixteen years of age my father took his younger brother and struck out to Miami, He told me he could not stay there and see his siblings and mother struggle any longer. He went south to find work and earn some money to help the rest of the family survive. This was in 1925.

My Mother on the other hand was born into a family where her father was a successful building contractor in Miami but was destined to lose everything in the crash of 1929. In 1931 when I was born the economy had been on rock bottom for two years.

My dad was very resourceful and tried many different adventures to make a living. He cut lawns did landscaping, had a laundry route , opened an old fashioned sundry store. My favorite as a kid was when he had a "Toms Toasted Peanut" route. He became the favorite of all the kids. He managed to save enough to put a down payment on a modest CBS home in an old subdivision, just off Flagler Street the main drag in Miami. Flagler and 63rd avenue was still a dirt road in 1938 when we moved there. My sister is just three years younger to the day than I am and had not yet began school when we moved to our new home. I had already started school and had to transfer to a completely different environment. Riverside Elementary where I began school was in town and was a typical Norman Rockwell atmosphere. I had actually enjoyed school until the transfer. These new kids were mostly poor and a very small percentage could even afford shoes. Fighting was the norm and every child had to establish his dominance over any new kids. The harassment never seemed to end.

Our refuge was after school and the protection of our neighborhood. There were twelve houses scattered over about thirty acres in a subdivision that had gone bust in 1929. We had wide streets with sidewalks and cast-iron lamp posts only they never got around to paving the streets. Some of the blocks had no houses and were fenced in with cows grazing on them. All the parents were very protective of all the kids and we couldn't get away with anything. I guess we had the original "Block Watch Neighborhood." We were way out in the country by any standards in those days. Plenty of snakes, rabbits and wild game in abundance.

We, all the people that lived there, developed a closeness that was really unique. The old family heads are all gone now and only us eighty year old kids are left but amazingly at Christmas the messages arrive bringing everyone up to date on the offspring newly arrived in the previous year.

Our yard was the largest in the whole group and just ended up being a gathering place for adults as well as the kids. Saturday night was pinochle or hearts for the men and I can still hear the racket they made arguing back and forth. For the kids our big yard was the background for all kinds of games, but the

Friday or Saturday favorite was the weekly fish fry. I don't know how it originally started but it was an almost weekly occurrence. We had a big Valencia orange tree in one corner of the yard and next to it my dad built a stone barbecue pit with a short chimney. He had a large rectangular pan about five inches deep that was for frying the fish and hush puppies. Unlike the mountains our source of fire wood for heating the grease was a handy supply of coconut husks. The women all saved their bacon grease during the week and all we needed was the fish when the weekend arrived. One food supply that is abundant in south Florida is the sea food.

Once, while eating lunch in a house under construction, I heard a new laborer from the north ask a long time black resident, "What does a fellah need to get by here in Miami?"

The old timer answered with a short pause, "All you really need to get by is a piece of string and a fish hook."

There was a lot of truth in that statement as far as the history of my family. I don't know how much our lives would have changed without fish as a staple. Our old stand by were black mullet. Just a few large ones would be plenty for our weekend neighborhood fish fry. It didn't take much of a tackle box to be able to catch them, and certain times of the year the canal two blocks from the house had plenty. They are vegetarians and even have a gizzard like birds. Biscuit dough as bait and very small hooks and small cork and a cane pole was all one needed. My dad had a trick of scattering oatmeal on the water to attract them to the bait. A pound and a half fish will take a bait as small as a green pea. It really takes a keen eye and a soft touch on the cane pole to hook one because of their small mouth and cautious feeding. Most of the old timers smoke them, but fresh caught fish are really delicious. There are now Mullet festivals all over Florida that attract the tourists.

There was a good supply of snook and plenty of bass, catfish and fresh water fish of all kinds in that canal. Truthfully though, my favorite was always the salt water fishes. Two of the favorites of the neighbors were when we caught a jewfish or my favorite was fillets from a barracuda. They claim they can be poisonous but we ate plenty of them, and no one in our bunch ever got sick.

On the night picked for the fish fry, the women would gather early with their contribution of bacon grease and usually avocado salad or coleslaw. Someone would bring the tea, and even ever so often their would be beer passed around. My mom prepared the fish and started a big pot of grits along side that pan of bacon grease. She used one half flower and half yellow corn meal to coat the fish after salt and peppering it. After the fish was all coated to her satisfaction she would mix in cut up onions, a little bit of baking powder and stir in enough butter milk to get the hushpuppies to the right consistency.

This is where my dad took over. He started cooking when the grits were creamy enough to suit him. Fish just don't taste right without a good helping of creamy grits. He pushed the pot to the back where they would stay good and warm and added coconut husks under the grease pan until it was hot enough. His unique way of judging that, was with a floating kitchen match. When it ignited the grease was just right. He would ease those filets into that grease and they would sink momentarily and then rise to the top. By the time they surfaced he would turn them over and that bottom side was already a golden brown. By the time he was half done cooking the fish he would start spooning in the hush puppies using the same floating method. Some of the invited people at first would claim they didn't like fish and the response would be. "That's because you never ate any of Myrtis's fish"

There were a lot of people converted to fish eaters in that back yard.

The very best fry we ever had was in 1947 when us kids caught a couple of hundred frog legs and everyone really had a treat.

My family was not limited to our back yard fish fries. My dad would drag us out of bed before daylight and we would go fishing off some pier or bridge and take what we caught down on the beach at daylight and have fried fish for breakfast. He had a favorite place south of Miami we would go in the evening. He would build a fire, place a grate and a piece of tin over it and then he would wade out into the mangroves and break of a mangrove root that had a bunch of oysters growing on it. He would lay that whole root on the tin and it would not be long before the oysters would start opening up. My dad made up a sauce to dip them in, but I got to where I liked them better right out of the shell. I'm sure my mom had something to go with them but I just can't remember what it was.

These and other activities such as catching shrimp, hunting rabbits or gleaming vegetables from the south Dade truck farms after they had been harvested were fun to a couple of kids. Food gathering always had a dual purpose although at the time I looked at it as entertainment. My dad had invented a way to put good food on the table and entertain the family with practically no cost. We never knew we were poor.

Reflection:

A smile happens in a flash, but the memory of it can last a lifetime.

Author Unknown

My Illustrious Athletic Career
by
William V. Bastow

Back in the early thirties all the little boys wore knicker-bockers and hi-top boots which came with a small, dull penknife in a holster on one boot. Today, such a dangerous concealed weapon would cause the school's principal to call in a heavily armed Swat Team to disarm the nine-year-old terrorist. Living in a North Jersey suburb of New York City, I was constantly bombarded with tales of the derring-do of the Yankees, Giants, and Dodgers. I don't suppose any of you are old enough to remember the Dodgers playing in Brooklyn!

Our family wasn't into those teams. We were kept up-to-date on the heroics of Jimmy Wilson with whom Dad had played church league basketball in Philadelphia. Jimmy was a star infielder with one of the national league teams.

But, I digress.

The game we kids played was "Mumbly Peg." A match during recess would attract vast cheering crowds of as many as four or five kids.

The game began by scratching a square in the dirt about two feet on a side. The object was to throw a knife into the square and, at the point of entry, bisect the square. The smaller of the two resulting sections became the target for the next player.

There were many variations in the throwing technique: there was the "Flip," the "Elbow," and others. My favorite was the "Slapsie." Eventually, one player would miss the ever smaller target, and the preceding player (usually me—he blushed modestly) was the winner. My ears reverberated with cries of "Billy wins again," and "Billy Bastow's a wizard!"

This sport is nearly as "edge-of-your-seat" exciting as cricket or tiddly-winks!

While I never made it as a high school "big-man-on-the-campus" due to my athletic prowess, my name is forever enshrined in the annals of my chosen sport: the Mumbly Peg champion of Roosevelt Elementary School.

Getting Old--Not All That Bad?
by
Naomi P. Bastow

Nobody I know, or have ever met, has very much good to say about old age. Euphemisms exist: Senior Citizens, Golden Agers'—can't think of any others right now. But the truth of the matter is old age may not be *all* that bad.

Senile. By the way, that word is not a synonym for "Nuts," as in: "My uncle Horace is really getting senile." The word means old. That's all. Senile just means old, and nothing else.

We all know the accoutrements of really old age—doesn't apply to people in their 60s and 70s, not to those kids--but to the authentic *old*, old; for octogenarians and non-agenarians, it can be pretty good.

Forget the arthritis, the quick and frequent trips to the loo—not always in time--; the forgetting of the name of your favorite movie actor, or, for that matter, the name of your next door neighbor but one. There is no point in laying out all the nasty and intrinsic side effects of being among the really *old* old, except gravity, of course, which causes everything to go south: jowls, bazooms, and other parts of the bodies of both sexes to sag and droop. (By-the-way, *old* old is defined as being eighty-five and older.)

For one thing, this wrinkling bit needs a little explanation. Once, when we were pleasingly plump and juicy, there were no wrinkles. Then, the years passed and we are no longer plump *or* juicy. So, as the fat disappears, the poor desolate skin loses its elasticity and just hangs there, forming, oh-my-God! wrinkles. What else could the skin do? I ponder that. Botox? *That's* against nature! Pussy cat, young is young, and old is old. As my daughter's second (of three) husbands would say "Case closed. Get used to it."

So, now, let's talk about the fun parts of being dinosaurs. First, is the wardrobe. You only need three pairs of jeans: one pair in the wash, one in the closet, and one on the body; a couple of pullovers or shirts completes the wardrobe. Shoot! You never go anywhere where you have to "dress up," so, a dressy dress or shirt and tie comes in handy for church, weddings, and funerals. Huddle House will take you as you are.

And that's just the beginning: movie tickets are cheaper; "Early Bird Specials" are everywhere (oldsters go to dine and then to bed early), and, if you have a "dicky heart," "bad back," or some other legitimate ailment—and who at eighty-five plus hasn't got one or another of these?—there is the disabled parking ticket that you can display. (An aside here: Don't never, *ever*, let relatives use your car and abuse your legitimate privilege for parking in order to save their lazy selves a few steps!—end of sermon.)

Also, less is expected of you. As an old geezer of eighty-five plus, do not despair if you have a flat tire on the country road. No, do not. Because as you stand there with the jack in hand, some young kid—or even a not-so-young kid—will stop and take that jack politely out of your brown-spotted hand and--Bob's your Uncle—he will have that sucker off and another in place in no time. Listen! These Southern kids have been well-bred to be polite and helpful to those in need. They vie with the Chinese in the reverence and respect for the elderly. God bless them.

Then, do not forget, if you still are able to travel, the discounts in car rentals and motels; or, if you are stay-at-homers, the 15% off purchases on certain days (Tuesdays at Belks, I think) in department stores.

Do you clip coupons? Buy one get one free? Look for discounts? Sure you do. It is all part of the mystique of being *old* old. I won't get into the joys of being able to spoil grandchildren, even under the disapproval of our non-spoiled children. How did we become so benevolent with age? I know that I'm a better grandmother than I ever was a mother.

I won't deal with the horror of *old* old age as it affects the destitute, the helpless, the uncared for victims of senility (remember, this means being old, nothing more); no, that is for another time.

So, this is just for those of us who can still sit up and take a little nourishment from time to time, make it to the bathroom--mostly on time—and who try to make some sense of what all those years had in the way of meaning.

We wake in the morning content to know there is one more day to repeat all the mistakes of the past, or, maybe, get over our hard-headedness and make the right decisions for a change.

At the very end, if I can be forgiven for a twist to the philosophical, or, for that matter, the Biblical: We often—but not always—reap what we have sown. That's it. And it's not so bad.

Fini

Reflection:

No one can look at a pine tree in winter without knowing spring will come in due time.

Author Unknown

My Gallus Gallusphobia
(Alektorophobia)
by
Naomi P. Bastow

I was five-years-old the first time it happened. I awakened in the dark to stark terror. The lower part of the bed was filled with bloated white chicken livers. My feet and legs were surrounded and I dared not move. Scarcely breathing, paralyzed, I lay there. Slowly, as full consciousness returned, I moved one foot experimentally. Nothing. I tried both legs, and when they encountered nothing, curled up tight, quivering, in a cold, clammy state of panic.

Next, it was chicken heads. Limp red combs drooped over half-closed white eyes. Hundreds of wrinkled heads filled my bed, filled *me* with mind-curdling horror. Enormous yellow scaly feet with curved menacing claws soon added a new dimension to my nightmares.

All through childhood, adolescence, and early adulthood, these dreams haunted my sleep at decreasing intervals. Eventually, they ceased; the fear of chickens, however, did not.

During those pre-depression days, my family lived in a spacious white clapboard house on five acres of land which my father farmed in his spare time. He also kept a flock of chickens.

Mind, we were country folk, and this was the 1920s; we had no indoor plumbing. My earliest recollection was of tripping out to our two-seater with the reigning rooster chasing me. I'd be trapped out there, bawling my head off, while that damned bird strutted back-and-forth in front of the door. Nobody could hear me way out there, and I'd be stranded interminably in privy darkness waiting for somebody to miss me.

Eventually, bored, the rooster would leave his post. I'd peek out...then run for it. Halfway between outhouse and house, he'd catch me--this demonic bundle of feathers, talons, and beak. Pecking and scratching, he'd fly at my head and arms while I screeched at the top of my lungs.

Day after day this went on. It seemed I spent half of my life in that outhouse. When my father learned of my dilemma, off came the rooster's head. I last saw Gus (for that was his name) on the dinner table.

Anyone brought up on a farm knows poultry doesn't come magically plucked, gutted, and prettily packaged in plastic. Dad, the unwilling executioner, would catch the designated victim, haul it protesting to the block, and chop off its head. Controlling his revulsion poorly, he would hold the creature by the feet and fling it away from him, where, headless, it would stagger to its feet and two-step this way and that, flop over, get up and waltz around again and again.

This drama was right up the alley of two blood-thirsty kids, and, as the blood spurted and the *Gallus* performed its macabre dance, we gaped in bug-eyed fascination. A ghoulish pair, my little brother and I were always on hand to witness the fun.

Later, in the kitchen, I'd watch in fascinated horror as mother pulled out the mound of steaming entrails. Nothing could have kept me away from the drama taking place in that kitchen; and my phobia was fixed forever.

I escaped the chicken threat when I became a student nurse in Philadelphia. Rapists, murderers, and other deviants roamed the city streets, but chickens did not. Ignorance *is* bliss, because I felt safe.

With a new profession, but with the same old fear, I returned home to the job of School Nurse and to the country of dairy, produce, and *poultry* farms. Afternoons found me making home visits, and sometimes, I'd be stuck, sitting in front of a student's house, unable to leave my car as hens and roosters strutted about...teasing...taunting. Sometimes, the student's mother would chase them away...sometimes, but likely as not, I'd have to slink away, mission *un*accomplished.

All this occurred many years ago. Although intact, my phobia went unchallenged as I lived in towns where livestock was prohibited, followed by four years cruising aboard a sailboat— no chickens at sea!

After my husband sold our boat, we settled in the woods of Maine beside a glacial lake. Surrounded by trees, our cottage sat on a promontory where—not five feet below—waves lapped ceaselessly against boulder-lined shores. Wind soughed in the pines, and the only other sound was bird song, loon call, an occasional owl at night, or the mournful cry, in winter, of coyotes across the frozen lake.

Then, tranquility was shattered. One day, as we returned from shopping, there, at the door of our cottage, feasting on spilled seeds under the bird feeders, was a flock of hens and one huge gold, black, and white rooster.

If the car had been on fire, I would not have left it. Nothing could have made me run that feathered gauntlet. My gallant husband shooed them away, and when they displayed a strong reluctance to leave, he threw a pebble which connected squarely with the rooster's backside, sending him squawking indignantly out of the yard and out of sight, followed closely by his fat, red harem.

Chickens thereby canceled my walks on the cross country road. There was, however, the lovely path around the lake's perimeter through a pine and spruce forest, past the rustic camps of the summer people.

Frequently, Chief, a rough-coated, foot-loose German Shepherd, with one ear which flopped forward, and whose face was as dolorous as any Basset Hound's, would accompany me on these walks. Patently neglected by his owner, Chief was left for days with no food, water, or attention. I had started feeding him some months earlier, and he had taken to spending long hours, a canine Sphinx, his huge body stretched out on the broken remnants of my tulip and daffodil garden.

Then, one fateful, sunny day, I started up the lake path and was quickly joined by a jubilant Chief who gamboled ahead, behind, and through the trees, taking investigatory side-trips to each cabin. We reached the end of the path and the last cottage where year-round residents lived.

Suddenly, I saw several hens scratching in the leaves. These people had never kept chickens before, but there they were. I wheeled about, calling: "Chief, Chief, come!" Hurrying away down the path, I called again: "Chief, Chief, come on boy!" But, Chief had spotted the hens. I stopped, and urgently called, and called again, but there was no deterring him now. He chased them gaily as they ran this way and that protesting shrilly. He caught one; it got away; he went after it again. I couldn't look.

Starting to run, I hastened toward home, an interminable half-mile away. I looked over my shoulder; Chief was coming through the trees fast, the hen, its wings flapping, in his mouth. I screamed at him: "Chief! No!" twice, three times, shrilly, hysterically. He dropped his burden, astonished. *Was this the same person who fed him biscuits and meat scraps and kept pans of cool water available?* Perplexed, he stared.

After a winter of deep snow and ice which had made daily walks impossible, terribly out of condition, I ran. *I ran*, and there, closing the gap between us, was Chief; the chicken, its head now hanging limp, wings wide-spread and dragging, held fast in his jaws—his prize.

I screamed. *My God! He's going to bring that thing right up to me. I can't...I cannot stand this.* I threw the stick I had picked up, and again Chief dropped his trophy. It didn't move. Now, I started running hard, seemingly covering no distance, no distance at all. My breath coming in short, ragged gasps, sobbing, half-crazed, I ran. My chest hurt; my lungs were bursting; the path stretched endlessly. I knew it would be but moments until Chief, and the loathsome thing he carried, would be abreast. I would die of fright...or go mad.

But, whatever Chief was doing to that chicken, he was doing it out of sight, and I ran on and on, near collapse. Then, unbelievably, the cottage lay just ahead. Just a few more steps. In *extremis* from terror and exhaustion, I stumbled into the house and slammed the door. I fell upon the bed, gasping, crying, half fainting. Safe. Safe, at last!

Just me and my Gallus Gallusphobia.

Reflection:

"I still find each day too short for all the thoughts I want to think, all the walks I want to take, all the books I want to read, and all the friends I want to see."

John Burroughs

Vintage 1939
by
Cathy Fiser

It was Spring I remember. Maybe that's why my mother decided on yellow; not a jonquil or butter yellow and certainly not cream.

These were the days when finances were tight. The depression was not in that too distant a past to be forgotten. This was to be "The Project" for the year. My mother loved sales and bargains better than anyone. Way back then, she was brought up in a household of four siblings with a single parent mother. Frugality was considered fine to practice and when it worked-- commendable.

Somewhere my mother had heard that firemen moonlight on their days off. So as soon as the idea of painting the exterior of our two story clapboard house was given the go-ahead by my dad...Away she went.

Unfortunately she struck out. The firemen either had other jobs lined up or were not off duty. Mother was one who liked to keep the ball bouncing, once an idea struck. Someone mentioned a "Handyman" in the neighbor hood who might be available. Like a shot, she was on the phone contacting him.

Meanwhile mother and dad had a few days to discuss another of mom's long standing and fondly hoped for, renovations. Several evenings were spent as mom laid out the ground work.

Dad finally said, "Alright if you want to put up with the mess."

In the meantime, Mr. Doonan, mom's contracted handyman, arrived. He stood about 5'4" in well-worn baggy pants, a short sleeve workman's shirt and leather shoes that turned up with a mind of their own. His three-day stubble and grizzled, graying hair seemed to grow together. On this particular occasion he had worn his teeth, but as the days commenced into serious work he skipped his dentures entirely. His features then gave the impression of a dried apple. He sawed and pounded, and clinching his corncob pipe helped his concentration. He was a dead ringer for Popeye's father and I felt like we had a celebrity in the house.

It was decided the car would be parked in the driveway, leaving the freestanding wooden garage available for Mr. Doonan's work.

Plan A called for bookcases to be built on either side of the fireplace. Six months before, my mother, with one of her "antiquing friends", while rummaging through a salvage yard, had come away with a prize. For thirty-five dollars she had carted home a beautifully carved mantle. We learned later that it had come from the home of Simeon E. Baldwin, who was then Governor of Connecticut. Heads must have rolled when it was discovered missing. We assumed it might have been carted off during a renovation of the governor's mansion. The dust and cobwebs had been swept aside, and this find was carried down to our basement, wrapped in an old blanket, where it was biding its time waiting for the renovation.

Meanwhile, Mr. Doonan swore softly into his pipe and slung fistfuls of nails around the garage when he miscalculated, which was often.

I was about eight at the time and I dearly loved to watch and dodge as he worked until I heard, "Come away from there and let Mr. Doonan work."

At last, he did finish the two bookcases with the cupboards below them.

My mother was delighted, now the "find" in the basement could be installed.

"Oh, before you go, could you put some paneling above the fireplace so it will all look like it all goes together?"

Dad didn't know that mother already had a plan in mind for a particular kind of painting to go on that paneling....But that's another story.

Mr. Doonan's shoulders sagged perceptively as he muttered his way back to the garage.

The next part of the "Renovation" was a pocket door to separate the cold breezes from our front door and the living room. This would then create a front hall.

Step by step my mother engineered her dream living room and Mr. Doonan stayed through the painting end.

It took several phone calls after that to entice him back to what was supposed to be the original project. Rumor had it that Mr. Doonan had gone on a five day bat shortly after his check had cleared.

The real story began when the two of them visited the paint store. My mother had brought home paint samples that were as close as she could find. Unfortunately, they weren't exactly what she had in mind. Two or three treks to the paint store resulted in getting the gallons of white paint and a small can of mixed yellow to add in. No centrifuges to whip up the paint in those days, it was manual or nothing. Wisely, the proprietor had added about six paint sticks. Over the next several days, Mr. Doonan concocted his brew, dipped in a stick and stood slack-kneed in front of my mother who pondered. No decision was rendered. Having come this far with the great restoration, she was not to be outdone in the final hour.

The next afternoon mother waited for Mr. Doonan and me to get into the car. Protesting that my valuable afternoon was being squandered, I slouched in the back seat. I always felt Mr. Doonan envied me that. Instead he was planted up front and tried to maintain rapt attention as my mother conducted a guided tour. I had no idea there were so many yellow houses. Somewhere between the second or third such afternoon tour, I suggested just white might be different.

This back and forth saga went on for over a week. Nails flew around the garage like a cat let out of a cage after a wild bicycle ride. Mr. Doonan's pipe was a stump of its former self. I figured murder was not at all unlikely.

So one afternoon when Mr. Doonan had shuffled off early, muttering all the way down the street, I decided to try and paint. I put in a little yellow and mixed until my hand ached, but I never got past eggshell.

Finally I decided to be daring and poured the whole darn can of yellow in. When I got that mixed it looked great! Nice and bright.

Mother was not pleased. Dad was puffing hard and almost chewed the end off his cigar

One last trip to the paint store for more white paint which was duly mixed and the actual house painting begin.

Mr. Doonan seemed to be the only one happy about the start. By the time he cleared the last corner he was nearly blind. Between the sun and the, "Nice bright paint," you could spot our house for at least five blocks.

We never did see any more of Mr. Doonan after he got his last check.

My Time, My Place, My Tranquility
by
Eleanore C. McDade

I was frozen in place...here it is, late Sunday afternoon, quiet and peaceful, not even a bird could be seen. Could they be roosting already? It's like being not only frozen in place, but also in time.

The wind...not even the wind was blowing. The clock on the wall seemed so loud all of a sudden. TICK-TOCK, TICK-TOCK, TICK-TOCK.

Gazing out the window I could see Blood Mountain to the southwest. It looked blue/grey against the remaining light of a winter day...as the sun slowly set in the west.

The woods surrounding the property were still and now growing dark and ominous. Night was creeping in and soon would engulf me. In these mountains, I do not venture out much after dark. Night sounds and darkness frighten me.

I have plants in my windows...they love the sun during the day and turn their leaves, straining to reach closer to the window for more nourishing rays. It is their lifeline of food. I supply their drink. Above the plants on my window ledge, the insulators from ancient telephone poles grow dark. They glisten bright viridian green all afternoon once the sun reaches the western sky. They are now deep cobalt green, as they appeared in the early morning hours when the sun was rising in the east.

My empty perfume bottles are also there with the insulators. They joined the "collector" status in my window once they became empty. They now reflect prism images on a sunny day. It is a busy window...capturing such a glorious view each day, plus reflecting the light which catches colorful rainbow images from my glass menagerie. The window is happy and smiles at me. It beckons me to come and see the view that it presents each day. Be it pounding rain or quiet, gently falling snow, I am constantly drawn to the window and the life transpiring in its midst.

Inside this comfortable arena, below the windows are bookshelves filled with my most favorite books and music...and there in front of all this scene is my Laz-y-Boy recliner, waiting for me and the comfort of its padded frame. I slide Mendelssohn's "A Midsummer Night's Dream" into my CD player, sink into my recliner, raise my feet up to a restful position and gaze out the window once more as darkness creeps in over the mountain. I then open the latest book I am reading and step into the world created by my own imagination.

Henry Wadsworth Longfellow wrote a poem entitled "The Children's Hour."

It begins....

"Between the dark and the daylight
When the night is beginning to lower...
Comes a pause in the day's occupation
That is known as the children's hour......and so it goes on...
The children's hour for me has passed, for they have grown
into adults and are gone."

As the sun slowly sinks down behind the mountain, I reflect on the day and this hour of peace and tranquility.

Reflection:

"Be not afraid of life. Believe that life is worth living, and your belief will help create the facts."

William James

The Passing of FDR

by

George Houdeshel

[Reflections on the death of FDR by George Houdeshel, 17 years old at the time.]

Radio newscasters spread the word quickly on Thursday, April 12, 1945, "President Roosevelt died in Warm Springs, Georgia today."

Initially, for me it created an emptiness—a void—followed by great sorrow. I remember walking up the street to visit with my long-time friend Tommy Taft. We sat on his front porch not saying much, but listening to the voice of the newscaster coming from the radio inside his house.

Roosevelt's death was not a total shock. The last picture we had seen of him was taken at the Yalta Conference in late February 1945. He posed with Churchill and Stalin. He looked poorly with pale skin and deep hollow eyes. The black cape draped over his shoulders looked like a shawl used by very elderly people. His report to the American people about the proceedings at Yalta had been his first public address when he acknowledged that he was seated. He stated that he was very, very tired from his 14,000 mile trip. It was after that radio address that he retreated to Warm Springs, Georgia, and it was there that he passed away. Warm Springs previously had rejuvenated him, but this time it was not to be. It was difficult to believe he was gone. He had been president for as long as I could remember even though he was not yet president when I was born.

The next day, Friday, April 13, 1945 I went to work. I was employed by the Monitor Controller Company down on Redwood Street in the heart of Baltimore. We were assembling huge electrical panels to be installed aboard Liberty Ships being built at the nearby ship yards. Our departments consisted mostly of female employees. There were four girls from "Little Italy" (a section of Baltimore primarily inhabited by Americans of Italian ancestry), three girls from Dundalk (a suburb of Baltimore with many Polish families), two hill-billies from West Virginia who had come to Baltimore for "war work" (they were of Irish descent), and two boys from the northeastern neighborhoods of mixed European backgrounds.

I don't remember much work being done that day. One of the Polish girls cried nearly all day, and no one could console her. She had clearly suffered a heartfelt loss. It was as if Roosevelt had been a close member of her family. The Italian girls huddled together and spoke Italian, so I didn't know what they were saying, but their expressions were of grief. The rest of us talked softly about our memories of the president.

Maryland, and especially Baltimore, was predominantly Democratic, but I had been raised in a conservative Republican household.

Mother never voiced her opinions much, except to say , "Roosevelt had gotten us into the war, and he had promised he wouldn't."

She remembered his "I hate war" speech given just before his election. She, of course, was worried about my brother Jack in the Navy somewhere in the Pacific, and I was less than a year from draft age.

My father was more outspoken, and very concerned about the Socialistic road Roosevelt was taking. To get us out of the "Depression" and now to "Win the war. "Roosevelt had made the Executive Branch of our government very powerful. He intimidated the Congress, and when the Supreme Court ruled against some of his boldest usurpments, he appointed additional members, so that it was stacked with men who would favor his New Deal politics. Most Americans didn't care as long as he was effective in lifting us out of the terrible depression and uniting the country into a win-the-war effort. But Dad was concerned for the long term. He foresaw the federal government getting involved and controlling more and more areas of our lives and eroding the role of local government.

He often preached, "We will be taxed more and more to pay for bigger and bigger government programs, and the value returned will be watered down by bureaucracy and politics."

On the international scene, Roosevelt had rallied our country to produce weapons for England and Russia before we entered the war, and to even greater production after Pearl Harbor. The 'Arsenal of democracy' was a phrase often heard at this time. He believed in Stalin and made concessions to him over Churchill's objections at the Yalta Conference. Part of Korea, two Chinese

Islands near Japan, and control of Eastern Europe were all conceded to Stalin. Some believed this decision was made as a result of his poor health.

Regardless of which side of the political fence you were on, nearly everyone I knew acknowledged that President Roosevelt was unexcelled in winning and holding popular support. He was most often considered a president for the 'little people' even though he was from a millionaire family.

President Roosevelt's death left everyone with a feeling of emptiness. The Germans, who, because of the time difference, received the word on Friday, the thirteenth, took this as an omen that things would now turn in their favor. The Japanese interrupted their normal broadcasting to acknowledge the president's passing with two or three combinations of soft sad music.

As the day wore on, the subject shifted from deep feelings for Roosevelt, his life and his death, to Vice President Harry S. Truman. How would Truman fill Roosevelt's shoes? No one believed he could or would. Truman was relatively unknown. A late comer to the Roosevelt camp, about all that we knew about him was that he had owned and operated a haberdashery in Missouri. The war was yet to be won and the post-war world would need strong American leadership. Now the great sorrow for the loss of President Roosevelt was mingled with anxiety about the ability of President Truman.

I believed Truman had performed commendably as vice president, but the lingering public admiration for the late President Roosevelt left Truman in a shadow which proved difficult to overcome. His work was cut out for him. He would definitely have to prove himself in the days to come.

Reflection:

"The only thing we have to fear is fear itself."
                              At his first inaugural address, FDR

Something Priceless
by
Philip W. Gatlin

Have you ever lost, found, or had returned, something valuable or what one might consider "priceless."

I have always been drawn to water, especially the ocean. As a native of Miami, I was intrigued with the stories of sunken Spanish treasures along the Florida coast. I often day-dreamed of finding 300 year-old gold pieces and rare artifacts. Living in Miami meant the ocean was a large part of my life, whether swimming, fishing or just relaxing. Beachcombing was a hobby of mine also and I enjoyed finding an unbroken seashell or occasional piece of unique driftwood. I never found treasure, but later in my life I experienced something that provided me with a priceless memory in a most unexpected place.

During one of my last business trips to Rio de Janeiro before retiring I had the pleasure of being a guest at one of the better hotels along the famous and very beautiful Ipanema beach. The hotel is not one of the large or more modern looking chain hotels Americans usually prefer, but it is my choice in Rio. The service, food and close proximity to my favorite part of the beach always drew me back when there on business.

Business trips to Rio can be expensive so it has always been my objective to make every day count while there. As a result I normally worked long hours with very little time left for rest and relaxation. Whenever possible at the end of a particularly exhausting day I look forward to a stroll on the wide sidewalk made of concrete and inlaid with beautiful hand-cut, black and gray stone. The sidewalk extended as far as the eye could see in both directions running parallel between the beach and main roadway. When the weather permitted, and darkness held off long enough for me to make the trip from the business center to the hotel, I would quickly take off my shoes, roll up my trousers and walk along the water's edge. The saltwater and cool soft sand restored my energy and soothed my tired aching feet.

My first workday of each trip to Rio was usually shorter than the rest of the week due to the long overnight, and mostly sleepless, flight from Miami. This particular trip was no different and I took advantage of the abbreviated workday afforded me by the local office. I returned to the hotel with enough remaining daylight for a relaxing walk along the beach. With a burst of energy in anticipation I hastened to my room and quickly removed my business clothes and donned my shorts and walking shoes. The elevator could not arrive soon enough and when the door opened to the lobby I rushed by the smiling desk clerks and crossed the busy thoroughfare. After briefly gazing at the surf I felt the cares of the world begin to slip away. Being a Florida boy I appreciate beautiful beaches and the rhythmic pounding of surf on the shore. I closed my eyes, inhaled the clean, salt-tainted air and wondered if Heaven had a beach. I fervently hoped it did.

The sun was setting fast and most of the locals still on the beach were gathering up their belongings and heading for home. I decided to by-pass my usual exercise that consisted of a fast-paced walk on the hard surface of the sidewalk. I did not want to miss the opportunity of feeling the surf on my feet in the now fading evening light. I quickly removed my shoes and without hesitation stepped onto the sand, still warm from the day's serving of sun.

Immediately I was overcome with a strange sensation that something unusual and exciting was going to happen. The image of me finding a diamond ring or some other valuable piece of jewelry flashed clearly through my mind that evening in Rio. I thought... that's it, I'm going to find something valuable on the beach today! People were always losing things on the beach. That's why others would spend enormous amounts of time scouring the beach for the lost treasures of those unfortunate souls who lost money or a keepsake. I began to carefully scan the sand at my feet as the advancing surf continued to draw me closer. Reaching the water's edge I turned and walked parallel to the shoreline, being careful to stay in the wet sand, but avoiding the advancing surf.

My thoughts turned to my wife who I so often left behind when the demands of business required me to travel for days and weeks at a time. I wondered what she might be doing right then and realized how much I missed her during these long business trips. I wished her here so she could enjoy, along with me, the beauty and excitement that was Rio. Moments as precious as these are meant to be shared. I continued walking with the thoughts of treasure now in the back of my mind.

As a huge wave retreated after violently throwing itself on the shore something caught my eye. At first glance the object had a small bright red appearance and seemed out of place on the sand as the wave washed away. I walked closer and soon realized the object of my attention was a beautiful long-stemmed red rose. Surely it was not a real rose. The partially opened bud and green leaves appeared too bright and perfect to be a real rose, particularly in this setting.

I knelt down in the wet sand and only after touching the object did I realize it was indeed a perfectly shaped and beautiful rose. I carefully picked it up by its thorny stem and brushed the sand off as best I could. I felt a warm glow as I admired the fresh bright colors against the contrasting hues of the sand. At that moment I wished even more for my wife by my side. I imagined we would carry the rose back to the hotel room and place it in a glass of water or perhaps press it for a lifetime souvenir of our visit to Rio. As the years passed, I would hold her in my arms and recall the rose we found on Ipanema one special day.

In the absence of someone with which to share my find, I began to wonder how the rose happened to be on the beach at this particular time and place. The swimmers, surfers and sun-worshippers had already deserted this part of the beach to head for their homes. Did someone throw roses from a passing ship as part of some celebration...or out of anger? Had a promising romance broken up over some silly misunderstanding or betrayal? I wanted to believe the rose found its way to that particular spot as the result of some gesture of love. The thought came to me that perhaps God meant for me to find that forsaken rose and reflect on its meaning. What is the meaning of "priceless"? Is it something held dearly by humans because of its value in earthly terms or something that cannot be measured in dollars or gold? As I held that single rose in my hand I was reminded of the gift God gave me at the cost of His precious Rose. The thorns of His crown and the Passion He endured when abandoned by the world spoke to my heart like no earthly treasure ever could.

After a few moments I gently placed the rose on the sand and stood up to look at it one more time before moving on to complete my evening walk. The sky was getting darker and I needed to head back, clean up and dress for dinner. It was only after I had taken a step or two and turned back for one final look that I realized what I had really found. In that instant I had learned another important lesson about life and the value placed on "things." A smile crossed my face as I looked toward the heavens. As I turned to leave for the day I thanked God for the lesson I learned on the beach that day and for giving me the gift of love.

Swamped in The Okeefenokee
by
Judy Abercrombie

I'd be done in '91...upon finishing the final course of my
Master's Degree. Daddy never made it past elementary, Mom
didn't attend high school – they'd both had to secure jobs early
in life. I wanted to prove we had the brains for it – just not the
time. This would be my final course before graduation at age
fifty - Wetland Ecology by a renowned (in her mind) professor,
Dr. Martin. Enrollment was limited to seventeen youthful
students, like a young 'hunk' named Neville. She said I was too
old for her class. By comparing her age to mine, I rubbed her
the wrong way, finally I was accepted by promising I'd achieve a
grade of 'B' or better.

Our syllabus included the five entrances to our great
southern swamp, where St. Mary's and Suwannee Rivers
originated. I diligently checked each entrance beforehand to
know what to expect and how to cope with it.

Seems swamp critters mated each year around July. Boy was
it noisy there! Mosquitoes and gnats were tenacious and the
romantic animal rituals were boisterous.

Our first adventure entailed serious water sampling of St.
Mary's River. Sleeping accommodations for us were sleeping
bags and, in my case, a bed roll beneath my truck. Food was
provided by our narcissistic instructor, who, sadly for us, was a
Vegan.

Vegetable juice, salad and wheat crackers 'passed' for supper.
After checking out nocturnal visitors to our camp, we settled
down as feasts for pesky mosquitoes and gnats in our natural
saunas. Breakfast was a repeat of supper, with a few slices of
sour grapefruit. Oh! for a cup of java and a honey bun, better
yet, bacon, eggs and hot buttered biscuits.

We sampled water, wading through brackish debris-filled
water near the campsite; after another pitiful lunch we were
back at it again.

This time however, proved more adventurous. Two local or
loco drunks (wrapped around small saplings) tossed up their
stomachs upstream from us as we sampled river water. Adding
to our stomach distress was a joy-filled camp meeting of
spirited Baptists singing and praising God's bountiful supply of

tantalizing victuals. Dressed in stinky jeans and tees (from brackish river water), my colleague and I tried to swipe a chicken leg but they shooed us off. Fact is, they tried to shoo us out of the 'ladies' restroom. Those high-toned Christian women were prejudiced against our using the same toilets. Or maybe it was because my associate was black and I wore a 'redneck graphic' butt-kicking tee shirt. What a day, and night wouldn't be much better.

That afternoon, Dr. Martin wanted us to raid gator nests so she could video their offspring. The squalling gator babies drew a crowd of male gators and I freaked, dropped our john boat (which I'd never navigated before) in gear and rammed Dr. Martin's boat. This knocked the video cameras into the darkened gator-infested waters and ticked our instructor to no end. I was again on her 'list.'

By the third morning, I really needed my caffeine. Waking Dr. Martin from her air-conditioned RV 'slumber, I begged for a cup of her steaming hot coffee, even offering to buy one. 'Negatory' on that, I was turned away. Dr. Eastling, (adjunct professor of geology and *Ms Hyde's* associate) awakened by the commotion, unzipped her sleeping bag and rolled from beneath the RV. Taking pity on me, Dr. Eastling offered me a cup of her own 'brew.' Eagerly, I accepted a unique cup of java from her thermos. Turns out it was ½ Folgers and ½ Bacardi Rum. How delightful! We parted with a 'don't ask, don't tell' agreement.

Next, we motored to Monkey Island, down a lily pad strangled trickle of water more appropriate for airboats than john boats. As usual, I was the captain. Each john boat held four of us. My study partner, Carla, and I were burdened with two 'stuck-up' teachers from Clay County Florida, who refused to offer any help. They filled our boat with suntan lotion, a personal stash of snacks and drinks (which they refused to share), and the plush seat cushions they perched on. After sticking my bare hands into murky water to free the propeller from slimy debris, I'd had enough.

Gators were dangerously close by on either bank (within touching distance) airing their gaping mouths and making hissing sounds. One of the two 'fragile' teachers squalled out like 'panthers' upon seeing those up-close reptiles. Thinking something awful had happened at our bow. I 'showered' down on our untangled outboard, slamming into some tall reeds by a

12-footer. He dove beneath our boat (you could hear the bumpety-bump of his hide on the boat's underbelly). At the exact same moment, an energetic "bowfin" landed in the woman's bare lap bringing out some choice words from her on my coxswain skills.

I didn't panic this time, just shut the engine off. After her 'cattawallerin,' I suggested she toss the fish back in if she didn't have a Georgia fishing license. Then, I allowed the boat to drift into more reeds, telling these she-devils that they'd power the boat if we were to leave Monkey Island, I was done!

Dr. Martin had led the way, making it to Monkey Island ahead of our entourage. Boy did I need to let out all the Gatorade I'd drunk. Tying our boat to thick reeds, I scampered into the only outhouse we'd seen during our entire trip.

It was stinky and pitch black inside. There wasn't time to check for reptiles or spiders and I didn't have time to fetch a flashlight. The seat did feel odd though, kinda like those cheap plastic padded toilet seats. Only, this seat was alive. Dr. Martin was on the pot and when I plopped into her lap, she started yelling at me again.

Well, that was the hardest 'A' I'd ever earned and it really was earned! She only allowed one other 'A' and that was to her pet student, Neville, who fetched beer for her on the sly.

Reflection:

"We gain strength, and courage, and confidence by each experience in which we really stop to look fear in the face ... we must do that which we think we cannot."

Eleanor Roosevelt

Flickerings
by
Zadie C. McCall

"Daddy really didn't want you to do this, did he?" Dawn asked, as she reversed the Neil Diamond tape.

Callie sighed, shook her head, and pressed her foot firmly on the accelerator as the gray Oldsmobile crossed the Georgia line into North Carolina. "No! Not particularly!" She pushed her short brown hair behind one ear. "But he would have done the same thing under these circumstances. It's not something that I'm looking forward to *myself.*"

"But why you, Mother? Wasn't there anyone else to make funeral arrangements?"

Callie hesitated, thinking exactly what to say. "No! No one! Joel lost both parents before he was four. He was raised by his Uncle Nate. Well, actually Uncle Nate was his great uncle, an old bachelor, who died while Joel was still in high school. Joel lived alone during his senior year."

"How sad!" said Dawn, looking out on fields filled with some kind of dainty, fringed, white flowers that looked more like a wedding than a funeral. "It's funny how you never told me about your first marriage until I was thirteen," she added. "And then you just brought it up out of the blue."

"Well, we were young and it didn't last long; not quite two years. Both of us should have tried harder." She glanced at Dawn, who pressed her lips in a thin line, folded her arms across her chest, and sighed.

"All right, Mother. Don't start in on me again. When I walked out on Charlie last week, it was final."

Callie frowned. They had discussed the separation up one side and down the other. Dawn insisting that if Charlie loved her half as much as his job, she would still be with him.

Callie pointed out Charlie's good, steady qualities. *"He does love you,"* Callie said. *"He just finds it hard to express."*

And Callie believed it was true.

Dawn relaxed her arms and turned her serious, gray eyes on her mother. "What happened with you and Joel? Why did *you* break up?"

He didn't love me Callie thought, but aloud she said, "Lord, honey, I don't know. It was twenty-some years ago." She thought a moment.

"At the time I felt he was stubborn and too tight with his money. And I never knew what he was thinking. But looking back on it, I know it was partly my fault..."

"Well, *you can be* a little stubborn," said Dawn matter-of-factly.

Callie laughed. "That's probably what makes me an effective teacher."

Dawn reclined her seat, and they fell silent as Callie maneuvered the curves that bent with the river through the Nantahala National Forest. Sunday picnickers dotted the shaded tables on the banks of the river, and teenagers on orange rafts dodged children on inner tubes in the shallows. The sun glinted on the dancing waters. It did not seem that anyone had died now or ever would again.

Just beyond Trading Post Corner, Callie turned left on a narrow blacktop road. The community in which she had spent four years of her life looked much the same, except for the satellite dishes; odd companions to the purple martin gourd houses in the side yards of the farmhouses. Callie's parents, missionaries to South Korea, had wanted her to spend the last four years of high school in the States, so Callie had lived with her Uncle Frank and Aunt Grace during that time.

It had not been a happy arrangement for any of them. Her uncle and aunt had just lost their only daughter to leukemia. Though little Jessie's belongings had been packed away and her room fixed up for Callie, the loss of the smiling, curly haired, three-year-old in the silver picture frame had permanently saddened Aunt Grace's face and had turned Uncle Frank into a man lost in his work.

Callie had not fit in with the local students. Neither had Joel Byers, the tall, quiet, intelligent boy who sat behind her in English literature.

Callie sighed. *Maybe we were just a case of two lonely people getting together.*

Now Callie glanced at the familiar half-smile, half-pout her daughter's mouth took on in sleep. She resolved that when this funeral was over, she'd try one more time to talk to her about Charlie.

"It looks as if we've stepped back into the 50's," remarked Callie, as she glanced around cabin #8 of the Moody Hollow Tourist Court near Adairsville. Pausing, she added, "Well, at least it's clean."

While Dawn went for ice and Cokes, Callie called home to let Ted know they had arrived safely. She smiled as she waited for the call to go through. It was wonderful to be married to a man who was secure enough to let her do things her way without making a fuss. It was good to know in advance that he would understand her sense of duty toward Joel and recognize, without criticism, the emotional attachment she might still feel for an old love. However, she had not told Ted about a problem with the funeral arrangements and wouldn't tell him now.

After talking to Ted, she made an appointment for the next afternoon with John Prather, the attorney who had notified her that she had been appointed executor of Joel's will. He had added that a notarized letter had been attached to the will requesting that Callie make specific burial arrangements.

"I sure hope you know what he meant by *specific* arrangements," Prather had said, "because the letter doesn't spell it out." Callie had not hesitated. Some conversations are not erased by the passage of time.

"Yes," she had said. "Yes, I remember!"

Callie sighed, removed her sneakers, and stretched out on the bed. She did not like breaking a vow, even one twenty-six years old, but she didn't see how she could keep this promise.

On the way to supper, Callie showed Dawn around Adairsville -what little there was of it. The house where she had lived with Uncle Frank and Aunt Grace looked as it did when she'd come back for their funerals, the only times Callie had been back since the divorce.

The school had not changed one iota, the same faded red bricks and the huge multi-paned windows. The grass needed cutting, which was usual for late June. *Which poet compared an empty schoolhouse to a ragged beggar?* She'd have to look that up sometime.

The old courthouse in the center of town had been converted to Haywood County Historical Society. The red brick Federalist building looked homey now that cream-colored curtains had been installed behind the aged, wavy glass in the narrow windows.

Callie remembered the building as being much larger when she and Joel Byers had stood shyly in its gloomy halls, applying for a marriage license. They had both been nineteen.

The grand tour of Adairsville over, Callie and Dawn finished a supper of overcooked vegetables, cornbread, and iced tea at Reba's Café. Callie glanced at her watch. She had hoped for a chance to see Maxine Nichols, and now was probably the only chance she'd get. Maxine would be at the funeral, but they might not have a chance to talk.

Maxine was the one person in Adairsville with whom Callie had kept in touch, and that being only an annual Christmas card and letter. Maxine had been a widowed neighbor to Joel's uncle. Greatly fond of Joel, she had been the closest thing to a mother that he had ever known. She had supplied him with homemade tea cakes and helped him make lopsided birdhouses and newspaper kites that seldom made it into the air.

Callie smiled to herself. Though her husband was open-minded about her former marriage, there was one thing that annoyed him; It was the post scripts Maxine always put at the end of her letters. They invariably mentioned something about Joel, something that sounded as if Callie should just forget this foolish second marriage and hurry back home to Joel where she belonged.

PS: *Joel bought a second-hand Dodge pick-up from Herbert Moss last week. Sure runs good.*

PS: *Joel's trying out that new yellow tomato they advertised in Gurney's catalog.*

PS: *Joel is thinking of starting a tree farm.*

Callie always read Maxine's Christmas letters aloud. Maxine wrote exactly the way she talked. Her letters were like sitting down for a chat in one of her unmatched kitchen chairs and propping your elbows on the clean, red and white checked oilcloth, while drinking hot coffee from mix-matched cups that somehow seemed like a perfectly matched set.

Callie had begun to look forward to Ted's wry comments as she finished the latest PS comments, which were supposed to be a continuation of Maxine's PS...such as, "*and both Joel and I*

114

remember how much you love yellow tomato sandwiches with lots of mayonnaise."

"Mother, why are you smiling?" Dawn asked, moving a limp piece of cabbage to the other side of the *blue willow* plate.

"I was just thinking about Maxine. You'll like her."

* * *

The minute Callie slowed down to turn in at Maxine's mailbox, she knew something was missing. At first she could not decide what it was but then realized that the potted plants and hanging baskets were gone from the front porch of the old clapboard farmhouse. The swing still hung at the left side, and the morning glory vines still clung to the strings Maxine provided them in exchange for their morning beauty and afternoon shade.

A tall, heavy-set woman with grayish-brown hair and shrewd-looking eyes answered Callie's timid knock.

"Hello," said Callie. "I'm looking for Maxine Nichols."

"Maxine don't live here anymore," answered the woman. She looked at the two women, frowned and then said abruptly, "She's dead. Who are you anyway, and what did you want with Maxine?"

In a shaky voice Callie started to explain.

"Hey, wait a minute," interrupted the woman, as she swung open the screen door. "I'll bet I know who you are. You're Callie Byers. You're the wife of that Joel Byers that got killed in that bad wreck day before yesterday."

"No. No. I'm not his wife. I used to be." said Callie. "But Maxine...dead? She was fine at Christmas. I had a long letter from her. She was fine..."

"Well, it was sudden," said the woman, her voice still blunt. "Heart attack. Always worked too hard, Maxine did. She was out there in the back yard feeding that mess of chickens she always kept, when she just keeled over. "That was back in February," the woman went on. I'm her half-sister. She left the place to me, seeing as how I'm her only living' relative. Surprised me half to death. We never did get along much."

I can see why thought Callie. "I'm sorry," she said softly. "I really liked Maxine."

"I reckon she had her good points," said the woman, clamping her mouth shut, but not for long. "Yeah, take that

Byers boy. Maxine thought the sun rose and set in him. He could do no wrong as far as she was concerned. I hate to speak ill of the dead, but to tell the truth, I never did see why Maxine set such store by him. Didn't amount to a hill of beans, in my opinion." She went on mercilessly. "I don't think the boy had a lick of common sense. Always startin' something and never carrying it through. Like that rock wall he started to put up around his uncle's old place and then just quit right in the middle. And that tree farm, they say he planted all them trees and then never cut the first one."

"We'd better go," said Callie, turning. She didn't think she could stand another minute of this woman's harsh voice.

"Oh, wait," said the woman, swinging the door wider. "I've got something for you. It's a box that had your name on it. I found it in Maxine's trunk. Come on in. I'll get it."

"I'll just wait here, thanks."

"Suit yourself." The woman padded off, her flip-flops slapping angrily at her calloused heels.

* * *

Callie waited until Dawn was asleep to examine the contents of the old cigar box. A small framed picture of Joel's parents and one of Joel as a baby lay on top. Underneath were a few old snapshots of Callie and Joel that had been made on a trip to Rock City. Beneath those was a jumble of old tax receipts, bills of sale, and even some cancelled checks from 1961, the year of their divorce. She glanced at Joel's cramped writing and flipped through the checks; an electric bill, a check for a hot water heater, one neatly labeled *Callie's new winter coat,* and one to a nursery. Callie remembered that coat. They had quarreled about it and *everything else* near the end.

Sighing, Callie flipped through the remaining papers, then caught her breath as she stared at the only letter she had ever written to Joel. Callie didn't touch it. Quickly she put everything back and snapped the lid shut. All these years she had wondered if Joel had ever received that letter. Callie couldn't sleep. She lay in bed and watched moth shadows on the thin drapes. The elusive wings flitted ever closer, then back, both drawn and repelled by the feeble light outside the cabin door.

On an August night such as this, she and Joel had lain on an old quilt on the hillside waiting for the meteor showers the weather forecast had promised. Though the west hillside overlooking Fawn Valley was Joel's favorite spot, he had not been keen on lying near the laurel thicket on a blanket in the middle of the night. What if someone saw them?

"So what? It's nobody's business," Callie had said impatiently. She had pouted until Joel had given in.

The first shooting star had blazed across the dark sky and disappeared in a flash.

As a second meteor streaked its golden tail across the heavens, she remarked, "Maxine says when you see a shooting star, it means that someone has died."

Joel was silent for a moment and then said, "When I die, Callie, I want you to promise me something."

"Don't be morbid," said Callie, raising up on one elbow. "You aren't going to die anytime soon I hope!"

"Well, just promise that if I die before you, you'll bury me wherever you are."

"Of course, I will, silly! What would you expect me to do? Dump you out on the side of the road?" She laughed and snuggled her head on his shoulder.

"Well, just promise," he insisted.

"I promise," she had whispered.

Now Callie punched her lumpy pillow and turned it over to the cool side. She sighed and listened to Dawn's even breathing in the other bed. What in the world was she going to do? She could not call Ted and ask if it would be all right if she brought her first husband home and buried him in their family plot. No husband would be that understanding. The idea was inconceivable even to Callie.

Tomorrow she'd just have to see about having the body interred in the old cemetery at Owl Creek beside his uncle.

Hot tears suddenly burned her eyes. It wasn't fair that Joel had burdened her with this problem. After all, when she left him, he hadn't even made an attempt to get her back. She had written him from Atlanta saying that she just wanted him to know that she was all right. She had purposely put a return address on the envelope.

He could have come after her. He could have sent a bus ticket. He could have phoned and asked her to come home. But he hadn't.

That had been the winter of 1960-61. She had written Maxine a short note about a month after her letter to Joel. Maxine had written back, begging her to come home. Maxine said that Joel loved her but just didn't know how to say it.

It had all been so ridiculous anyway, thought Callie. Now she could not believe how immature they both had been. They had argued over this. They had fussed about that. She had pouted; Joel had clammed up.

But the last straw for Callie had been the argument over, of all things, Christmas tree. She remembered that it was a Saturday. They had mailed the packages to South Korea and had finished their meager shopping spree in Freemont, and were driving home in Uncle Nate's ancient pick-up, when she saw a tree lot and asked Joel to stop.

"We have plenty of trees at home," he had said, rocketing past. "We certainly don't need to *buy* one."

"But I only want to look," Callie wailed.

Sighing, Joel slammed on the brakes so hard that the wrapping paper flew onto the floorboard. He turned around at a nearby gas station and sped back to the tree lot.

Callie had always loved trees and had immediately spotted a six-foot Colorado blue spruce.

"Oh, Joel," she breathed, "let's get it. I know that twenty five dollars is a lot to pay for a tree, but just this once, let's splurge! It could be my birthday present, too. You do remember that day after tomorrow is my birthday, don't you? Isn't it the most beautiful Christmas tree you've ever seen?"

"No, Callie. You said you only wanted to look. We have plenty of cedars at home."

Callie had never liked asking anyone for anything. But to ask her own husband for something and have him refuse, after she had been so careful with the grocery money, was humiliating. Besides, she knew that the hardware store had given him a Christmas bonus. With face burning, Callie had climbed into the truck and slammed the door. If Joel had tried to cheer her up, it might have been different. But he hadn't. He'd acted as if nothing whatsoever had happened.

On Sunday afternoon, Joel had gone into the woods and brought back a perfectly shaped cedar, nailed two boards across the bottom, and set it in one corner of Uncle Nate's dreary living room.

They decorated it in silence.

And the longer the silence had lasted, the more it seemed to Callie that if he really loved her, he would have gone back to get that tree, or at least he could have said he was sorry they hadn't got it.

That night Callie read a library book, and Joel just sat there thumbing through his seed catalogs. *Like some eighty year old man,* she had thought angrily. *Probably getting ready for the highlight of his Spring, a new stringless green bean or something.*

On Monday when Joel went to work, Callie packed a suitcase and asked Uncle Frank to take her to the bus station in Freemont. He reluctantly agreed. "I don't know what the problem is," he said, "but you won't solve it by running away. Why don't you just come on back with Grace and me for a few days?"

Eyes brimming, Callie shook her head.

Even now, Callie could hardly bear thinking about the months that followed. She had written the letter and waited for Joel to get in touch. When he hadn't, she had decided the marriage was over and had filed for a divorce, which was uncontested and granted on grounds of incompatibility.

Bitter tears wet her pillow. Joel, who had not reached out to her when she needed him, had no right to reach out to her now in death.

At last Callie's eyes closed to the flickering shadows on the drapes, and she slept.

* * *

When morning came, Callie decided to get the whole thing over with as soon as possible. Right after breakfast, she called the minister of Owl Creek Methodist Church. Luckily he could see her within the hour.

She immediately liked the young Rev. David Kimsey. The kind expression in the brown eyes, under a shock of unruly brown hair, put her at ease. As they sat in his slightly shabby, toy-strewn den, one of her worries melted away.

"Will there be space for Joel beside his Uncle Nathan Byers?" Callie asked.

"Oh, no problem at all with that," replied the young minister.

"And this is just a thought," he added kindly, "if you feel uncomfortable with the idea of selecting clothing, a casket, and

119

so forth, considering the fact that you have been away so long, the church has a committee for handling...uh...unusual situations. I know the ladies on the committee would see to it that everything is done properly.

"Mr. Byers was a member here, but seldom attended. However, he could always be counted on to help with a worthy cause. He was very well thought of, but just kept to himself. But you probably know what he was like," he added.

Callie nodded gratefully. The funeral was set for the following afternoon at Owl Creek. The Rev. Kimsey and his committee would handle everything except expenses.

Once the decision to bury Joel at Owl Creek had been made, Callie relaxed a little. After all, what other choice had there been? It was a promise no one would expect her to keep, even if they knew about it.

The meeting with John Prather also ran smoothly. Callie clutched her purse as he read aloud the letter attached to the will. His mellow voice ended the short paragraph with "*should contact Mrs. Callie Vinings, who will make specific arrangements for interment.*"

"Yes," said Callie, loosening her grip on her purse. "That has been taken care of."

When the terms of Joel's will were read, it was not surprising that the property was to go to the Methodist Home for Children in Raleigh. However, Callie was astonished to hear John Prather's voice add, "*with the exception of the twenty acres lying to the east of a line running from land lot #230, commonly known as Fawn Valley. I, hereby, leave said parcel to Callie Vinings.*"

* * *

"That's wonderful," exclaimed Dawn as they discussed the day's events in the car on the way to Uncle Nate's old house. "Maybe we could build a summer cabin on your land. I love it up here. It's beautiful and so cool! Can you imagine how hot it is at home right now?"

"I know it's beautiful here, but I don't know about a cabin, Dawn. This is a part of my life that I've put behind me."

"But, Mother, just because you remarried doesn't mean that part of you won't always remain here." She was silent for a moment and then added, "As much as I love Charlie, and I *do love him,* it doesn't mean that I won't always remember Jeff Hawkins." Jeff was the first boy Dawn had ever been serious about.

"All this has opened some old wounds. Wounds that I thought had healed."

"Would it help if we talked?" asked Dawn, in a near-perfect imitation of Callie.

Callie laughed. "No, thanks." She had never told anyone about that last quarrel with Joel.

The farm had changed very little. They walked around in the yard. Only the half-finished rock wall was new, and the spindly maples she and Joel had planted at the back were huge now. The clothesline was still tied to a stake on one end and to the June apple tree on the other. Callie couldn't believe that Joel had kept Uncle Nate's old truck. It was parked under the shed. She ran her hand over the dusty hood.

Callie climbed the back steps and crossed the sagging wooden porch. Uncle Nate's farm tools still hung on rusty, square-headed nails driven into the wall. Peering in the kitchen window, she was a girl again, once more sitting at the familiar, rickety breakfast table. The green Depression glass sugar bowl and the big square salt and pepper shakers still sat in the center of the table.

A feeling of sadness gripped her. "Let's go," she said, "unless you really want to see the valley."

"Oh, but I do," Dawn said. "Let's at least go have a look." She hugged Callie. "It'll do you good, Mother. We've both been under a lot of stress, and a walk will be nice."

At the car they changed into sneakers, and Dawn followed Callie up the worn path. They paused beside the vegetable garden with its neat rows of cabbages, onions, beans, and tomatoes.

Three blue bird houses perched atop the stakes at the east side of the garden fence. Wild flowers nodded in the uphill draft as they started their climb.

The trail rose sharply. Callie, ready to push past any remaining nostalgia, forged ahead, but her daughter lingered behind taking it all in and chattering enthusiastically. "I still don't see how you could have left this place, Mother. Just feel that refreshing breeze!"

Turning to look behind her, she continued, "And what a terrific view of the farm! I wish I had brought my camera." She put her thumbs and her middle fingers together to form an imaginary frame. "The barn and that rock wall are at a picture-perfect angle from here."

Callie, who had reached the crest of the hill, suddenly caught such a sharp breath that Dawn jerked around to see what was wrong.

"Mother, what is it?" She rushed to Callie's side and gasped at the scene before them.

Callie let her breath out slowly.

At least a hundred Colorado blue spruce trees dotted the hillsides in grand array, obviously never meant for tree farm formation! Their blue-green spires reached skyward, the thick branches seeking no decoration, needing no ornamentation to gladden the hillsides.

A breeze whispered through the blue-green branches which freely gave up their fragrance. Mother and daughter stood silently for a long time. Then with face glowing, Callie said, "You're right, Dawn. A part of me *is still here.*"

Callie walked among the trees. She heard her daughter ask what kind of trees they were, but she didn't answer. She was searching for just the right spot. Perhaps near the laurel thicket.

The End

Reflection:

Remember, brilliance has no deadline!

Unknown Author

Animal Stories

Posing For an Art Class
by
Sonny Boyer

It was in the early spring that I had a strange experience. My mate of two years was comfortably sitting on four eggs that she had proudly laid last week.

It had taken us almost a month to dig out our cool home, under the turf of a big field that bordered a large lake. We had picked a spot to make our entrance that was next to a flat rock. There were several cows that used the field, and we had to be careful that one of them did not accidentally cave in our entrance and trap us underground. The foxes and raccoons were always trying to dig us out, so we had dug several false tunnels to mislead them.

We had designed the tunnels so that in a real heavy rain, if we developed a leak, these false chambers would act as reservoirs to trap the water. We knew that in this type of sand the water would dry up quickly.

Our sand pile in front of our home made a good perch for either of us to guard our children. Close by, was a row of wooden posts that also made good guard towers. Sometimes these posts were used by the other birds. We have seen blackbirds, meadow larks, and occasionally other types; but our greatest danger was from the hawks that constantly patrolled the area. I and my mate have learned to scream very loud to warn each other of any danger that was in the area.

There is plenty of food for us in that field and our eyes are so good that we can hunt day or night. One of us always stays very close to the entrance so we can be in the tunnel to protect our children.

The day my strange experience started was in the late afternoon, about three hours before the sun went down. A young human that I had seen many times before, was coming on his metal wheeled machine down the path that went alongside the wooden posts. He and another young human usually went to a large tree and stayed for a couple of days, and then would leave. This time he stopped, laid his machine down, and walked straight to our home. I screamed to warn our mate. I didn't know what he was up to, for he bent over and did something to our pile of sand. He started backing away from our mound. I could see he had not damaged it, so I had no idea what he was doing. He kept backing away and I knew he was far enough that our home was out of danger. He was carrying a stick with him and when he was well away, he just sat down in the grass and sat real still.

I stayed on the post for a long time and periodically would scream to see if he would move.

My curiosity got the best of me and I had to go to the mound and see if my mate was safe. I flew and landed close to the mound. I called softly to my mate to let her know I was there. She cooed back so I knew she was safe. I hopped up on the mound to see if the human was still there. He was standing up and then he jerked the stick backwards. I felt something tighten around my feet and I couldn't get loose. I was able to fly, but the string that had trapped my feet was drawing me closer to the human, and I was screaming and awfully scared. He drew me to him, and grabbed my feet with one hand and pulled my wings in close to my body with the other. He talked to me softly and I soon realized he was not going to hurt me.

He carried me to his machine and placed me in a wire box where I could barely stand erect. He took me to the place where he slept and we waited for morning. When morning came we traveled inside a bigger machine that made a lot of noise, but the human sat my box on his lap and continued to talk softly to me.

We arrived at a large building and entered a room with many young humans; they all wanted to look at me. The one who caught me reached in the box, and snapped something around my foot, and lifted me out into the open. He gently sat me on a perch that had a bowl of water on one end and a small pan at the other. Whatever was in the pan was some kind of food, but I was too nervous to eat. My throat was so dry that I could not resist the water, so I took a long drink.

An older human came into the room and all the young ones, including the one who had caught me, sat down and began trying to draw me on a piece of paper. The one who caught me instructed everyone not to move fast, not to make loud noises, and I would not become frightened. He was right, I was feeling better already. The older woman instructed the younger ones that I would only be there for the day; and after school the one who had caught me (Sonny) was going to take me back and release me at my home. I knew my mate was panicking and I was very relieved to know I would be going back. The children were amazed when I would look all around the room by turning my head, without moving my body. Most of the time I just stood very still, staring out into their young faces. One child thought I was stuffed and not real, until I turned and looked directly into her eyes. The young people would leave when a bell would ring and a new group would arrive and take their seats.

The older person and the one who caught me, remained with me all day. Between classes Sonny would tempt me with some of the food. In the beginning I would snap my bill at him and warn him with my most ferocious look. He was not intimidated by my looks, even when I grabbed his finger when he put the food too close. I did get a taste when I did that and I decided to take a small amount. It was rather good! Everything I did during that day brought ooos and ahs from the young ones. Even when I took time to preen my feathers, they all thought I was wonderful. I looked all around the room and there were many strange things that I had no idea what they were. The objects that fascinated me, were the windows and the invisible barriers that even kept the wind from blowing.

At the end of the classes, true to his word, Sonny lifted me off of my perch and put me back into the wire box. We traveled in the big yellow noisy box back to where he had slept. He got out his wheeled metal machine and we headed back to the lake. He laid the machine on the ground, opened my metal box, and placed me on his finger; as if it was the perch that I had been standing on in the class. I could not bring myself to fly at that moment; I just stood there gazing into his eyes. I did not know how to thank him for my freedom, so I remained perched there looking at him. When I did fly, I just flew to the next post and stood there for a long while looking into his eyes. I could feel the apology for what I had been through, and I accepted it as I flew to find my mate. I saw young Sonny many times after that, but I never felt again that there was any danger, and always greeted him with my scream.

Friendship
(Lessons on Life From Morgan And Dudley)
by
Jean A. Nethery

Diane brought Morgan to the dog park most every day. Morgan was a ten-year old spotted Basset Hound whose ears nearly touched the ground and often got wet when he drank from his water bowl.

Today was Jennifer's first visit to the dog park with her spirited two-year old rescue dog, Dudley. Dudley had arrived during an ice storm, skidding all the way to the front porch of Jennifer's house. He was a yellow Labrador who looked up at her with mischievous brown eyes.

"Chow," said Morgan as Dudley came up unannounced to examine Morgan's body parts.

"Did you say that there was food around?" asked Dudley.

"What do you mean? questioned Morgan. Ciao is another word for hello. And, please don't get so personal on a first meeting." said Morgan. This was day one at the dog park and the beginning of a genuine friendship.

Day two began when Jennifer let Dudley out in her fenced back yard. He was nowhere to be found 15 minutes later when she returned to let him in. She called and called, but no Dudley. Ten minutes later the doorbell rang and Jennifer opened the door to find Dudley pulling a frail old man who was desperately grasping the dog's collar. Jennifer thanked her neighbor and immediately yanked Dudley inside. Looking out the back window into the yard she discovered a big hole under the fence where Dudley had escaped.

"You bad dog," she scolded him. When Morgan and Dudley met at the dog park that afternoon Dudley bragged to Morgan about his escape and adventure. Morgan shook his head and exclaimed, "You dumb dog. Don't you know that you are supposed to come when you are called and that you don't destroy property? You'll be lucky to get supper tonight." Dudley looked chagrined and went off to think about what Morgan had said.

Day three at the dog park began with Dudley chewing up Sabrina the poodle's tennis ball. When Morgan came up to Dudley he said, "Where'd you get that ball, Dudley?"

"Sabrina put it down and offered it to me," said Dudley.

"You're lying, Dudley. I saw you steal it from Sabrina. Don't you know that stealing is wrong? You're never going to make friends when you take something that rightfully belongs to someone else."

Several weeks passed and Jennifer was becoming more exasperated with Dudley and his poor behavior. She discussed it with Diane who really didn't have much in the way of advice to offer. "Labs are active dogs," Diane replied.

The next time both dogs were at the dog park Dudley got into a snit with two other dogs. Neither of them paid any attention to Dudley so he decided to take a swim in the forbidden pond, which was next to the dog park on private property. Fish and ducks occupied the pond and all of the dog owners knew that it was taboo to allow their dogs to go there. Jennifer had previously warned Dudley that the pond was off limits. Nevertheless, Dudley saw Jennifer looking the other direction and dashed for the pond.

Gasps were heard from all of the dog owners as Dudley, quite pleased with himself, jumped in and began swimming around trying to catch a duck. At this point Jennifer yelled to Dudley to come and raced over and attempted to leash him as he darted past her, heading for the woods next to the dog park. He ran fast and then hid behind some mountain laurel until all of the dogs, except Morgan, had left. Then he raced back, rolled in the dirt and peed on Jennifer's pant leg.

"You stupid Lab," cried Morgan. "Won't you ever learn that you don't break rules and irritate Jennifer, who saved you as a rescue dog from a bleak life of torture? You really are a dud, Dudley."

"But none of the other dogs would play with me and I really wanted to take a swim and sample one of those ducks," explained Dudley.

"We must be kind to our loved ones, listen and make an effort to accept other dogs even when they are different from us. Wag your tail more, Dudley. Look happy. When was the last time you gave Jennifer a big lick across the face?"

"I guess that you're right, Morgan. I really want to be accepted. It's just that it's really hard to be good."

Days went by and Jennifer and Dudley tried once more to go to the dog park. "I wonder where Diane and Morgan are?" said

Jennifer to Dudley. No one at the dog park knew where they were either. Dudley played nicely with Sabrina and when two other dogs came up to him he joined in to play and chase balls.

One of the other dog owners said to Jennifer, "Dudley really is a well behaved dog now. You have a real winner!" Dudley overheard the comment and felt very proud of himself.

A week later when Jennifer and Dudley returned to the dog park Sabrina's owner said, "Did you hear what happened to Morgan?"

"No," said Jennifer.

"Morgan had a stroke and died in his sleep." With that, Dudley stopped what he was doing, crouched next to Jennifer, and laid his head on her foot in mourning. Morgan had been the only friend that he had ever had and now he was dead.

Morgan had come into Dudley's life at a time when he needed him. He had given him guidance and support until his untimely death. He would always remember Morgan. Dudley's needs were met and Morgan's work was done.

"Come, Dudley," said Jennifer. Dudley obediently followed Jennifer's instructions. There would be no more digging under the fence, running away or snatching a ball without permission. He wanted more than anything else to be a good dog and please Jennifer. With that he sat down next to Jennifer, gave her a big lick across the face while she clipped the leash to his collar and trotted home right beside her.

Reflection:

Jealousy is bad for the soul; it is energy poorly spent.

Unknown Author

Ginger
by
Faye A. Brown

Bringing his truck to a complete stop on the dirt and gravel road; Billy was about to pull out onto Skeenah Gap, when he noticed two large hound dogs who looked as though they may be after something. Glancing over into the grass, along the road side, he could see a small animal that looked as though it may be trying to escape the dogs. Stomping on the gas pedal, he swerved off the road, onto the grass where a small spotted fawn lay exhausted.

Quickly, hopping out of his truck and running over to where it was, Billy scooped the trembling little creature up into his arms. It wasn't a minute too soon, as he saw that the dogs were in close pursuit behind them. Turning toward them he stomped and shouted at the dogs to chase them away.

Holding it against his chest he could feel the fawns little heart racing a mile a minute as he carried it over to his truck and wrapped it in one of his old flannel shirts, before placing it on the front seat of his truck. Wow, he thought to himself, what a find!

Billy, a single, nice looking young man in his early twenties, lived with his parents in the North Georgia mountains. He often drove his old model Ford pickup truck along the back country roads just to look at the deer and wild turkeys that were so plentiful in the area.

As he watched the young fawns with their mothers (in the pasture land where they came out from the woods to feed on the tender grass), he often wondered to himself what it would be like to raise a young fawn and watch it grow up into adulthood.

Since he was a small child, he remembered his parent's friend, telling about the deer he raised on his farm in Texas. In later years, he listened to Uncle Raymond, a one armed man in his sixties, almost cry as he told about his pet deer. It was caught in a fence by his horns, had a heart attack and died before Uncle Raymond was able to free him with only a left hand. These thoughts were only fleeting ones and as he was driving along the road, He remembered that he hadn't even thought about Uncle Raymond's deer for a few years now. He just knew that today, he would rather go for a lone drive through the back country than to go into town where all of the celebrating with fireworks was taking place on the vacant lot, across the hill side near McDonald's Restaurant. The town's folk of Blairsville were celebrating our Day of Independence. Billy was also celebrating in his own way. He had a tendency to stay away from crowds and rather liked the privacy of being alone with the wild life that he so enjoyed.

He had only driven about a mile from their cottage in the woods before coming upon the small fawn.

He had hardly had time to even start looking and certainly wasn't expecting to find anything today. Billy hadn't prepared himself for this find. What would he do with it he thought to himself? Leaving it behind for the dogs wasn't an option. He knew that he should report it to the Department of Natural Resources, but they may not even be open he thought as he was driving back to his parents house. The tiny fawn, with its large frightened eyes, was watching Billy's every movement. Glancing over at the beautiful little critter, with cinnamon colored fur, speckled with white spots, he couldn't help thinking what an innocent little creature it was. He had always dreamed of raising a small fawn, but this one couldn't be more than three or four days old. He would have to buy formula and a nursing bottle. What if the little thing didn't like a bottle; what would he do then? There were many what ifs on Billy's mind as he carefully drove over the bumpy crooked road, over hills and around the sharp curves back home.

Calling his family out to look inside his truck, Billy just stood there with a serious smile on his face. His family was full of questions as they asked, "where did you find it"? Is it a male or female? He hadn't had time to examine it yet but it looked to be in good health and after a closer inspection, looked to be a little doe.

"What are you going to name her?" Mrs. Hatcher asked.

At first puzzled by all the questions, Billy said, "I like the name of Ginger for a little girl. She looks the color of cinnamon spice, but I like Ginger." So Ginger it was!

Billy ask his mom if she would look after Ginger while he went to the hardware store to get a bottle and some powdered formula to feed her with. He would have to keep her alive until he could report it to the DNR. He wasn't gone long before returning with the powdered formula for goats and sheep. The

Hatcher family was soon engaged with the care of a very young fawn. The sun was setting as Billy began making a bed for Ginger in the corner of his room. They had hardly noticed that darkness was setting in. Suddenly, they were brought back to reality, to the sizzling and booming of the firework display in the east, towards town. The town folks weren't the only ones celebrating this forth of July celebration. You would think it was Christmas time at the Hatcher's house. Everyone was so concerned about the baby deer being cared for properly. It was a time of excitement for the entire family and they were very surprised at how well she adapted to the new nursing bottle.

This was a new experience for Billy. He had to mix the formula by directions, and after warming it, had to test it on the inside of his arm, just like he would if it were a real baby. The real experience would come later on as Ginger became lonely for her mother.

Billy contacted the DNR after a couple of days and explained the situation to them. They told him that it was illegal to have a wild animal locked up without a permit, so Billy left the basement door open so that she could come and go as she pleased.

Bears had been known to visit the area very near the house on several occasions, so Billy called for the dog to sleep with them. Daisy belonged to his nephew and was half Lab and Border collie, but she had the markings and characteristics of a Border collie. She thought she was the boss of the mama cat's kittens. When they crawled out of their box onto the floor, Daisy would herd them up like cattle and put them back into the box. Billy's family often wondered if the mama cat appreciated her help or was annoyed by such a boss hog.

Within a few days, Daisy had appointed herself guardian over Ginger. They slept together and licked face. Ginger was adorable and she and Billy were bonding very quickly. Billy was losing quite a bit of sleep and like any new mother, wondered if he would ever get a whole nights' sleep again. The training went very well. After each feeding, Billy walked around in the yard with Ginger following closely at his heels. She soon learned that it was time to use the bathroom on their walks.

At night, she seemed to be missing the closeness of her mother, so would jump upon the bed. She liked to be stroked and scratched as she slept next to Billy. She nudged him in the back for more scratching.   Many times he was so tired from the several feedings throughout the night, that he didn't even mind her being next to him on the bed. Billy pulled the covers over his head, tucking them tightly around him. It didn't take Ginger long to figure out how to pull the covers off his head. Taking them between her teeth she would soon win out.

Poor Billy, half asleep mumbled to himself, "This is too much!"

Ginger was growing bigger and stronger each day. Her spots were beginning to fade some and spreading further apart. She and Billy went for daily walks in the woods and they sometimes spent several hours down at the small creeks that are also called branches. There she nibbled on the tender grasses and fodder. She began to drink water from the branch and didn't require so much milk from her nursing bottle. Billy and his family had noticed an older doe deer hanging about, near their house, which was a natural habitat for deer. One day Daisy and Ginger were engaged in a game of chase together when Ginger stopped abruptly and looked at the large deer who was watching them. Ginger trotted off toward the deer only to be stomped at and chased back. Poor little Ginger didn't seem to know what to do. She timidly rotted back to Billy; her human mom.

"It must be the human scent on her that the deer smells", Billy told his family.

He knew that he must refrain from touching Ginger so much now for the big deer to accept her. He had mixed emotions about

Ginger leaving with her deer family but wanted her to be a healthy and happy deer. He also knew that grown deer can be dangerous around people and dogs and the way she was growing, that day may be near.

Daisy seemed to stay near her when Ginger was out in the woods alone. They played together in the yard, running circles around one another. One day as Billy stood nearby watching them play; He saw Ginger kick her two little hind legs together and off she went toward the big deer. Billy always had sensed that the old deer nicknamed Scar, with a white streak down her face, was Ginger's real mother. After all, It wasn't that far through the woods to the area where he had found her. It did seem strange that only one deer was hanging nearby without a baby. There were several deer in the area, and the older ones all had babies. The day Billy had been dreading finally came and he felt both, relief and sadness at the same time, as he watched Ginger and the old deer walk off together.

His mother reminded him of the baby squirrel he had raised when he was only twelve years old. Billy remembered the day that he had found *Squirrely* helplessly laying on the ground beneath a large oak tree where he had apparently fell from a nest. A few months later, while riding on Billy's shoulder, *Squirrely* suddenly leapt onto the trunk of that same tree and away he scampered. Billy stood looking up at the tree in shock and finally realized that his little friend had reunited with his animal family. It was a sad day for Billy as he moped around, remembering that he had fed him with a medicine dropper and carried him around in his shirt pocket until he was big enough to sit upon his shoulder. That also was a very sad day for Billy.

"You'll get over it," His mom told him, "Just be happy that Ginger has a real deer family."

Unlike *Squirrely,* Ginger didn't leave entirely. She still came around for her bottle occasionally. She was easily detected amongst the group of deer feeding in the clearing behind the Hatcher's house. Her fur coat wasn't as neatly groomed as the other young deer. Even the fur comb that Billy had used to comb her with didn't compare to a natural mother deer's grooming. She was detected afar by her scraggly fur. As the cool fall weather approached, she began to get her darker winter coat and turned out to be as beautiful as any deer in the small herd. She attracted a young buck and was soon with 'child' or fawn. The Hatcher family watched her belly enlarge during the spring months and guessed that some time in early July would be her delivery date.

One morning Ginger failed to show up. It was later in the afternoon when she did arrive and it was evident that she had recently given birth. Feeling compassionate about Ginger giving birth to her first born, Mrs. Hatcher walked down into the valley to give her some shell corn. She lightly scratched Gingers head while she ate and quietly talked to her, giving her praise for her delivery. Ginger seemed to appreciate the support given to her.

Billy began watching daily to see if Ginger would bring her new baby down into the clearing where she came to eat corn; but she never did. She seemed to understand that she must keep her baby away from the dogs and humans. Occasionally the family could see a fawn upon the hillside, while Ginger came down into the clearing to eat. One day while visiting neighbors next door, Billy saw a video they had made of Ginger and her baby in their heavily wooded yard. Within a few months she and her baby disappeared. The Hatcher family didn't know if they had left the area or had just blended in so with the herd, that they couldn't be told apart.

After the passing of several years, Billy and his family often wondered if the deer coming into their yard now, were off-springs of Ginger and her baby.

Photograph by Faye A. Brown

Reflection:

"Ask, and it will be given you; Seek, and you will find; Knock, and it will be opened to you."

Jesus

A Kidnapping That Went Awry
by
Faye A. Brown

It was mid-July in the North Georgia mountains where the Hatcher family lived. The foliage on the hardwood trees was very heavy at this time of the year, making it difficult to see up the hill.

Daisy, their family dog, was barking non-stop, up on the curve near their house. She often seemed to bark just to have something to do and the Hatcher's thought this was one of those times.

This was the second or third day that she had been near the same spot barking her head off, slightly interrupting the unusual quiet of the woods. Finally, after becoming weary of so much barking, Mr. Hatcher decided to investigate. He was only there a short time before walking back down the hill where Mrs. Hatcher had waited.

He said to her, "Come here, would you like to see something?"

The two of them walked back to the curve and finding nothing there, Mr. Hatcher a bit surprised, said to his wife, "It was right here."

"What was right here?"

"A little deer, it couldn't be more than a week old."

Noticing a swarm of flies above the ferns a short distance down the hillside, Mrs. Hatcher said to her husband, "I see a swarm of flies over there."

Upon a closer inspection, they could see that the flies were after the small fawn.

"That doesn't seem right." She told him. After watching the small animal for a few seconds, with its frightened eyes blinking at them, they decided to let it be.

Calling Daisy to go with them, they walked back to their house.

Later in the afternoon, after their son Billy returned home from work; Mrs. Hatcher told him about the fawn. Billy started to walk up the road. Near the curve; Daisy ran up ahead, as if anxious to show him what she had found. She was a bit too eager and the fawn tried to escape her invasion. Billy immediately recognized there was something terribly wrong with it. After watching it stagger further down the hill side, he could see that It didn't have any balance. He called for his mother to come get Daisy. After entangling itself in a brush pile, Billy was successful in getting hold of it. He carried it into the basement where he slept, to inspect the dehydrated little creature.

Shaking his head in despair, Billy told his mother, "I don't know about this one".

The flies accumulated on puncture wounds to the head and body where the skin had been torn off in several places. It was obvious that a Bob Cat or Coyote had attacked it. Billy picked the fly larvae off and with peroxide, cleaned the infected wounds. It appeared to have fluid on the brain from all the swelling surrounding its small head.

"This is why his equilibrium is off," Billy told his family.

Billy had raised a small fawn four years earlier and not expecting to raise another, had thrown the old nursing bottles away. He asked his mother to watch after the fawn, while he went to the local feed and garden store to purchase another bottle and formula. Mrs. Hatcher had been a nursing assistant for several years before moving to the mountains. She realized that the fawn would not survive much longer without quickly getting some fluid into it. She got a wet wash cloth and began to moisten its mouth and nose. Gently prying the broken jaw slightly apart, she was able to dribble small amounts of water down its dry throat and moisten it. She knew that keeping this animal alive would be no small task.

After awhile, Billy returned with the formula and a bottle. The kind salesman at the feed and garden store had also recommended some ointment for the wounds. Billy had found the people at the hardware store to be very caring persons while tending the first little fawn.

After carefully preparing a regular babies nursing bottle, Billy spoon fed it into the fawn's mouth. The entire family was up most of the night helping to get enough formula into it to keep the fawn alive. They knew that first night would be crucial to its survival. Its sex didn't seem important at first; keeping it alive was Billy's main goal.

However, after discovering that the fawn was a buck; Billy was excited. "We'll call him *Buckie*", he announced to the family.

Within a couple of days, Buckie was taking four-ounces of milk at a time and seemed to be filling out at a fast rate. The Hatcher family realized that Buckie was older than they had at first thought. The challenge of raising Buckie was much more than that of raising the first fawn named Ginger. It took Buckie a while to get his balance back, so he at first used the bathroom in the floor until Billy could build him a box. The box was a low, square, four-foot frame that had a rubber lining in the bottom. He filled it with cedar shavings and Buckie seemed very comfortable in it, but Billy's room didn't smell so nice!

Being an outdoorsman and loving to hunt, Billy had always wanted to study the behavior of a young buck deer. He occasionally did some taxidermy work for his friends and had several wall mounts, hanging on the basement walls.

What will Buckie think of all the deer mounts on the walls, he thought to himself?

He knew it would be impossible for him to see them before his head healed. It was a slow daily process with all the family involved in nursing Buckie back to health; but that day did finally arrive. Billy was so excited that he called his family down into the basement to see Buckie standing upright and walking without staggering and falling.

It was now time for the outdoor training! Billy walked down the hill into the clearing where other deer came to eat, with Buckie following. He was like a little toddler just learning to walk. Each day his spindly little legs were growing stronger. Occasionally he would trot a few steps and then gallop across the field. Within a few days he was nibbling on the tender grasses in the valley behind their house.

Billy sat cross legged on the ground and watched him walk around and feed himself. He couldn't help but feel a sense of pride that he had helped this little deer get back on his feet. Buckie also seemed proud and acted as though he wanted to show off for his human mom. One day, as Billy was sitting on the ground watching, Buckie clicked his hind legs together, up in the air and ran a circle around him. Billy's heart almost stopped as he did it again, this time running a larger circle around him.

It was as if he were showing off and saying, "Look at me, watch me go!"

Billy couldn't help but smile as he watched the little fellow frolicking around enjoying himself. Billy wondered if he would just start running and never return. He was anxious to see him develop into a normal healthy deer but knew that he wasn't quite ready to give him up. Besides that, Buckie's broken jaw had grown back crooked and he also knew that it needed more time for healing. Just incase Buckie decided to run and keep going, Billy felt that he should get better acquainted with the territory of the woods, surrounding their house. They began by making daily trips across the hillside and down to the creeks. He was soon learning to drink water from the creeks. Billy tried to teach him all of the things that he had noticed the older deer teaching their young. He combed him daily searching for ticks. Unlike Ginger, the first little fawn that he had raised, who could be detected afar by her scraggly fur; Buckie could be detected by his crooked jaw.

Buckie needed a protector so once again, Daisy, the family dog, appointed herself as guardian. She was always nearby while Buckie was roaming in the woods near the house. Daisy made her daily rounds in the mornings to ward off any predators that might be near. Buckie was growing more independent each day and his bottle feedings were becoming more irregular. Anytime he showed up in the yard, one of the family members would prepare a large bottle of eight ounces of formula for him. Buckie seemed to enjoy his bottle too much and would nudge it with his nose, as if he couldn't get it fast enough. It was delightful to see him enjoying it so much with it frothing all around his mouth. Billy wondered if he would ever out grow his love for the bottle. A day came very soon though, that made Billy glad that Buckie did still enjoy his bottle.

One day after Billy and his dad had left for work, Daisy was up on the curb barking nonstop again, the same way she had barked when discovering Buckie. Mrs. Hatcher had seen Buckie only shortly before in the ferns on the curve. She was getting ready to go into town to do some grocery shopping so she stopped her car on the curb on her way out, but she didn't see anything unusual, so she drove on. Everything seemed normal as the family returned home. They were sitting out on the back porch to relax, after supper. The sun had set and it was growing dark, when someone remarked that Buckie hadn't come for a bottle that afternoon. Billy's first thought was that he was eating

140

more grass and fodder and may be weaning himself. A couple of weeks had passed and the Hatcher family often wondered what had happened to Buckie. It was strange that he didn't even show with the small herd that came around everyday to feed in the small clearing behind their house. The family joked about what Daisy knew about this situation and even discussed how they wished that she could talk.

One day a neighbor boy asked Billy if he ever found his deer. Hum, thought Billy, *how did he even know that I was missing Buckie?*

"What do you know about Buckie?" Billy asked the teenager.

Stuttering at first he said, "I think I know where you can find him!"

"Where?" asked Billy.

At first the boy was hesitant to tell, but knew he would be in big trouble with Billy if he didn't. He had been threatened by his buddy if he told. Billy told the boy to get into his truck and ride with him to the other boy's house.

"I can't" he said as he began to back off. "He told me if I told you that he'd whup my _ss".

Billy was growing a little impatient by this time. Speaking in a more authoritative tone, Billy told him to get into the truck. The young man timidly got into the front seat of the truck and Billy handed him a warm bottle of milk.

"Here, hold this," he instructed him.

After driving across the ridge for nearly a mile, they came to a house with a young deer closed in on a screened in porch. Billy confidently walked up to the screened porch, spoke to the woman and her son as he opened the screen door and told them that it was illegal to have a deer locked up. Buckie ran toward Billy and followed him out to his truck. Billy got the bottle and Buckie went for it, nudging it as if he couldn't get enough.

Looking back at the woman and her son, he said, "You know that I have raised this deer."

"I don't know anything," she scowled back at him while her teenage son walked back and forth cussing Billy for every thing imaginable. They also had a few choice words for the young man sitting in the truck. Billy opened the rear door of the cub cab truck, and when he gave Buckie a little nudge, he leapt into the back seat. Handing the young man the bottle to hold for

Buckie to drink from, they quickly brought him home where he belonged.

The dumb woman and her son made an anonymous call to report Billy for having a deer locked up. What they didn't know, was that Billy had already reported having a deer and it wasn't locked up. Within an hour a young officer, who was performing his duty, came to check it out. He and Billy walked out a ways into the woods and sure enough, Daisy led them right to Buckie.

Daisy and Buckie were licking one another and the officer couldn't help but smile as he watched the two of them together. He told Billy that he may have to come get the deer and relocate him. Billy agreed that it would be fine with him, but he didn't want him locked up on that porch where the boys had plans to raise him to eat. No one ever came to remove the deer.

If Daisy could have talked, she would have told Billy that while the Hatcher family was gone, the boys had driven their four-wheeler down a back road in the woods. They slipped up near the house and caught Buckie. They tied his feet together and were driving fast across the ridge. Daisy had followed for a ways but they were going too far, so she turned around and came back home. It was a plot that went awry as the two teenage boys had planned at first to take the deer to the other boy's house.

When it became apparent that the mother of his buddy wasn't going to let the young man raise the deer, he became angry and decided to tell.

Young Buckie was happy to be back home where he belonged and followed Billy about in the yard eating acorns. He soon took up with a couple of does and blended in with the herd.

Billy could pick him out of the group by his crooked jaw and button antlers. By the next rut season, Buckie had developed into a nice little four point buck and was off to find another herd to run with.

Thus preventing an inbred herd.

Hobo, a Dog of a Lifetime
by
Bruce R. Sims

Hobo began his life as the runt of an unwanted litter of half-breed puppies. His mother was a cinnamon colored Chow and his dad was a black Cocker Spaniel. Hobo took after his dad, which meant he would never be a very big dog even if he had not been the runt. He would have to make up for his lack of size in courage.

During my first four years of marriage to Jerry, I spent one year in Morocco. The rest of the time we lived in apartments and moved several times. It was not a lifestyle favorable to owning pets. We finally got a little house in the back corner of an 80-acre field. Two-acres were our very own. Now we had room to spare. A family with puppies wanted to get rid of them as quickly as they could. He was barely big enough to lap milk when Jerry brought home this tiny ball of black fur. I don't know why she decided to call him Hobo, but it turned out to be a very fitting name. We took good care of Hobo and he grew up not knowing he was a dog. He thought he was our child. He got all our attention and was a quick learner. He was going to be a house dog and we didn't want a dog that would mess in the house. One of the first things I taught him was to let one of us know when he needed to go out. He would go to the door and sit. If he wasn't noticed right away then he would bark. He would also bark on command. The command was "Speak, Hobo." It took some patience and repetition for him to learn, but he was smart. He also quickly learned what "No" meant.

A few years later, I attended the Air Force Sentry Dog Handlers School and learned several commands that I never taught Hobo. I never worked him on a leash and all his commands were vocal.

No matter how far he had wandered, a yell of "Here Hobo Here" would bring him running.

I believe that dog could smile. He just exuded happiness. He was not a hunter, in fact I never saw him chase anything other than a cat. He was just a pet, and loved people, with one exception. That was in the car. Hobo soon came to believe that he owned the car. We started taking him with us as soon as he was big enough to climb into the back seat. He liked to have the rear passenger side window down so he could stick his head out as far as possible. He learned what was safe the hard way. On this particular day, Jerry had kept the car and had to pick me up after work. Hobo showed his happiness to see me. We were on our way home and Hobo was leaning out the window as far as he could. Suddenly, and for no apparent reason, out the window went Hobo. We weren't going fast and Hobo was not injured, but coming back to the car, I have never seen a dog so ashamed. I noticed that he didn't hang out quite so far after that.

Hobo liked attention and would sometimes cross over the seat into the front and try to get a little petting.

Jerry taught him to get into the back again by telling him "Over Hobo" and he knew to jump back to the back seat.

About once a week Jerry picked up a maid to help clean house. The maid or anyone could ride in the car as long as we told Hobo it was "Ok".

The maid got a kick out of how well he obeyed when she told him "Ovah Hobo Ovah."

Jerry started working at Georgia Cigar and Tobacco Company and Hobo had to stay home. We didn't know how this would work out. He understood that I left every day and he couldn't go. But how would being left alone work out? He didn't like it. He was just not used to being alone. It wasn't long before he came searching for us. He learned that we often visited the Smiths. Bill was my fishing buddy. If we went to the Smiths and didn't take Hobo, in a few minutes he would show up there. He also knew what time we came home in the afternoon. The Smiths lived about a half mile from us. Theirs was the first house after turning off the paved road onto the dirt road where we lived. We learned to always look in the Smiths yard because that is where Hobo would be waiting for one of us to give him a ride home. The Smiths liked Hobo and thought he was smart. Sometimes the weather was bad and Jerry didn't want to let Hobo in the car with his muddy feet. There were two alternatives. We could tell hobo to "Go home" and he would run along beside the car for a ways until he could take a short cut and arrived in the yard about the same time as the car. The other was to let Hobo ride on the outside of the car. We taught him to jump on the hood of the car on command. He would spread his feet to brace himself and enjoyed the breeze. We did not drive fast for fear of slinging him off. Jerry went a step farther and taught him to go from the hood of the car to the roof simply by reaching out of the window and patting the roof of the car. Jerry liked to show off before our neighbors and arrive home with her dog riding on the roof of the car.

I don't know why, but everyone did not like Hobo. There were only two neighbors on the road where we lived and one who owned the property where Hobo took the shortcut. At least one of them thought the dog should stay at home. Maybe Hobo chased their cats or scared their chickens. They apparently decided they would teach him a lesson. One evening he came home looking bedraggled and kind of dragging around instead of looking alert and proud as usual. I saw that he was licking himself in a couple of spots. My examination showed that he had been shot with birdshot. A couple of pellets had barely penetrated his skin. I picked the shout out with tweezers and gave the wounds a generous swabbing with alcohol. In a few days, he was his old self again. Hobo was absolutely fearless. There wasn't anything in his learning process to teach him fear until he was shot with the shotgun. Few dogs came into our yard but no matter how large or small, he sent them running. Bill Smith invited me to go fishing on his mother-in-law's property. I gladly accepted and as usual, took Hobo who was hanging halfway out of the rear window. As we drove into the yard, a large hound came toward the car. He was barking and the hair on his neck was bristled up. We were not welcome. Bill said "Ug -oh, I forgot to mention that the hound is a mean dog. Maybe you better leave Hobo in the car." Too late! The car had hardly stopped moving when the hound was close enough Hobo flew out the back window and landed squarely on this back. The hound didn't know what hit him. Instantly he had a ripped bloody ear. He retreated under the house and Hobo took over the porch. We never saw the hound again as long as we were there.

It was time to move to Texas. I had joined the U.S. Border Patrol. Hobo was one of seven dogs. Jerry had two Chihuahuas that she kept in the house. I had two Beagles. Hobo was the family pet. I had a mixed breed German Sheppard named Lassie that was gentle. We let her have one litter of pups and kept one which was a beautiful white dog and looked to be a full-blooded German Sheppard, although he was not. Seven dogs were too many so we gave Lassie to my mother-in-law in Mississippi. The young German Sheppard would make a good watch dog for a junk-yard owner who had a five year old grandson. The dog would become his pet and guardian. The others would make the trip to Texas.

The first place we lived was a duplex in the city of Harlingen, Texas. It was not a good place for dogs. At the first opportunity, I rented a house in the country a few miles from Harlingen.

It was a dead-end road and the paper man turned around in our driveway every morning early when he delivered our paper. One morning in the fog he ran over one of the Chihuahuas. But Hobo was street smart and knew to stay out of the way of cars. Hobo and I learned that the danger to him was a pack of wild dogs that lived in the thickets at the end of the road. They roamed the area causing all kinds of problems.

Hobo was usually at the door waiting to see me off to work every morning. I wondered where he was. He might visit the neighbors during the day but he usually saw me off, and either met me or was waiting for me to get home. When I got home that evening, Hobo was laying by the front door. He was almost dead but somehow dragged himself home. I looked around to see where he had come from and what had happened to him. A quick examination showed numerous puncture marks on his neck, ears and chest. Also, his rear legs had been bitten. This was much more serious than the few shotgun pellets I had picked out of him before. I swabbed out every puncture wound I could find and applied alcohol. When I came home from work the next evening, Hobo was still barely able to move but I saw that he was going to survive.

I knew Hobo had been in the orange grove beside the house. I went out in the grove and found the spot where the wild dog pack had attacked Hobo. When the wild dogs bit hobo on the back legs, he had sat down to protect himself. They had made a ring around him and when they finished their attack, they left him for dead. He managed to crawl home. Hobo needed my care and was sore and stiff for several days.

It wasn't long before I found an empty house on Tamm Lane. I noticed it while on farm and ranch duty. It was a large ranch-style house with weeds growing in the yard and a dirty swimming pool in the back yard. I found out that the owner was working in Kingsville, Texas, and she was eager to rent her house, just to have someone living in it so vandals wouldn't destroy her property. We moved in and I cleaned the pool and irrigated the yard.

After we moved, Jerry soon took a job as a secretary at an elementary school. Hobo would be at home alone again like he had been in Georgia. Hobo was a people-oriented dog. He soon made friends with our nearest neighbors. My duty hours at that time were from 5 am to 3 pm, so unless I worked overtime, I got home before Jerry. Hobo soon learned our schedule. Since the neighbors lived farther up the road, Hobo couldn't hitch a ride home. He learned to come home at the right time to meet us. Hobo wasn't destined to enjoy his new surroundings very long.

Tamm Lane was not a paved or much traveled road. Fate stepped in. One day about 3:30 pm I pulled into the driveway. I looked for Hobo and saw him coming from the neighbor's house. He was coming at a trot with his tongue hanging out in that familiar happy expression. When he was 50 yards from home a car came speeding by. I wondered what could be the driver's hurry. I watched my street-wise dog get as far over to the edge as he could get. He gave the car the whole road. I couldn't believe my eyes as the driver deliberately swerved almost into the ditch to hit Hobo. He gave a yelp as he was struck. I was in uniform and carrying a pistol. It was my first impulse to jump in the car and chase down the idiot who had deliberately hit my dog and shoot him. My second impulse was to see about Hobo. My second impulse won out and I ran to the ditch where Hobo lay. Hobo looked up at me with those big brown eyes, not understanding what had happened to him. He could raise up on his front feet but his rear legs flopped over to one side. I could immediately tell that his back was broken.

When Jerry came home and saw what had happened, she was just as heartbroken as I was. I examined Hobo and he didn't seem to be in any pain. The broken back had deadened the back part of his body. I fixed him a bed on the patio and went to work the next day. When I came home he was my first concern. He had lost control of his bowel and bladder movements. Gnats had found him and he couldn't escape their torment. He was never going to get any better. There was only one thing to do. He had to be put to sleep. It was the hardest thing I had ever had to do. Since he was a puppy he had trusted me with his life, now I was ending it. I carried him into the Vet's operating room. I held him in my arms and tears ran down my cheeks as the Vet prepared the lethal shot. I said goodbye to my pet, my partner, a part of my life, as the Vet inserted the needle while Hobo stared at me with those big brown eyes.

I am not ashamed of those tears which did not stop until Jerry tearfully joined me in burying Hobo in the backyard. I will not forget you pal.

Reflection:

The really happy person is the one who can enjoy life, when he has to take a detour.

Author Unknown

"We Can Prove It"

By
James Goode

It began as a day not unlike most others in the Detective Bureau. Captain James Beach was the first to arrive, had read all reports, and was assigning follow up investigation to the detective teams as they arrived.

Sergeant Jackson and I were given a more or lass routine assignment. A request had been made by a Georgia sheriff to check out an address in our city in a effort to locate a fugitive. The address as it turns out, was a rooming house that was managed by a very cooperative woman.

"Yes our fugitive rented a room in the house. He was at work and most often came in by six o'clock."

After more conservation, more details, room location, etc., we followed the familiar routine informing the midnight shift and they would "Take him off the roost"

Case closed? Well yes, but there is more.

As e turned to leave I remarked to the woman that I would like to have the little dog that was following her around the house . We both agreed that Fox Terriers and Rat Terriers were probably the most intelligent of all dogs.

Jackson and I were suddenly put on "Sanity alert" when the woman announced that her dog could talk, but apologized for having to encourage the dog with raw hamburger meat.

All of us (maybe even the dog) knew that the test must be given. A small portion of raw ground meat was held over the dogs head, while the words "Want some" were repeated over and over by the woman owner. It was obvious the "Talking" was not a simple task for the dog. After several unrecognizable sounds, much straining and shaking, the dog very plainly came out with "Want some."

Yes we heard the dog talk, but a serious problem existed. Who would believe the story that we would tell to everyone we met? The solution came to us. We realized that a tape recording of the dog talking would add a great degree of veracity to our story. We were told that more ground meat was needed for the tape recording session.

In route to the Detective Bureau to pick up the tape recorder we stopped at a small meat market on the north west corner of South street and Parramore for the ground meat. As the two of us entered the door the store owner hurried toward us holding a typewriter in his arms.

We listened to a time worn story. " A strange had brought the typewriter into the store wanting to sell it for ten dollars. Felling sure the typewriter was stolen I bought it to turn over to the police. I was just about to phone you when you drove up."

Jackson and I bought the story. (We also believe a hen carries a snuff box under her wing.)

On we went to the Detective Bureau with a typewriter and a pound of beef. After generating a report on the recovered machine and a notice to the midnight shift, we checked out a tape recorder we headed back to nail down the "Talking dog."

During our absence of maybe two hours, great tragedy had struck. We were met at the door by a grief stricken woman who, between sobs, told us her dog had been hit by a car and killed.

A day or two later, the story of the "Talking dog" had been widely discussed and most viewed the incident with skepticism.

In the presence of Jackson and several other detectives, I remarked, "Well, we didn't get to tape record the dog talking, but it doesn't really matter because Jackson and I both heard him talk. Right Jackson?"

Jackson replied, "I have no idea what you are talking about."

Paul and Christy Goings, Living with Multiple Sclerosis

Lucky In Love
by
Paul and Christy Goings

Paul and Christy Goings share a love that could warm the coldest heart. Their home, complete with a dog, fireplace, and accessible deck, is nestled in the Appalachian Mountains of North Caroline. Married for five years, Paul and Christy share the fairy-tale romance on which dreams are built. Their life is not a fairy-tale because they both have Multiple Sclerosis.

Christy attended Montreat College in the Blue Ridge Mountains. During her junior year she was struck with dizziness and visuals problems. After her eye doctor found nothing out of the ordinary, she went to a neurologist in Atlanta. Within a week, Christy was diagnosed with MS, the same disease her Mom had been diagnosed with just a few years earlier.

Despite her health problems, Christy earned her degree, with a concentration in youth and adolescence. "The day of my graduation my eyes were really messed up. But there was no way I was going to let them mail me my college degree. I was going to that graduation ceremony."

After graduation, Christy worked with adolescents with disabilities , which she found extremely fulfilling. Three years later, optic neuritis and cognitive issues began to interfere with her job.

"I would work for a short time, then I'd have a flare up, work again flare up again one right after another" she recalls thinking I am way too young for this, I want to work longer.

But it was not to be. By the time Christy was approved for short-term disability, cognitive and visual symptoms made it necessary to apply for long term disability. Christy was 24 years old.

MEANWHILE, THREE STATES AWAY

Paul Daniel Goings, a 1981 Mississippi State University graduate, was working as an ornamental horticulturist in Jackson. Then, in late 1996 at the age of 39, Paul began to have peculiar seizures.

"My speech would grow garbled. My left hand and my left leg would get weird for about fifteen seconds," Paul explained. "Then everything would return to normal. A short time later, an MRI and lumber puncture confirmed that I had MS. I was glad because now I knew what was weird about me."

Physically, MS hit Paul hard. Always the comedian, he describes himself as a "wall hanger with basketball eyes," referring to his gait and nystagmus (rapid involuntary, rhythmic eye movement.)

"I came up to North Carolina to visit a friend and just fell in love with it." Paul says, "It was beautiful and affordable, so I decided to buy some land. I think in the back of my mind, I was preparing for the worst. I bought a house and in 2000, I moved up here.

A short time later, my MS progressed to secondary-progressive."

Meanwhile, to "get his mom off his back," Paul attended a local MS support group meeting.

BOY MEETS GIRL

"Our local MS support group meets at a downtown pizza place. "Christy remembers that there were usually about ten of us, sometimes as many as 15 show up. "One night, I arrived early and was sitting at the table drinking coffee when Paul walked in with his cane; I introduced myself and got him a cup of coffee. We talked and hit it off wonderfully. I needed a really good friend. Neither one of us could drive at night so we talked on the phone for hours and wrote each other letters. Over time, our friendship just grew."

Paul's version of their meeting has a somewhat different twist.

"I walked in, and there was Christy drinking a cup of coffee. I finally saw what the big deal was about the support group meetings. The meeting hadn't even started yet but I was already feeling much better. I should've listened to Mom sooner.

BOY MARRIES GIRL

Following a brief engagement, Paul and Christy were married on June 29th, 2002. The night of their wedding, they stayed in a honeymoon suite with the biggest bed either of them had ever seen. "It was a great honeymoon and it was our first real date because neither of us had ever driven at night."

"If Paul had not proposed to me when he did, I was going to ask him," Christy admits.

"If there comes a time when he can't ever get out of bed, I'll be there, right beside him."

"I love this young lady" Paul says. "It did bother me that I couldn't carry her over the threshold to begin our new life, but she said it was no big deal." I had to believe her on that one.

"Most of my problems are cognitive and most of Paul's are physical, so we really complement one another," Christy said.

Paul and Christy are grateful to their local Center for Independent Living for providing a scooter for Paul and bathroom modifications. Paul and Christy enjoy woodworking, even though Paul can only use his right hand, he managed to make a nice CD rack and is now working on bathroom cabinets. Christy enjoys reading to Paul by the fireplace. They enjoy watching comedies, getting together with friends, and doing research on the computer.

"When you find a true friend, that person will stand beside you no matter what. That's what I found in Paul." Christy said.

"You have to understand that we clean up real good," Paul adds, teasing again. When Christy and I go out, people look at us and think, "dog-gone, those two must be in love they are so lucky! Luck had nothing to do with it. Christy and I are very blessed."

Happy Anniversary
by
Paul Goings

Yes, today marks our number three,
When you hung up the Weaver name to join me on the tree.
1095 days alive and well on the tree,
Full of phrases and jokes hitherto unknown to thee.

There were pundits and skeptics, who laughed in their own
abyss,
But the wedding of two M.S.er's, standing as one is simply bliss.
Though each day is a challenge to the newlyweds,
Just give us a prescription to fill our needed meds.

Through good days and bad, I love my wife,
For without her I would not have a life.
She fulfills my wishes,
And even does the dishes.

Christy you are my partner in dirt,
And hope you do not mind a quick flirt.
For we have a task to complete,
To move and compress some dirt and plans to delete.

I love you dearly my bride,
And think of you in glowing pride.
For you are the one who completes my life,
YOU ARE CHRISTY LYNN GOINGS, MY WIFE!

My Dove
by
Paul Goings

Feeling old at forty-four,
I swung open the door,
There sat a little dove.

God has blessed me from above,
A tender wonderful woman,
Who accepted me as a man.

Little did we know,
Through the letters we would stow.
From strong friendship to love,
I fell for my beautiful dove.

On the day, April twenty-third,
I asked the most important words,
She accepted me as her groom.

Let's get married in a special room,
One with candles and flowers,
Assembled in symmetrical towers.

A room full of love,
For my special dove.
My beautiful dove,
The recipient of my love.

My gorgeous purple dressed wife,
The essence of my life,
I said I DO my precious dove.

She said I DO my precious love.
We exited our special room,
She walked hand in hand with her groom.

Man and wife,
What a wonderful life,
GOD'S TWO LOVE BIRDS.

Christy
by
Paul Goings

My angel I love dearly,
Blessed with many spiritual gifts.
Her beauty is heart-warming,
Her eyes bluer than any ocean.

Her petite size hiding an extraordinary love,
Her heart like the universe.
Omnipotent and always expanding,
Her effervescent smile brightens the darkest day.

An unbelievable strength she shares with me,
Fighting our M.S. together.
I love my Christy,
She gives me love and happiness.

She pushes me when I need pushing,
She compliments my accomplishments.
She gives me strength when I am weak,
On June 29th, she will be my wife.

With God's leadership, guidance, and love,
Paul and Christy will have a wonderful life.
Brought together by God, their love for one another exploded,
Two people who never expected a marriage.

But thankful for our special gift,
Life eternal together.

Some Things Are Great And Small
by
Christy Goings

Some things are great and small,
Others have it all!
You are one of those,
Whom I have chose.

Your honor and devotion,
Are always set in motion.
I'll love you to the end,
Nothing can make me bend!

Thank you for your love,
As peaceful as a dove.
Our day is coming soon,
When we shall find our room.
I love you, Paul, and that says it all!

M.S.-erized
by
Christy Goings

Thursday was a great day; I even walked the dog for the first time. All Paul told me was to let the dog (Merit) know I was in control, and he would obey. My legs were working, my eyes were without grey spots and my brain was cognitively acute. Thursday was a great day.

Friday was much different in that my computer crashed. My operating system and software seemed to be non-existent. My husband said that if I were a computer, my hard drive had crashed!

Saturday was worse, my software was loaded, but I was missing something. Paul and I went round and round but I couldn't understand. I read and prayed to God in the early hours of Sunday and I loaded the operating system--God.

So I arose Sunday morning, with my personal computer fully loaded and I booted up. None of the *"garbage-in, garbage-out"*; I felt good and went to Sunday school. GOD IS GREAT and HE is the operating system we all need.

Idell M. Shook, Our Resident Poet

With Her Elements of Style in Poetry & Prose

A Page From My Life
by
Idell M. Shook

My identical twin sister and I were born toward the end of the Depression. We were small but survived under the loving care of our parents and older sisters. We grew up, graduated from Hayesville High School and married first cousins. She had four children and I had three, and life moved along. Our husbands worked hard and we worked outside the home too. Our children grew into teenagers and we grew older.

Tragedy struck on November 14, 1980 when our sixteen-year - old daughter and four other people were killed in a car accident. I thought my heart would never mend and even now a memory can make my heart bleed again. Ten years to the month, my twin sister Odell died from cancer. Again, another part of me was gone. But life went on.

Our two other children graduated with degrees. My eldest daughter is a Medical Technologist and my son is a Machinist. I have lovely grandchildren who call me Karate-granny. I have worked at several different jobs in my life, retiring from Walmart after sixteen years and four months, in early two-thousand. That was when I started writing prose and poetry. I have sold three-hundred copies of my poetry book. This was much to my surprise and pleasure. I am grateful to the Lord for the anointing He bestows on my writing.

Tragedy struck again on August 23, 1997. I came home from work and found my husband of forty-two years dead on the floor from a third heart attack. Again my heart was shattered. How could I pick up the pieces when I didn't even want to? I had lost three of the dearest people in my life. Why was I left behind. Was I to walk among the headstones and wonder who would be next?

Soon after retirement, I thought it might be me, but once again the Lord spared me. So I picked up my pad and pencil and write of the mysteries of life, glad to be alive.

Sometimes people ask me why I write about sad things. I remind them that life is not always happy and pretending so is not facing reality. All of my life has not been sad. I write light poetry and prose also. I will share some of them later. Events in life shape our thoughts and spill into our writing. I write these thoughts because they have been such a part of my life, and now leave a void that is hard to fill. Sharing my thoughts with others has brought me a lot of healing tears. For this I am most grateful. It has also shown me that I am a survivor. That, like a tree, I can bend with the storms of life. When the storm passes I can rise again.

I am not the only tree in this life, or in this book.

Alone
by
Idell M. Shook

Like my heart,
your side of our bed is empty
and sleep is not for me.

You are gone,
never to sleep here again.

Death flew in on silent wings taking you away,
leaving me behind
in a lonely bed.

Porch Memories
by
Idell M. Shook

I took a walk to the old home place of my late husband Dee Shook. As I neared the house, the porch invited me in. My thoughts took me back to the age of eighteen, when I first sat on the porch with my husband and his family.

I remember a swing at the end of the porch, and a blue hydrangea bush blooming nearby. A mighty poplar tree, at the front of the house, gave its shade to the family. A grapevine grew in the yard, bearing its fruit. My lips soon matched the blue of the grapes, as I tasted their sweetness.

The can house, filled with jars of home-grown fruits and vegetables, bore witness to the labor of the family. Wooden boxes were filled with wheat from their fields. The smoke house was full of hams they raised on the farm.

As I looked at the old house, sunlight bounced off the shutters and reflected through the windows. The sunlight warmed the room; the memories came out to play. The old house gathered them to her bosom. I will gather a memory while they linger, one for you and one for me.

Let's go inside, and look back in time. Warmth greeted me as I opened the door. Flames danced in the fireplace. Nestled in the hot coals was a Dutch oven, and the aroma of baking cornbread filled my senses.

My father-in-law, "The Chief," as his grown children called him, rested in the corner of the couch, watching the evening news with Tom Brokaw. Mama Shook sat in her favorite chair on the other side of the fireplace. In the wintertime, you could hear the ringing of her hammer as she cracked out walnuts.

As each new day broke, The Chief rose first, bringing the fires to life. Soon, Mama Shook would go into the warm kitchen with the needs of her family on her mind. The aroma of coffee,

162

mingled with the smell of frying ham, eggs, gravy, and biscuits filled the house.

What biscuits they were! My mother-in-law would knead a mixture of home-grown wheat flour, lard, baking powder, soda, salt, and buttermilk into a smooth mound of soft dough. Then she would take her fingers and pinch off a piece of the dough, the size of a country biscuit. She shaped the biscuit in her hands, placed it in a greased pan, row after row, until the pan could hold no more.

In past years, five children joined Mama Shook and The Chief around the table. Grace was said, and the food was served. After breakfast, The Chief left for work at Ritter Lumber Company. Mama Shook tended the home and waited for the return of her family. The Chief came home from work at five o'clock with a tired body, an empty lunch box, and a contented mind. He had labored hard, and it felt good to be home with his family.

The Shook home was full of love and laughter. Guitars and banjos played as voices rose in song. All was well.

My husband and I stayed in the mountains and built a home nearby. The other Shook siblings married and moved away to work and rear their families. After their retirement, they returned to the porch at the old home place in the mountains, to search no more.

As I leave the porch, my eyes search the hills for what has been and will never be again. The swing still holds its sacred place. The can house stands as if to say, "You may need me again." Clusters of ripe grapes beckon my lips. The poplar tree, tall and proud, holds its age in its arms. Ancient shade caresses my face.

But time has moved on. Guitars and banjos lay silent. Voices stilled. The old house void of life.

Leaving the yard, I walk down the steps my husband built for his mother. The steps lead to the road and beyond. The road is more traveled now, but so am I. I look around one more time, move into the road, and walk back to my place. My heart is warmed by the good memories. When I hear the porch call again, I will go and sit with my memories, bask in the sun, and hear once again the music, the laughter, and the voices.

Rambling Thoughts
by
Idell M. Shook

I take up my pen and begin to write. Talk about a frightening experience. This is it! Why would a person choose to bare his soul, risk criticism, rejection, and the possibility of never being published, to put words on a piece of paper? There are millions of words already out there, why write more? Why do I go to writing classes, critique classes, etc.? Nobody can tell you the words to write. They can tell you what not to do, and the rest is up to you. I read my work in these classes when I can get up the nerve, and my trembling hand and voice doesn't shake the paper out of my hand.

As I write I peer over each and every word. Will it work? Maybe; maybe not. I search for a different word. I like my first choice better. What do you think? It is best to ask writers because others will say, sounds fine to me, when I know it needs more work.

Why do I write? I write to see if I can. I am still waiting for confirmation on this, but I keep writing.

Then I sleep on it. Tape recorder, pad, and pencil by the bedside. The dream might come tonight for the perfect novel. Those elusive thoughts might jell at the midnight hour, or the moon could spill its secrets, sending them down to me in the moon dust outside my window.

Regardless of what the night brings, when the morning comes, the tide changes, the sun comes up, I write again just to see if I can. I come up with some lines and I laugh or cry. Then I put them away. In a few weeks, I look at the work again and if the words still move me, I work on it and see where it goes. Now and then I read my book of poetry, *Rivers of My Heart,* I wrote and published. Tears fill my eyes, but joy fills my heart that I have written simple poetic words to touch people's hearts.

Higher Plane
By
Idell M. Shook

I write poetry in the early morning.
I write poetry in the gathering dark.
I write a lot of poetry
and still I push the pen
across the page.

I must glean my mind
like Ruth gleaned the fields of Boaz.
I must not leave a word unsaid.

I will leave this earthly life
to take my heavenly flight.
No words needed there,
on a higher plane I will be.

I will leave my words behind
and hope they speak to you
as they spoke to me.

When I read, write, and share, the fear subsides, replaced by a feeling only a fellow writer understands. And sometimes I will get up enough courage to submit an article and wait for an answer.

So I suppose, in spite of fear and aching muscles, I will ramble on. I hope you will too and good luck to all of us.

Photograph by Leeann Shook Wildman

The Midnight Hour
by
Idell M. Shook

The sound of the rain on Sam's roof is like the beating of a drum. Pounding and pounding. On and on the sound goes, piercing his ears and his senses. He usually enjoys the sound of the rain and the smell of the rain. But this is different. This is too much rain. Soon there will be nothing but water; and he will be a part of it.

He turns on his side, facing the window. He usually retires early and sleeps late. He likes the darkness. It usually gives him freedom from his thoughts, but tonight he can't turn them off.

He thinks of his marriage of fifty years. Although his dear wife died two years ago, she is often in his thoughts. After her death his grief was unbearable. He had no desire to suffer like that again, so he lives alone.

He thinks of the death of their only child, and the thought is heart-rending even after ten years. At times he and his wife fought the storms of life, and the death of their child was one of the worst times. When they should have been close and strong for each other, they drifted apart. Each weathered the lodss in their own way. Time helped though, and their marriage held.

But, oh what a storm! He has lived near the water for many years, but never witnessed anything like this. The lighting stalks the sky. The thunder is like clashing cymbals. The clouds are pregnant with water. The wind whips the trees, and they bow in submission. He is under a dark canopy, with no silver lining.

He sees a movement at the window. What is it? Could it be a raven seeking shelter from the storm?

"Quote the raven, nevermore!" drums in his mind. He has to know what is at his window!

He eases from the bed, slips to the window, and peeps out. He jumps back as if a stone has struck him; so great is his shock. Water, water, is everywhere with nowhere to go.

He crumples to the floor, his limbs loose and limp. Fear grips him and he shakes like a wet puppy. His senses become a pool of jumbled thoughts. Quietly he waits. When death crashes through his window, and claims him, he is ready.

A Visit With Mama
by
Idell M. Shook

My Mother is now 101-years-old and lives in the Chatuge Regional Nursing Home. I visit her to make sure she is warm and comfortable. I find her playing with the fringe on the shawl draped around her frail stooped shoulders.

"Hello Mama," I say.

She asks, "Who are you?"

"Your daughter Idell," I answer as I give her a piece of banana bread.

We try to talk, but that is a thing of the past. I stoop down to see if her ankles are swollen. I wash her eyeglasses for her almost sightless eyes, and then wash her pretty face. I comb her long hair and pin it up, remembering the years when it was jet black, and laid in waves around her face.

I hold her work-worn hands in mine. The skin is thin, and memories wash over me of how those little hands worked to feed her family. The skin is beginning to thin on my hands too, bringing me closer to my mother. The bond beginning at conception, between a mother and daughter never ends. I trace the veins in her hands, as if to walk through life with her again, wipe the tears from my eyes, and wonder how many more visits we will have together.

Reflection:

"Do not go where the path may lead, go instead where there is no path and leave a trial."
Ralph Waldo Emerson

Day of Tears
by
Idell M. Shook

On 09-11-2001, an unknown enemy flew our skies,
bringing death and destruction.

Too cowardly to face us, they came
in on wings that were not their own,
plunged into the twin towers, one by one,
a maniac at the yoke.
The Pentagon is next.
Another plane to its target.
Smoke billows, people flee,
a horror movie it seems, but it is real.

The calls go out, 9-1-1 they dial,
help us they cry as a fireball fills the air.
People scream and run for the streets.
Some will never run again.
What we thought would stand,
fell, and lay in a heap at our feet.

An eerie silence fills the land.
The enemy has attacked.
Not on the beaches of Normandy.
Nor the hills of Korea.
 Or the jungles of Vietnam.
It's on our own soil.
Breaking our hearts,
but not breaking our spirit.
They tell us the enemy
lived among us.
We knew him not.

How could we be so blind?

Harold Fights On
by
Idell M. Shook

He stands tall and proud,
and then like a bolt of lighting
his body is ravished
by mantle cell lymphoma.

His body weight melts away like snow,
forty pounds, or so they say.
His red hair is no more.
But he fights on.

His face is weathered
and racked with pain.
His body bears the marks of needles.
Like Job he has lost so much.
But he fights on.

More trips to Atlanta,
more chemotherapy.
The pole that holds his bags of life,
is his life-line between life and death.
It serves as his staff
as he slowly moves about the room.
And he fights on.

Will he win or lose?
Time will tell.
In the silence of the room,
Harold fights on.

Silence
by
Idell M. Shook

I step inside my empty house.
Silence greets me,
wraps me in its cold arms,
rides upon my back.

Tears of grief fill my eyes,
overflow,
and lie in a puddle at my feet.

The Master's Touch
by
Idell M. Shook

Winter
the trees are barren.
Reminds me of Sarah,
Abraham's Sarah.

Spring
the trees are green.
Isaac sleeps in Sarah's womb,
Both touched by the Master's hand.

Grief
By
Idell M. Shook

Grief is sharp as a knife,
piercing as the cold,
heavy as lead
as it draws the
life from me.

Grief is a pain I bear
not by choice,
but it comes
in a whiff of Old Spice.

His empty chair,
the silence of the house,
the smell of cigarette smoke.

Grief lies with me,
gets up with me,
gnaws at me
like a dog with a bone.

Grief may be short or long.
But inside,
where God resides,
hope springs eternally.

My Little Mama, Dollie MacDonald
by
Idell M. Shook

Mama stood four feet ten inches tall
with twinkling brown eyes, glasses on her face
and a hat on her head.

She was small in stature, but strong.
Raised seven girls.
She walked for miles, a load on her back,
her keys around her neck.

Hot or cold she worked for shelter and clothes.
There was no end.
When night came she combed and braided her hair
and waited for a new day to begin.

Mama had a double portion of faith and courage.
She rose with faith, walked the hills with grace.
Echoes from the hills renewed her strength,
and she faced another day.

Poetry

Highway To Heaven
by
Ellie Dobson

As I sit on my mountain top,
I watch the changing colors
Of the Blue Ridge Mountains.
Hearing the streams rush by,
The beauty of this place fills
My senses with new found joy.
The sounds of nature are like
A song singing to me,
and is music to my ears.
The smell of wild honeysuckle
and mountain laurel
Tell me I have found my place.

I walk into the cool damp forest after a rain,
Watching the clouds skipping,
across the mountain range.
Like ghosts that are late for an appointment.
The trees blow in all directions,
 swaying to and fro.
 I hear the birds calling to one another and
squirrels are fussing at each other.
I pick blackberries and eat my fill.
Sighing with contentment,
I know I have found,
 my Highway To Heaven.

The Forest Speaks
by
Ellie Dobson

Into the woods I walk,
on a very hot day.
I stop and listen to,
what the woods have to say.

The slight breeze softly,
whispers my name.
 When I hear these sounds,
I know I'll never be the same.

The magic of this moment,
 envelops me like a cloud.
And the mystery of the woods,
close in on me like a shroud.

Long forgotten voices whisper to me,
it will only be a short span of time.
Peace, Joy and Happiness,
Will be waiting for me, at the end of the line.

A Town Remembered
by
Ellie Dobson

A train whistle blows in the distance
And it's such a lonesome sound.
It reminds me of my childhood long ago
In a friendly railroad town.

It was a small town where honest people
Worked hard and long each day.
And cared for one another
In a very special way.

There were two churches in this town
Well attended - rain or shine.
And a small business center
At the end of the streetcar line.

I used to walk a mile to school
With many friends I liked so much.
But all of us went separate ways
And we failed to keep in touch.

Now gone from the town are the people
And what was has ceased to be.
The houses have all been leveled
And replaced with industry.

I often think of friendly folks
In that town of long ago.
And I feel a touch of sadness
When I hear the lonesome whistle blow.

Spring Deer
by
Nadine Justice

Well hello little deer.
Where have you been?
I've missed seeing you
pass by my house again.

Surely by now you see
we're closely related.
Your family and me
could never be gated.

Like you, I'm scared too,
my deer little friend.
Not so sure about you
but know where I've been.

On your sad face
my own story I see.
So, I found this place
where we can all run free.

You knew it was this lady
who, on cold frosty morns,
left out for you and baby
those rare treats of corn.

Spring is in flurry
and food's aplenty.
No need to worry
'bout your wee family.

You all roam together;
now you number five.
Have you ever seen another
sitting here by my side?

No, it is only I
who waits all alone
unless you come by.
The lonely lady
in her house near the sky

Visit me in Spring this year
and when Winter rolls round
I'll be waiting for you here;
a kindred spirit you found

My Neighborhood
by
Juanita J. Schneider

My neighbors from every window I see
The lush green leaves upon each tree
Standing tall they hide the sky
Except above me where I lie

The morning sun filtering its light
Through the trees upon our site
Morning feedings, they all appear
turkey, rabbit, squirrel and deer

Hummingbirds quickly make flight
Upon the red feeders they do alight
Yellow finch flitter to and fro
Spilling seed down below

In this beautiful mountain place
If I could fly up into space
Like an angel, I could see
Neighborhoods from sea to sea

Sharing their life upon the land
Giving neighbors a helping hand
Joining together a fruitful blend
Of many people who say 'Amen'.

Tribute To The One I Love
by
Judy Abercrombie

When I was just a little girl, I had a special place,
With my loving folks I dwelled, no dangers did I face.
In dark and dreary moments, my father eased my fear,
And mother soothed every hurt and wiped away each tear.
Now my folks have passed away, in Heaven they reside,
Yet I am not alone down here, my husband's by my side.

He eases my anxieties, knows what I need the most,
I'm proud of my companion, though wishing not to boast.
His smile dissolves the many woes that may come my way,
Just to glance upon his smiling face, brightens up my days.
My youth is gone and I am in the downward stage of life,
I thank the Lord that he's my husband, and that I am his wife.

We know not when our time is up or when we'll have to part,
If it be he instead of me, he'll live on in my heart.

Poetry Is Music
by
Judy Abercrombie

Poetry is music
brings lyrics to my ear
Expressing joy or sorrow
And sometimes just plain fear.

It speaks of things that could have been
And those that still might be
Of places closest to my heart
And those across the sea.

Whatever it may bring to me
As writer or beholder
Uplifting as a butterfly
It lights softly on my shoulder.

A Bodacious Bosom
by
Judy Abercrombie

She'd been a cute little girl - those who knew her would attest.
But, alas, by third grade, she had no discernible breasts.
While other girls shopped Sears for *Triple 'A's'* and such,
This poor child shopped cap guns;
bras didn't interest her much.
Mother came to her rescue - her figure she'd alter,
By laboriously stitching a homemade boob halter.
How quickly the young girl's figure seemed to grow,
Mom inserted her shoulder pads - no one would know.
At the local square dance, the girl danced as she pleased,
'Til, those shoulder pads fell to the floor with all ease.
The girl and her date made for a hasty retreat,
As foam rubber pads entangled their feet.
As years went by and the young girl matured,
Certain parts wouldn't grow - there was no such cure.
Now, mother would install a modern device,
A blow-up contraption, that'd be twice as nice.
It was prom night...oh, what a great night!
Things would just have to be perfectly right.
Her date brought a corsage - how great would that be.
But, what happened next, no one could foresee.
The pin on the flower poked a hole in her top,
Flat-chested and tearful, the girl's life seemed a flop.

Postscript: After years of friendship
and possibly more, the young man
never returned.

180

Solstice
by
Lorraine M. Orth

We wait upon the winter solstice
A whole new season lay before us!

Mother Nature has rung the bell
Of winter's cold she does foretell

With rusty leaves upon each bough
Summer's warmth is gone for now

Bucks and does with white flags high
No longer are they oh so shy

They romp and play in the autumn sun
Rutting season has begun

The hunter's sound of a cracking gun
Bring thoughts of tasty venison

Bustling squirrel's chestnuts find
Dry Kudzu brown stays all entwined

November's days are cold and short
First frosts and snow do they court

So snuggle by the hearth's warm glow
Relax! Enjoy! Forget each woe

Long past is the summer solstice
A whole new season lies before us.

Old Age Approaching
by
Sonny Boyer

At first the thought is kind of scary
It tells me not to tarry

The things I used to do with ease
Always seem to hurt me in my knees

My daylong wanderings through the woods have stopped
A porch swing, a cool breeze is the way to rock

The things I planned are mostly finished
Ideas and projects are all diminished

The ones not finished are harder to complete
Yet I continue on like time can't defeat

I'm jealous of the time I have for tomorrow
To waste this time will arouse my furor

Talking to a machine I just won't do
My time left is short, too many other things to do

For one who looked at taking one pill a chore
Now it's climbed to where I take twenty or more

The doc describes my heart with confusing phrases
When all he's saying is it's up to God's praises

Every morning as I awake to look around
I give Him thanks for one more round

I was remiss at failing to notice all the beauty
As I went through life trying to do my duty

Those tomorrows are all up to Him
I still enjoy them as life starts to dim

Fifty-One Years Together
by
Sonny Boyer

Christmas for partners is a challenging road
Christ the protector sets a bewildering goal

Fifty one years of bliss and trials confuse a couple,
But ducking and weaving teach you to be quite supple.

At first you are convinced that this is the one
With the first spat it's *what have I done?*

Making up brings back that temporarily loss
As you find it's not important who's the boss

Children bring about an unknown power
That bonds you closer by the hour.

Hard times and good test God's contract with you;
Satan never quits with his temptations all new.

As you rely on faith and ignore the bad,
The years rush by some happy, some sad.

When you look back over your shoulder,
Suddenly you realize it's almost over.

When it's now down to two old farts
Losing most of their parts

When you buy a car, and it's fleet and strong,
with power hundreds of horses strong,

and it's motor hums with a joyful song,
and you speed up as you drive along,

when speeding serves an inner need,
an urge for power that you must feed

when to "slow down" signs you pay no heed,
you are driving with Mercury, god of speed.

When you have served the gods well,
and when at last your life is through

and you descend to Hades, now called Hell,
Pluto or Satan waits for you

Photograph by Ellie Dobson

More Yesterdays Than Tomorrows
by
Sylvia Turnage

The path of life stretches far,
like a railroad track.
It climbs up hills, crosses wide rivers,
sometimes runs through dark tunnels
with no ray of warm sunshine upon it,
no light except a headlight,
revealing just a little of the track ahead.
Other times it crosses fields
with ripe grain blowing in the wind.
The track runs beside a placid lake,
where birds flutter gaily in a game of tag.
It passes through neighborhoods
where children laugh and play.
It runs beside the cemetery
with tombstones marking places
where loved ones have been laid.

I look at the crossties on the track.
Those behind me mark my yesterdays,
those ahead my tomorrows.
Look! How many more crossties
lie behind me

than those that lie ahead!
I must redeem the time,
make every day count.
There are lessons I must teach
the young ones who don't know.
There are memories I must make,
some of them to warm my heart
in the winter days ahead,
some to embody my spirit in loved ones,
to live on after my body has gone.

Yes, there are many more yesterdays
than tomorrows left for me
on life's lengthy railroad track.
But when the track has ended
and my spirit is set free,
there'll be no need for marking time;
I will live eternally.

The Cloud Watchers
[children's poem]
by
Zadie C. McCall

The Cloud-Watchers lay in the meadow green
All on a summer's day,
And waited for dragons to rear their heads
To frolic and dance and play.

But a Viking ship came sailing,
Sailing the blue, blue sky;
Yet before the two could clamber aboard,
Wild ponies came thundering by.

The ponies fattened and changed to sheep.
The sheep soon drifted apart
As the Cloud-Watchers lay mid the daisies
And waited for the next show to start.

I Know The Trees
by
Zadie C. McCall

I know the trees
Their bark, their limbs, their leaves.
Tall stately poplars showing yellow,
Black gums flashing crimson.
Who will transform first?

Dogwoods flaunt their scarlet berries,
Sassafras bushes wearing orange mittens
Dance with the fiery sumac
In the autumn breezes.

The faithful hemlock whispers,
"I change not.
I will provide your scented wreath
For the door
Come Christmastide."

Yes, I know the trees,
Their bark, their limbs, their leaves--
A gift from my mother.

Summer In The North Georgia Mountains
By
Jean A. Nethery

Blooms of mountain laurel fade and drop to the ground. Spring is over and the heat of summer is upon us.

Kudzu, lying dormant during winter, shoots out leaves from heavy stems, weaving its way up trees and telephone poles, determined to have its way.

Trees leaf out and shades of green gradually sneak up the mountainsides, replacing the grays of winter.

Hikers, carrying heavy backpacks, pause to drink from a mountain stream, while a doe and faun nibble on newly emerged tree leaves nearby.

Hummingbirds and butterflies flit from place to place in search of water and nectar.

Blooming sourwood trees attract noisy, buzzing bees, gathering food for honey. Blackberries ripen along roadside and people emerge from cars, like ants, to pick the juicy, black fruits for jams and pies.

"School's out," children shout as they head to the pool or baseball diamond.

Motorcycles and bikers maneuver curves as the beauty of the mountains lures tourists.

Campsites overflow with visitors cooking hamburgers over camp site grills and happy children congregate to see who can spit a water melon seed the farthest.

Nearby, under a tulip poplar, sits a bearded man strumming his guitar; people, familiar with the tune, smile and begin singing along.

It's Friday night and one Courthouse Square is alive with families hurrying to catch that Bluegrass Concert in the historic courtroom.

On Saturday the Square is full of antique cars or local crafts while tourists and locals saunter by, munching on kettle corn or fried green tomatoes.

Newly mowed grass attracts our senses and makes us wish that summer will never end.

Vegetable gardens provide beans and tomatoes for the table and zucchini to give away.

People gather for lunch at local ma and pa restaurants enjoying the mountain air, sweet tea and a barbeque sandwich.

Violent storms appear suddenly from over the mountain and dogs take cover in a nearby shed or under the bed.

Lightning causes the power to go off and reminds us what life was like before we had so much.

The heat subsides and suddenly it is fall; forest animals take cover as hunters quietly move about in search of food.

Jackets and mittens reappear and yellow school buses alert us to the fact that school has begun and "Vacation is over."

Enjoy it while it lasts!

Make The World Turn
by
Rhonda Kay Brigman

Everything in my life bears your touch
Going through my world daily
Mixing up your love and emotions
Fixing them on you and me.

Piecing the hours and minutes together
Spending my day dreaming of you
Bringing the day to an end finally
As I wind up in your arms once again.

Inevitably we blend our spirits into one
Caressing each others bodies and souls
Breathing up each others aroma
Making the world turn in ecstasy.

Unfaithful
by
Rhonda Kay Brigman

Together in union at last
Fulfilling a little girl's pretendings
Initiating and closing in family leadership
From role-models copied for generations.

Everything transforming in dreams
Finally face-down pretending free-flowing desire
Even butterfly's silky bodies have discipline
These days border his disgrace.

Gray Wind
by
Rhonda Kay Brigman

Drab and dreary
Overcast and gray
The sky tells us rain is coming
And a weather front is near.

Winds blowing limbs
Leaves rumpled and crisp
All tell the story of Autumn arriving
Cool days and nights ahead.

Time for flannel
Coverlets and throws
Prepare to bring in winters dawning
With warm fires aglow.

Homes hearth beacons
Warm and cozy
We hear the families gathering
Hearts filled with love.

My Fall
by
Rhonda Kay Brigman

Turning leaves dry and yellow
Tell me its time to begin raking
Leaves, brush, and earthen debris
Letting me know the change of season.

Cooler days and nights have fallen
Giving us relief from warm summertime,
Allowing us to breathe the fresh air anew
Alerting us to begin readying our winter's nest.

Pulling out the fleeced worn covers
Stirring up our warm cups of brew
Making our homes full with coziness
Setting our days up for family and joyous holidays.

The Car
by
Rhonda Kay Brigman

Glass embracing sun-streaked air
Metal bent and strained
Against the highway rubber burned
The drive only moments along.

Love
by
Rhonda Kay Brigman

....let Love be part of everything you do
....let Love be part of everything you give
....let Love be part of everything you hear
....let Love be part of everything you say
....just let Love be!

Mid-Life
by
Rhonda Kay Brigman

Well-learned observation ends in treasures
Ancient words gleaned
Both lived and measured in countless repetition
Sometimes fifty-something life is altering.

Safe Heaven
by
Rhonda Kay Brigman

Heaven floats in a cloud
Lights in the Sun to wait
And elsewhere nothing but strife
Northern Stars seem safe.

As I Awake
by
Rhonda Kay Brigman

In the quiet of the morning as I first awake,
I thank God for a good night's sleep.
Drinking in the break of day's beginning,
I take a deep breath to prepare myself as I shake,
The last realm of sleep from my eyes I keep.

My mind begins to wonder at the dreams of the night,
And I thank God for His keeping me safe and warm.
Dressing in both clothing and thankfulness,
I know blessings await me as day unveils itself in light,
The new day's adventures begin to form.

The Pagan Gods Are in Your Veins
by
Dorothea Spiegel

The pagan gods are in your veins.
They hold us still with long forged chains.
They bind our bodies, mold our brains.
The pagan gods are in our brains.

When you hear the rattle of the war-cloud's drum,
When you feel the pre-storm blood-lust rise,
you hear the hammer of the mighty Thor.
You see the sword flashing in the skies.

For Thor is the god of thunder and war,
the Teutonic god of thunder and war.
He shouts to us now as he shouted before,
"Go to war, go to war, go to war."

When you sniff a breeze from a tropic shore,
or laugh in the face of a nor'east gail,
when you thrill at the sound of the ocean's roar
and long to stand at your old ships' rail.

When you love to play in the waves white spray,
or gaze from the shore at the distant blue,
or swim with the fish in the deep, green dark,
Neptune the sea god is calling you.

When you dream of a woman, the right one for you,
And you haven't met her, but this one will do.
For her skin in the moonlight is silver and pearl,
You are thinking of Venus, no flesh and blood girl.

You'll make love to Venus in human disguise,
not knowing the difference, for Venus is wise.
And you will believe that you've found your prize,
when Venus has placed her spell on your eyes.

Sonnet to Mama
by
Dorothea Spiegel

These are the times that we remember best
The times when even dreams for us are real
We were too short to wear our mama's dress
But wore it playing dress up, made a meal
With little cookies served on dolly's plates
And teacups full of sugar water tea.
Are these the memories we need today?
I think there's something there we need to see
A time for mimicking our mother's life
And fitting in the customs she had learned.
They help behavior when we deal with strife.
In dreamtime there've been times when I have yearned
To be like mama, but I cannot be.
One person only I can be, that's me.

Tsunami
by
Dorothea Spiegel

Tsunami--- A word we only learned this year
We knew that earthquakes sometimes must be feared
And tidal waves-- we'd heard about them too,
That earthquakes cause them. This we all knew,
that big waves come across the sea, "Pacific"?
Not peaceful, no, it should be named "terrific."
We say "tsunami" now, not "tidal wave,"
And watch a film of lives that were not saved.
We try to think how orphaned children feel,
Trying to live in land no longer real,
No landscape that they knew, no family near.
Where are they---all that they hold dear?
"Tsunami"--- a word we won't forget,
And hope some how these children's needs are met.

Christmas For Children
By
Dorothea Spiegel

Erika likes her building blocks, she dumps them on the floor
grandpa picks them up again and puts them in the bag,
Hides it behind the Christmas tree. Erika finds it there,
Erika likes her building blocks, she dumps them on the floor.
"Isn't it nice to have the family over here this year?"
"Erika sure has grown a lot, I hope this sweater fits her."
"Erika come sit on my lap and we will read a story."
Erika likes her building blocks, she dumps them on the floor.
"You have to store the blocks away. She's too young to build."
"Let's try on the pretty dress that Auntie Linda made."
"Erika, come see the dolly Santa Claus has brought."
Erika likes her building blocks, she dumps them on the floor.
The family gathers 'round the table, grandpa says the prayer.
Erika eats a little bit, then climbs down off the chair.
"Come eat some more, dear", the anxious Grandma pleads.
Erika likes her building blocks, she dumps them on the floor.
'Oh, look, it's just begun to snow. Come, Erika, and see!"
"No," says Erika as she tries to put blocks in the bag.
"I almost fell~~I stepped on blocks. Who bought them, anyway?"
Erika likes her building blocks, she dumps them on the floor.

After School
by
Dorothea Spiegel

School was out: it was three-thirty
I heard the words, "ain't she purty?"
As I walked by the corner store
Where boys hang out. Three or four
about my age, grade six or seven.
I am tall but only eleven.
I heard some bad words, then Big Talker
Said, "Follow her, you could stalk her
like the guy on TV last night.
When you catch her, maybe she'll fight."
No, she knows me I live next door."
"Well then whacha waiting for?
Follow her, go along with her.
When you catch her, you can give her
a kiss." If he should grow bolder
Like he'll be when we are older,
gee a kiss would be outrageous.
I hope he's gonna be courageous

Experiences

My Kids
by
Laurie Boyer

I started teaching in 1973 at Kinloch Park Jr. High, near the Miami International Airport. It was the same school my husband had attended as a kid, when most students were too poor to wear shoes. By the time I arrived at Kinloch, 90% of the student population was Hispanic. I had no problem teaching students who could not speak English, I just assigned one of my top students to help them and we went on from there.

Some of my methods would not be accepted in today's politically correct environment, but they worked for me. I had one of my husband's old wool socks half full of all-purpose flour and tied with a rubber band. To stiffen students from continual tongue wagging or to regain their attention, I threw the sock (like a softball) at the offender, leaving a white spot. Attention regained, we would laugh and I would continue my lesson.

Later, after my class, other kids would say "Oh! Mrs. Boyer got you!"

Whenever I had to be absent, I told my students that substitutes were like company come visiting at their home. It was not the time I wanted them to act-up. I would forgive them for acting up with me, but not for acting up with a sub. I also made a seating-chart for my subs with specific instructions for them to inform me truthfully regarding the behavior of my classes. Compliments brought some form of treat or reward. Complaints brought retribution. When I was absent, kids who did not behave in other classes were angels in mine. I was very proud of my kids!

Marcy was the first student to make a unique impression on me. I had given a test in his class and I was grading the papers. When I got to Marcy's paper, every space had an answer comprised of 4-6 letters, making absolutely no sense. (kyse, vuntw, plmug)! Puzzled, I went to inquire among his other teachers. I learned that Marcy was in special education and was being main-lined in my class. **Marcy could not write words!** I gave him special credit for copying pages in the text book, or notes off of the blackboard. I assigned my best student to help him. I always gave him a D1A for his report card grade. D barely passing, 1 maximum effort, A excellent behavior. By the time

198

Marcy was in his third year in my class, he was getting 5 or more answers correct on each test. When he graduated from junior high school, he came to me with his heart broken,

"Mrs. Boyer, they're going to keep me in special education classes in high school."

I explained to him that Special Education would help him be successful and when he got ready to find a job I would always give him a recommendation. *Marcy always attended class and always tried his best. Not everyone can be the store manager; someone has to sweep the floors.*

Juan Carlos came to my class in the middle of a term. My students were very impolite when he entered the room and no one wanted him to sit next to them. When he left to register in his other classes, I gave my kids holy-cain for how they had treated him and I threatened "God help them," if it happened again. Juan Carlos had large ugly scars in his scalp and he was as jumpy as a grasshopper. Also his skin was always ice cold like he had stepped out of a refrigerator. I learned he had been an honor student through the fifth grade; then he developed a brain tumor. After multiple surgeries he landed in my 8th grade class. I soon learned he could not do the work, but man HOW HE TRIED! I realized he would not live to graduate from high school. One day when Juan Carlos was absent, I decided to confide in my class about his condition. I told them that I trusted them not to betray my confidence. I asked them to consider how they would feel if it were them. I said he would never have a sweetheart that he would never go to prom, or graduate from high school. I asked was it better for him to sit home waiting to die, or come to school and get something out of each day? I asked them to protect him from other kids who would make fun of him. I told them that he did not know that he was terminal **and they were not to tell him**. My confidence was well placed! They protected him throughout the day shared with him, and treated him the way they would have wanted to be treated. Juan Carlos got a B1A for his grade. Without discussing it with other teachers, I found that each of them gave similar grades. It was a kind and gentle white lie; one that did no harm and brought happiness to a boy with a very short life span.

I taught at Kinloch six years and then we moved to Georgia. I landed a teaching job at Lakeshore High School in College

Park, GA It was a beautiful school in a beautiful neighborhood. I was surprised to find it had a 97% black student population. The principal was a good disciplinarian and the students were very well behaved. Many a night I worked in my classroom until nine or ten p.m. with no fear for my safety. The custodial crew always looked out for me.

One of my first confrontations at Lakeshore occurred when one of my students wanted to use the restroom immediately after lunch. I refused to let him go, as he had had the opportunity to use the restroom during lunch. Later the principal told me when he had been a kid, he needed to use the restroom and his teacher had refused him. He went to the bathroom in his clothes and never forgot the humiliation. I always remembered after that to choose mercy over discipline.

One of the most exciting terms of my teaching career involved a biology class that had four students who had such friendly rivalry with each other; they were constantly trying to outdo each other. It was so much fun to watch who got the next top grade. I could hardly wait until that class period came around. The following year Robert, a young man in my class, was notorious for disrupting his classes. Typical grades were an F until midterm and then he started coming on like gang busters. His grades climbed to high C, low B, and high B. At report card time he had earned a low C, and I was as proud of his grade as if it were an A. I found out one of my former best students was tutoring him. He wrote me a card, saying, "Mrs. Boyer, you showed me I can make it out of Red Oaks." Red Oaks was thought by some to be the ghetto of Atlanta. I will always treasure Robert's card. This is what teaching is all about; to change the course of a youngster is a real thrill!

Jody had been absent several days. When I called her home her mother told me she had been raped at the bus stop, on her way home from work. I told my kids **only** that she had been injured. We raised enough money to send her a bouquet of flowers. When she returned to school, I asked to speak to her in the hall. I told her that what happened to her was not her fault, that she was as pure and good a girl as before her attack. I told her she did not have to confide in me, but **that it was important for her to find someone** she could trust, someone she could confide in; someone she could share her pain, her anger with. It was most important that she not keep her feelings inside, that she releases them. I told her not to confide in people who asked her questions, seeking the dirty details. She was not dirty, and she never owed anyone, including future boyfriends, an explanation about the attack. Jody and I exchanged Christmas cards for many years thereafter; unfortunately we have lost contact with each other.

Alan was a student in one of my low ability science classes. He hated to read aloud and would complain when I would select him to read. I told him that everyone in the class was a poor reader and the only way to improve was to practice. **I was there to help him**, no matter how small or large the word. We **practiced sounding out** syllables. He had been a student in my class a couple of years when he was absent several days in a row. When I called his home his Dad told me that he had applied for a job, but was unable to complete the application form. I told his Dad to tell him to come back to school, that I had a letter waiting for him. When Alan showed up the next day I presented the letter I had prepared for him. In it I said that Alan had difficulty with reading and writing, but that in the two years that I had taught him he had improved significantly. I said that he attended school regularly, absent only when he was very ill. I recommended that anyone who took the time to show him what they wanted him to do would be very satisfied with his performance. I included that if a hundred dollar bill was laying on the classroom floor, that Alan would not touch it and he would be sure to inform me it was there. The next week, Alan came to class with a grin from the right to the left ear. He had landed a job with the City of Atlanta Recreation Dept. and he was one very proud and happy young man.

Lakeshore was changed from a high school to an elementary school, so I had to move on. I taught at Tri-Cities High, North Springs High, and spent my last six years teaching at Milton High, in Alpharetta, GA

Matt entered my science class in the ninth grade. I soon realized that he and one other young man knew everything I was required to teach, so I put both of them in independent study in the library. They still took the class tests and passed each with flying colors. In the tenth grade, Matt was a student in an accelerated biology class. He came into my class one day and told me that his Dad had lost his job, and he had just been diagnosed with brain cancer. Since there was no job, there were no medical benefits to cover his treatments. A week later I wrote his parents a letter. I told them that Matt had confided to me about his Dad's illness. I wanted to assure them that I thought Matt was an extraordinary young man, and they had done an excellent job raising him. Despite his tender age, Matt was so well grounded that if he lost both of them that day, that he would land on both feet, able to do with his life what they both hoped for him. My prediction proved accurate.

Each quarter in addition to tests and major exams, I always required a major project. I was not looking for projects where students spent the most money, but where they used imagination and uniqueness to demonstrate our studies. In the fall I required a leaf project (where at least twenty families of leaves were identified, including scientific name and common name), or a three-dimensional cell project (where you could identify the organelles of the cell by the touch of each cell part.) During the winter quarter I required a genealogy project that included a minimum of three generations, including siblings, cousins, aunts and uncles, and grandparents on both sides of the family. Finally in the spring I required a wildflower project (twenty separate flower families, scientific names and common identities). In some families everyone in the family as looking for wildflowers. When Matt turned in his wildflower project, he had **species from five states**. I was flabbergasted. It excelled any flower project I had ever received. Because of his Dad's illness, his family had gone visiting all the family relatives to say goodbye while his father was still well enough for the trip. So Matt had collected and identified his flowers as they journeyed. I kept up with his progress throughout high school. **He excelled in all of his classes**, taking accelerated AP classes and when he graduated, he earned enough scholarships to pay for his complete college education. Matt was on his way to the rest of his life!

During the same time period, Steve was in my classes. For the class project that term, I had assigned a science fair project. Steve found a neighbor who worked at a science laboratory in Norcross, GA He came up with a project about abnormalities of blood. He won first place in his sophomore, junior, and senior years. Although I was not his science teacher during his final two years, he continued the pursuit, and won first place in the Fulton County Science Fair in his senior year. When he entered in the Georgia State Science Fair, a project inferior to his won first place. The professor from UGA did not believe that a kid could produce a project that was as complex as Steve's without unauthorized assistance. We were crushed with disappointment, but I told Steve that he was a winner no matter what and that nobody could stop him from becoming what he was destined to be. Years later, the week that Steve prepared to marry his high school sweetheart, his Dad died of spinal meningitis. His younger brother was his best man and as I watched the wedding ceremony I could feel the presence of their father at that service.

Julie was a member of the same grade. Their project in the fall term of her sophomore year was a three-dimensional cell (plant or animal). Julie's was so accurate in detail, so imaginative in materials used, that no one ever came close to her cell project. Although I did not get to teach her, other than that one term, we stayed in touch, each term in succeeding years. After she graduated from college, Sonny, my husband, and I had the pleasure of attending her wedding, one of the most elaborate events I have ever enjoyed. Through the years, Matt, Steve, and Julie have stayed in touch through Christmas cards. I have watched as their children were born, and each year as they grew.

Last summer we got an email; "Julie has a brain tumor, PRAY FOR HER!" What! Who! Which Julie? Her Mom responded immediately. GoGo (the Mom) kept us informed as Julie and Bret, her husband, searched for the very best surgeon they could find. The tumor was on her pineal gland, in the center of her brain. It was a category 3. They picked M.D. Anderson, a renowned center for the treatment of cancer located in Houston, Texas. During the ten-hour operation, her family informed us three times as to her progress. Through Caring Bridge, a medical informative website, we followed her recovery, her therapy, the love that her husband, parents, and sister had for this special, wonderful young woman, a ray of sunshine to every person who knew her. GoGo was the leading cheerleader in Julie's recovery, encouraging every step in Julie's battle to regain her health; stepping aside to allow Julie and Bret treasured privacy. Six weeks after surgery Julie went home to spend Christmas with her beloved sons; to return after the holidays to Houston for proton radiation therapy. Talk about solidarity, when Julie became self-conscious about her hair loss, her whole family shaved their heads.(Mom, Dad, Husband, Sons,) The whole cotton picking

Our First Georgia Mountain Christmas
by
Juanita J. Schneider

This would be our first winter in the Georgia mountains, actually our first winter season in forty years. We moved from the blustering cold of northern New Jersey to southern Florida in November 1965. The locals gave us the name of 'half-backs'.

Early in December of 2004, we went out into the woods surrounding our new home. The afternoon chore was clean up the fallen tree branches and pull up the small pine saplings that continually spring up around our home.

I called to my husband Rick, "Can we keep our eye out for a nice pine tree to use for our Christmas tree? Remember, we sold our artificial tree when we moved from Florida".

After another twenty minutes of our 'clean up' session; I heard Rick yell "Honey, here's one! How do you like this tree"?

I stopped picking up branches stretching my back as I stood up, and looked over towards my husband of nearly fifty years, holding up and proudly showing off his new find. "Well, what's that?" I replied. "Are you serious?" Proud of his new find he replied "Yes, of course! This tree will be perfect."

"Ha...you are so funny." Smiling at my mischievous hubby I stated "Well, maybe it will work out just fine."

Decision made, we had picked out 'our Christmas tree' that would enter our home and brighten up this special Christmas season.

Although the pine was slightly crooked and a little on the short side, it did have a few pretty, but scraggily branches. Yes, I must agree this would do just fine.

We carried our treasured tree into the house, set it up on the counter top, put on a few strands of tinsel, a few colorful berry ornaments and proclaimed "This is our own little 'Charlie Brown' Christmas tree. It's perfect!!!"

A Visitation

[Personal Experience Article]
by
Ellie Dobson

This story is about a dream, one so real that I actually felt I was in it. I had to force myself to wake up so I could write it down. It was a struggle to wake up out of this dream because I felt so at peace in it.

I was walking in a deep dark forest, a familiar place much like the pathway to Tray Falls of Helen, Georgia. I remember thinking this could be a scary place because of the way the trees formed an arch over the path. Then I began to feel as if something or someone was watching me. I felt no fear, just curiosity. As I looked off to the right of me, I heard laughter. All of a sudden, my Jennifer and Bradley jumped out of the forest and happily grabbed hold of my hands. They began to walk with me. We were all so happy to see each other. They begged me to let them show me all they could do. At that point, all three of us began to be lifted up into the air, in a floating state. We were lifted upward, where the color of the sky was a mixture of blue, pink, lavender, yellow and green. They sat me down on a cloud and laughingly said, "Watch what we can do". They flitted in and out of the clouds, darting around playfully chasing each other. They continued laughing, as they were having the time of their life. I remember experiencing complete peace, happiness and contentment as only the grace of God can offer.

After a while they gently lifted me back down to the pathway in the forest.

I cried, "No, please let me stay here."

Jennifer and Bradley wrapped their arms around me and said we will all be together soon but you must stay back on earth. You are still needed on earth; the rest of the family needs you. You are a powerful force in their life. Time will heal all wounds. You and what you have to offer are greatly loved by them. Everything that you have seen and experienced here will be waiting for you, when your time comes to join us. Be strong and know that God and His Angels are always near. Lean on God. See you soon!

Then the forest was damp and dark again but now I felt no fear. I was filled with peace and happiness because I had a chance to visit with them, hear their message, and know that they were with God.

Jennifer's Mother and Bradley's Grandmother

Reflection:

"Save your rejections so that later when you are famous you can show them to people and laugh."

Meg Cabot,   American Author

My Life As a Table
by
Jean A. Nethery

My story begins a number of years ago when I was cut from a forest, sent to the lumberyard and made into a door. No one looked at me because I was slightly blemished, warped and finally put in storage ---away from all of the other doors in the retail shop.

Nevertheless, one of the office employees took me home one night and said to his wife, "Now wouldn't the newlyweds like this for a table. Just think what they could do with this beautiful piece of wood."

"Sounds good," the wife said, and they made preparations to deliver their gift.

The newlyweds appreciated their gift and thought long and hard as to what kind of table they needed. They were now proud new owners of a small four room house and were in need of a coffee table for their living room. The Mister went about putting a nice new maple finish on me, attaching short legs, and suddenly I became a coffee table. My main function was to hold newspapers, coffee mugs, textbooks and sometimes feet. Since the Mister was now in graduate school, there were lots of late night study sessions and conversations around me.

About the time I was feeling comfortable with my new role, a baby was born into the household. Since I can't remember names very well I'll call her Willow. I found myself used even more now. I held baby bottles, soiled bibs, baby food and love thrived all around me as the Mister and the Missus were now a family of three.

As scratches and stains started appearing on my surface another baby, I'll call Walnut, arrived. Soon after that I was loaded into a U-Haul trailer and hauled off; first, to a brick house in Maryland, and then to a more permanent location in New York State. It was here that I really shined! The Mister took off my short legs and put long legs on me for a breakfast table. Did I stand tall! Benches were stained to match my new walnut finish and the Missus made bench pads (for the deacon's benches) to compliment me. I was the gathering place for the family and friends. It's a good thing that the Mister and Missus planned ahead and bought extra long benches, because two more babies came along---a girl, Chestnut and a boy, Acorn.

Breakfast was a madhouse when the family would all dine together slopping cereal, milk, toast crumbs and coffee all over my beautiful finish. Sometimes the cat felt sorry for me (if the Missus didn't get me cleaned off right away) and licked my surface. Boy, did the Missus ever get angry when she saw that cat walking on top of me.

After school, I became a haven for conversations about school and family problems. I learned to keep a lot of secrets. Peanut butter and jelly, Kool-Aid spills, and tears of joy and sadness dampened my top. I was in my prime because I was there for all the family. Often 4-H meetings were held around me. A pie crust was sometimes rolled out on me, as well as pizza crusts. In summer fresh produce was brought in from the garden and family members would stem strawberries or string beans on me. When large batches of cookies were baked, they cooled on top of me; along with homemade jams and jellies. Sometimes I became a typing table when the Mister or Missus had a letter to type. The Missus found solitude sipping a cup of tea, while hemming a dress, or planning what to have for dinner. I was there for all the family!

I recall one time when the man from the lumberyard and his wife visited and the cauliflower was ready for harvesting. Everyone sat around me cutting up twenty-one heads of cauliflower for the freezer. I think that my original owners rather enjoyed seeing me put to good use, but I must admit that to this day the smell of cauliflower makes me sick!

Soon the family outgrew the house and I was loaded onto a large moving van and padded well. It was a short ride but a lot more comfortable than a U-Haul trailer. By now the family was very much involved in school, church and community activities. A larger table was bought for the kitchen and I was moved into a family room; I then became the Missus' sewing table. She would conduct sewing classes in my midst, and scissors, rippers and pins were tossed on top of me by amateur 4-H seamstresses. My surface soon began to look worn. Nevertheless, I was there where I was needed.

One day I noticed boxes being packed, items discarded and knew that it was time for another move. The family didn't seem too happy about this move. This was a forced company move for the Mister and just when everything in life seemed perfect, things were soon to change.

Sure enough, I was loaded and unloaded twice for this move and I was now ostracized to the basement, where I became a laundry table. The Missus folded clothes on me and my surface continued to show wear and tear. By now, Willow and Walnut had moved out of the house, and I only held laundry for four rather than six. What had happened to me? No longer did I have the glow I used to have. Was I losing purpose? A flood in the basement even warped my legs, which were now starting to show signs of age.

About the time I was feeling pretty down, I found myself being loaded once again into a moving van, and hauled off back to the Midwest. It was my longest trip, but those movers cared for me well, and I survived the move just fine. In fact, the Mister decided that I should no longer be in the basement and I was upgraded as a computer table in his office. Wow, modern technology! I longed to be a part of that! One has to change with the times.

I was a part of the Mister and Missus's lives even into the wee hours of the night! I was in my prime again until one day, the Mister came home with a new computer desk, and I was relocated to the attic. I spent several years there loaded down with canning jars, empty boxes, items which the other children would take back and forth to college; frankly, I gathered a lot of dust. I wasn't too happy and then something serious happened.

The children had all moved out, and the Mister and Missus decided to have an "Empty Nest" Sale. I was hauled down to the garage and a sign was placed on me first for $5 and then crossed off to $2. I was sure unhappy and I wished I could trip the Mister or Missus for even considering selling me--- especially for $2. That was an insult! Aren't older things supposed to increase in value? What had happened to me? I thought that I was a part of this family! After the final day of the sale the Missus looked sad, removed my sale sign and I was moved back to the attic.

I remained in the attic for some time while the Mister and Missus decided what to do with me. In the meantime one of my long legs had cracked. It wasn't too serious, but one day the Mister came up and started working on me. I got a new leg and a refinishing job. I was hauled down to the center hall, and a baby-changing pad was put on my back. Did this mean what I thought? Yes, Walnut had married and not one, but three babies were expected. I sure had a new lease on life. From a lowly coffee table, I had now risen to the occasion for the next important stage of my life. I would become a changing table for the three new babies!

What joy those triplets brought to the household whenever they visited. Occasionally, a wet diaper was left on me and my surface didn't always smell as nice as homemade cookies or spilled jam. But, my mission in life was to change with the times; three babies were being changed around the clock, on my top, whenever they visited. Well, nothing is forever and as you might have guessed, those babies grew into toddlers, and soon there was no need for me again. I started to lose my lease in life.

"What do we do with the table?" said the Missus to the Mister one day. They both had computers now and desks to go with them. There was no use for a laundry table, a coffee table, or a sewing table.

"I know," said the Mister one day. "We need a place for the paper cutter and odds and ends in the office closet."

Oh brother, now I had to go into the closet. This meant that I had no heat on my back in the winter and summers would be hot and stuffy. But, life goes on! I'd weathered quite a few storms and, at least, I was being used for something.

Several years went by. I did have the chance to emerge from the closet and become a changing table again (for a short time) when Acorn and his wife presented the family with a new little "nut". And then, another move! This time the move was to the South and I was transported to the lower level of a new house, where sunshine and the view of mountains reflected on my top. I decided that life wasn't too bad. The Mister's jars of screws and nails, sheets of sandpaper, hammers and pliers were placed on my exterior. I was to become a tool bench.

Life is a journey. Sometimes you are up and sometimes you are down. Blemishes and warps don't mean that you can't still have purpose and significance. The secret is to be willing to rise to the occasion and change with the times. I think that this mission is just right for me now. Wood shavings sometimes cover my top, and a little 3-in-1 oil spills on me occasionally, but I am there for my family and always will be.

A Morning Symphony
by
Jean A. Nethery

It's morning, even though the sun isn't up yet. There's no need for an alarm clock. Last night's wailing sounds of the coyotes are only a memory. The symphony of sounds begins with the nuthatches' rhythmic pecking on the bird feeder, sounding like a wood block from the percussion section. The opening movement of the symphony---the allegro movement--- has begun. Sounds from nature are coming so fast I can't keep up. I hurriedly throw on a pair of jeans and a sweatshirt. A first glimmer of light shines on the horizon as the sun begins to poke its face into my view. Fall has arrived in its entire splendor.

I plug in the coffee pot, unlock the door and quickly call my dog for an early morning walk. Slowly the adagio or second movement of the symphony of sounds begins to emerge. The hummingbird feeder magnetically attracts skittering hummers, fighting for their place to fill their tummies for the long flight south. The morning fog in the valley below rises like a down comforter floating to the heavens. The katydids of summer fade out as the chill of fall beckons. The morning dew puts a glaze on everything while spiders attempt to design their webs in perfect artistry. In scherzo a red fox scurries across my path seeking cover. Fading grasses weave like drunken soldiers attempting to stand up straight. Acorns and butternuts gently fall like a spring rain, causing me to move to the center of the path to avoid getting hit. Could there be a snare drum nearby?

The color red appears on the sourwood tree above as well as on the ground where the blushing Virginia creeper sneaks into my path.

A family of quail parades by, searching for insects and seeds.

Fading goldenrod scatters seeds as a gentle wind softly caresses each plant. Orange toadstools glow in the early morning light and quickly disappear after their magnificent performance. My dog looks up with pure affection, but also disappointment.

The walk is nearly complete. The last movement of the symphony will soon end, but the impact of the sounds and sights will remain.

I pour that first cup of steaming coffee and greet the day.

My brain and body are ready for whatever lies ahead.

Photograph by Juanita J. Schneider

The Baseball
by
Ralph Kwiatkowski

I wasn't ready to die! I just retired a few of years ago and have a large *"bucket list"* of things I still want to do. One of which, is to attend a World Series game.

Growing up, I was surrounded by serious baseball fans. I lived in Toledo, Ohio. The closest pro-team was the Detroit Tigers; however, the Cleveland Indians, Cincinnati Reds, and Chicago teams White Sox and Cubs were not far away. Toledo had its own team, the Toledo Mud Hens. The Mud Hens were a Triple-A farm club of the Baltimore Orioles and played in the International League.

In my early teens, I was a member of the "knot-hole gang". As a member, I got in to see the home town games for twenty five cents. Living within walking distance of the stadium, I saw many a game. Even saw Mickey Mantle when the Yankees sent him to their minor league St. Louis team for rehab. In those days, baseball was in my blood.

After I retired, I lived in the Atlanta area and took in as many games as I could. The Braves were having a good season this year and made the playoffs. They had their best chance in years to make it all the way to the World Series. If they made it, I wanted to be there!

Until a couple of days ago, I didn't believe in out of body experiences or ghosts or spirits. It is now October 15th and I am one, lying in a bronze casket at the Pleasant View Funeral Home. I am not prepared to listen to what my visitors have to say but I hope they won't say something absurd like, "Doesn't he look good? Almost natural!" But they are saying it; again and again!

I haven't worn a suit and tie since Uncle Joe's funeral last year. After I retired, I vowed never to dress up except for weddings and funerals. I guess some things haven't changed!

Well, so far no white light or dark shadow lingering around to lead me to some unknown destination. Seems like heaven and hell don't know that I'm dead, or they just don't care. Maybe neither wants me, or maybe I've been relegated to Purgatory to repent for past sins. I have the feeling that

Purgatory might be like going back to the minor leagues for retraining.

Here comes my wife. She always cries at funerals; guess it comes naturally. I'm sorry for not saying goodbye dear, but it all happened so fast I don't even know what happened. I remember being at the game, then nothing; not even a blur! Nothing was functioning. No breath, no pulse or heart beat! I was dead as a door nail!

Now as I look at you one last time, I think, "I'm sure going to miss you honey." You've been a good wife, my best friend, and a good and caring mother, not to mention the best cook in the family. I remember our wedding day. You were as beautiful as any princess that ever walked down the aisle! Remember how we celebrated the whole weekend before leaving on our honeymoon? We had a lot of good times too throughout the years watching the boys grow up; all of those baseball and basketball games, swim meets, vacations at the beach and of course, the grandkids!

Here comes your brother-in-law Eddie, better known as "*Fast Eddie*"! He's always looking for a sucker to take advantage of, and before they realized it, they've been had. I never did like him; he's a hard person to understand. I guess the feeling was mutual. "I'll give you ten to one odds he hits you up for a loan before they close the lid on this box, AND make sure he doesn't take the baseball like he did from dad during last year's playoffs!"

Oh my, look whose coming! It's your old flame. I forgave him once for meddling in our affairs but now he's back. Just beware! He's been in and out of trouble ever since you left him. Three marriages, two divorces and one dead spouse! I hope he disappears like a bad dream!

For some reason, no one ever asked why I was holding a baseball. I guess they all knew I was a baseball "*junky*" and why not take along a souvenir.

"Look, *Fast Eddie's* back!" This time he's taking a closer look at the baseball in my hand. I wonder why he is so intent. He asks, "Is this a generic baseball or a real souvenir?" As he rotates the ball between my stiff fingers, he discovers that it was autographed by Chipper.

Eddie says, "I sure would like to have that in my collection".

My wife replies, "No way! It was a souvenir from his last game and the least we can do is to let him keep it."

Now I don't remember getting a ball during the game. All I remember is that it was the last game of the play-offs and if the Braves won, I'd be going to my first World Series. The game was tied at the end of nine and we were in extra innings with the Philly's. After a couple of scoreless innings, the Philly's scored a run. In the Braves half of the inning, Raphael, the utility infielder, led off with a pinch-hit single and stole second. The next two batters struck out leaving the entire season up to Chipper. We needed one run to tie, two to win. With a 3-2 count, Chipper hit two long foul balls along the third base line. I thought, *"If he could only straighten it out a little, we might have a chance."* Then with a solid crack of the bat, everyone in the stadium was on their feet. The center fielder raced to the wall leaping as high as he could but the ball disappeared for an apparent home run.

We had won the game! The fireworks went off as they did for all home game victories. I was so excited that I was going to the World Series that I passed out. It's the last thing I remember. I'll have to find someone to fill me in on what happened next.

I've always heard that when you're out of body, you get a good perspective of everything and everyone. It's true! Everyone has a different aura around them; some are bright and strong like my wife's. Others' aura are faint and weak like her old flame's. Fast Eddie's was stronger than I had anticipated. His aura had a faint glow but pulsed like a warning light. From my new perspective, I now understand that he secretly supports several charities and isn't as stingy as he puts on to be.

Just as everyone was leaving the funeral home, I saw a figure coming closer and closer. I finally realized he was not in the real world, but in my new world. He introduced himself as my guardian angel and that he too was a Braves fan.

Even though I hadn't seen him before, he said, *"I've been around all your life!* There were times that I wished I wasn't a Braves fan, but I couldn't do my job right if I remained impartial or didn't root for your team."

I asked him if he could fill me in on what happened, and he said he would be delighted.

He said, "It's like this. As the runners were rounding the bases and everyone was cheering, you had a heart attack and died. In all of the excitement, no one saw the left field umpire wave off the apparent home run. Someone in the stands had leaned over to catch the ball, and the umpire called fan interference. He ruled it a ground-rule double and only one run counted. The game was tied again and continued two more innings. The Philly's finally won in the fifteenth inning 4 to 3. The Braves season was over as well as any trip to the World Series."

I asked, "Can you tell me about the baseball and Chipper?"

"Well, as the excitement died down, 911 was called and the game temporarily suspended until they got you on the stretcher and out of the stadium. In the meantime, the fellow that interfered with the ball threw it back on the field. I don't think he wanted a souvenir that would remind him of keeping the Braves out of the World Series. When Chipper found out that you were taken to the hospital, he got a ball, autographed it, and had it delivered to the ER. As a final gesture, they put the ball in your hands."

The angel continued, "I know you weren't superstitious during your life, but do you realize your demise came in the thirteenth inning, on Friday the thirteenth, at thirteen minutes past the hour? Coincidence? Maybe! Just something to think about!"

"Time to go," he said. "My assignment is just about complete. Earth as you know is just a testing ground to see if you were worthy enough to take the next step." He told me that I had been a challenge during my most of my life especially through the teen years. Keeping me out of trouble wasn't always easy. Now, he's relishing having some time off.

The angel continued, "You really got lucky! You were scheduled to have a fatal accident next month. Your car was going to get hit by a big truck. What a bloody mess that was going to be!"

"Look at it this way. Untimely though it was, you died a happy death on Chipper's apparent home run, ***and you got to keep the ball! Who says you can't take it with you?***"

Hello Mom, It's Me!
by
Ralph Kwiatkowski

It was a Saturday early January 1996 and a cold wintry day. My wife Dianne had just discovered that her birth mother was living in Fort Wayne, Indiana. A break she had been waiting for a long time. Who am I? Where did I come from? Questions we sometimes contemplate in our spiritual lives and every day by someone who was adopted at birth.

Dianne had been adopted at age three months by Erma and Ed in Toledo, Ohio in March of 1946. Ed was fifty-one years old and considered too old to adopt a child as the normal life expectancy was somewhere in the sixties. Erma was thirty-three and still considered young enough to adopt a child. The adoption went through and the records "sealed" to protect all parties involved.

Raised as an only child, Dianne often wondered if she had siblings and what her birth mother was like. As the years went by, the wonder grew more intense. Finally at about the age of fifty Dianne started to make some inquiries into the adoption.

The big break came when it was discovered that those supposedly "sealed" records were no longer sealed. It appears that someone had appealed the process and won a class action suit. It opened the door for anyone requesting a copy of their original birth certificate. The certificate of course, would contain the mother's given name and place of birth. Dianne's birth mother now had a name, Lily June, Continental, Ohio.

Her mother no longer lived there but it was a starting point and the search went on. After searching the county records to no avail, she found out that one of the volunteers at the county library was into genealogy. Through obituary notices we discovered her last name. The volunteer had put a notice on the bulletin board at the library asking if anyone knew the whereabouts of Lily June. Fort Wayne, Indiana was the only lead.

After some hesitation, we decided to call the information operator in Fort Wayne to check for a listing. Fortunately for us, Lily June's husband had passed away a few years before and the phone was now listed in her name. Now we had a number, but should we call? Was this the right Lily June? If it was, it certainly would be a shock. Would the call be accepted, welcomed or would she say *no thanks, I put that out of my life years ago.* Well, nothing ventured, nothing gained, so let's take a chance. Better to find out one way or another where we stand.

I made the call and June answered. I asked if she had ever given up a child for adoption and she said yes. My response was "I'm the husband of that child", and we chatted for a few minutes. I then asked if she would like to talk to her. After a short pause, Lily June said "yes" and I handed the phone to Dianne. They talked for about two hours. At one point during the call, someone came into the house and Lily June said, "Guess who I'm talking to? Your sister!" "You mean Ruby?" she said. "No, your oldest sister!" Ravenna then joined the conversation for a while. Dianne had just talked to one of her sisters for the first time in her life, a bonus on the first call. After the pleasantries, it was agreed that we would meet someday in the future, but nothing set in stone.

Three weeks later, a very close uncle of mine died and we were on our way to Toledo for the funeral. The best airfare we could get was flying into Detroit and renting a car for the fifty mile trip to Toledo. What an opportunity to meet mother June! We called and explained the situation and asked if it would be ok to visit Fort Wayne after the funeral. No objections so far, so the meeting was set.

How do you handle such an awkward situation? It was decided that since we didn't know our way around town, we'd meet at a Burger King. Whoever got there first could relax with a drink while waiting. Anticipation can be a nerve racking experience but something as important as this was something neither of us had experienced before nor since.

We arrived first, June and Ravenna were not far behind. We each got a drink, sat down and introduced ourselves. We visited for about a half hour or so and then asked where we could go for dinner. It just so happened, that mother Lily June had planned a surprise for us to meet the rest of the family. She had reserved a meeting room at the local country buffet restaurant. There we met the rest of the family which included another sister and her husband, three of the four brothers, their wives, and a dozen or more nieces and nephews. The eldest brother lived in Springfield, Ohio at the time and was not present.

We practically met the entire family that first day. Getting to know them all was a welcomed experience. We got to know everyone and enjoyed the evening very much. It seems that mom Lily June had told everyone about having given Dianne up for adoption and wondered if they would ever meet. The hidden past was now open for all to grasp, no longer a mystery but a welcomed reality. We spent the night with brother Randy and his family, and experienced a rare feeling of peace and contentment. The next morning, we drove back to Detroit for the flight home ,promising to return in the fall for the annual family reunion. Dianne's been invited to all of the reunions since and not missed a single one. She has been accepted into the family as the long lost sister.

In 2002, Dianne had the opportunity to spend her first Christmas with her new family in Fort Wayne. It was a "Hallmark Christmas" complete with ten-inches of snow. Mother Lily June and all of the brothers and sisters were there. Later, mother Lily June visited us in Georgia to meet her other grandchildren. We took several vacations together and enjoyed every minute of them.

Mother Lily June and Dianne kept in touch often after that first meeting. Weekly phone calls and little gifts were sent back and forth for no special reason. They might have been something found on sale or at a thrift store, but something to know that you were thought of and remembered. The ten years Dianne and her mother shared were more precious than gold. A time which will last forever!

Mom Lily June passed away Thanksgiving 2005 weekend. *All* of her children were there.

A Little Bit of Sweetness
by
Ralph Kwiatkowski

Many years ago, when I was a bit younger, before I discovered girls, certain shapes and figures played an important part in my development. Some were athletic in nature like the baseball for instance. It was round and hard and you could either throw it or hit it. My brother and I used to play catch out in the front yard and if we could get enough kids together, we'd choose sides and get up a game of sand-lot baseball at the old abandoned school yard.

The old school yard was in our neighborhood only a few blocks from where I lived. The school yard was fenced in on two sides since it was located along a busy thoroughfare. In the corner where two streets met, there was a backstop to keep foul balls from getting into traffic. That backstop was a real asset because when we didn't have all the positions covered someone on the batting team would have to be the "catcher" and when he batted, the backstop became an invisible player. As I remember, there were a few trees in the outfield but they never got in the way. I spent many hours there playing baseball on that dusty field. Even took home a couple of broken bats and skinned-up knees for mom the bandage.

Now getting back to shapes; take for instance the football. A football is oval instead of round like the baseball but you can still throw it and play catch with a friend. You can't hit it with a bat, but you can kick it almost as far as you can throw it. The same gang that played baseball in the summer also played touch football in the fall. Those were the good old days growing up. We were just a bunch of kids having fun and staying out of trouble.

As I grew older and discovered girls, that girlish "hour-glass" shape caught my eye. You know there's something about an hour glass. It has curves where there ought to be curves! A place designed to put your hands to get a firm grip on things. I just think it was meant to be. The shape is somewhat unique. It is hard to describe but anyone who has seen one will easily recognize it.

To this very day, that shape continues to bring fond memories. I can still remember the first time I held her firmly in my hands and tasted her sweetness. When our lips met I longed for more. Her lips were wet and sweet. Nothing in this whole world could be as refreshing and as stimulating as that first experience. As I grew older, she never lost her attractiveness.

She has remained a loyal companion throughout the years. She has always been there to greet me after a hard days' work and has accompanied me on many business trips, vacations and other special occasions. On an ordinary day, she was there to comfort me when I needed something to pick me up.

To this very day, I'm still captivated by her figure and have never been let down. Holding her firmly in my hands I long to remember that first experience and the sweet taste of her moist lips. I remember getting energized every time I experienced her. I hope that she will never change!

Over the years her shape has changed a little but the old familiar one is still the apple of my eye. She's not quite as curvaceous as she used to be but her sweetness remains. I guess I'm very lucky to have met her at an early age. I believe that true loyalty over a lifetime is rare and should be prized so tonight I think I'll celebrate. I'll take her in my hands, and gently put her sweet lips to mine and enjoy another *Coke*!

Santa And Rudolph
By
Ralph Kwiatkowski

There was no one more berserk one Christmas Eve than Santa. It happened many years ago but I remember it as though it was yesterday. I was starting to party before our work was finished that Christmas Eve, and Santa went on a tantrum throughout all of the North Pole looking for me. I had never seen him that mad before that night.

My name is Rudolph and I'm one of Santa's reindeer. Yes, the famous one with the red nose! I wasn't famous when Santa had his tantrum and I didn't have that red nose yet either. Santa's rage was my fault but that's life. Whether I like it or not, I must admit to my poor behavior. Just like you, I have good days when everything is going my way; and not so good days when nothing seems to go right.

Santa occasionally has a bad day too; however, it's a secret we keep to ourselves here at the North Pole. Santa is the only employer up here. He's our livelihood. Without a job working for Santa, I'd be out on the tundra with the rest of the reindeer scavenging for food all winter, and the open range is not a fun place to be especially in winter. Polar bears are always on the hunt for food and food is scarce. Normally I can outrun a polar bear, but when I'm tired and weak, I'm just as vulnerable as the rest of the reindeer. What I fear most is the man with the gun. It is impossible to outrun a bullet as many of my relatives have discovered to their dismay. So in winter, I'm happy to have a job, food and a warm stable to sleep in.

Now let's get back to Santa. Most of the time, he is a jolly old man singing all day and directing the elves in the toy shop. He also spends some time planning for the next Christmas trip around the world. I had been in Santa's stable for about six or seven years doing my best to keep in shape during the off season. One year Santa had a different idea. He thought I could stay in better shape by taking some practice "Christmas runs" in mid season. Besides keeping in shape, I could learn my position which, at the time, was at the back of the team. This was a difficult task for me. I thought I was born to be a leader so it was hard being at the back of the team. Some of you know exactly what I mean!

One fourth of July, it was my turn to fly next to Comet and co-lead the team on our exercise trip. I did all right. As we circled the North Pole, I locked-in on the North Star, and set my internal *GPS* for Santa's workshop. No matter where I was in the world, I could find my way back home.

Comet and I took off for Russia, the Netherlands, the Swiss Alps, Iceland and the Arctic Circle. We had a ball! Comet informed me that on Christmas Eve, Santa has a plan that he's been following for many years. The reason Santa can travel as fast as he does and deliver all of those presents is that he travels north to south, then back again, and not east to west. In this manner, he can keep up with the changes in the time zones. Now this sounds a little strange, but Santa works 24 hours on Christmas Eve and every one of those hours is between midnight and one o'clock. Santa realized that if he could keep up with the time zones, it would be the same time wherever he went. It was always between midnight and one in the morning. Staying on time was easy up north where the time zones are close together but further south, the zones are wider and we had to work harder and faster. I soon realized Santa's job was not easy and to cover the world in 24 hours was a team effort.

I remember exercising everyday that year from summer into late fall. I also studied the world atlas in detail and discovered that the international dateline was located in the Pacific Ocean west of Hawaii. This is where one day changes to the next. To keep within the first time zone, I started in northeastern Asia (Russian Siberia) then due south along the western side of the international date line all of the way to the south pole.

Turn right and enter the next time zone. Heading north we traveled through New Zealand, the Philippines, and Japan back to the Arctic Circle. With each turn, we entered the next time zone. To stay on schedule, the trip from the North Pole to the South Pole had to be completed in one hour or less. The same was true for the return trip north. Each round-trip took two hours. Any deviation from the schedule would make Santa late, and he was a stickler for being on time.

Now that you know how Santa makes it around the world in one day between midnight and one o'clock. I ask that you keep this a secret because if the Grinch knew Santa's route, he might try to steal Christmas and there would be many, many, many disappointed children around the world.

Well, when Christmas Eve finally arrived, I wasn't feeling very good. I had the "Asian" flu. Since Asia was the starting point, Santa had to find a substitute for me. Santa's elves loaded the sleigh and he took off for the part of Asia nearest the Arctic Circle. I'll bet you didn't know it, but the Russian Eskimos in Siberia are the first people on earth to get their Christmas presents from Santa.

Now, while Santa is off flying around the world, the elves are packing Santa's bags for the next round-trip. Every time Santa flies over the North Pole, he gets a new bag of toys and off he goes with presents for children in another far away country. This continues throughout the night.

Since everything was going so well, I found time to celebrate while Santa was gone on one of his trips. The elves and I hit the spiked cider and eggnog a little more than we should have. Soon Santa's bags were not as full as they should have been and he was running out of presents sooner than expected. Some children weren't getting all of their gifts. After a few trips, Santa was really getting frustrated and disappointed with the crew back home at the North Pole but he had to keep going. There was no time in his plan for him to backtrack.

You must remember that every time Santa entered a new time zone, it was always twelve o'clock midnight and he had only one hour to complete all of his stops in that zone. At one o'clock he needed to enter the next time zone which was again twelve midnight.

Over the ocean, Santa didn't have as many stops as he did when flying over land. Not too many people live on the islands. Therefore, if he was a little behind schedule, he could make up some lost time. On one north bound trip over the Atlantic, Santa's only stop was in Iceland so when he got back to the North Pole, he had time for a short break. However, Santa was disappointed not having a full bag of toys ready when he returned.

Santa's Ho, Ho, Ho turned into a Bah! Humbug! He started to look for his elves. He wanted to know who was responsible for not filling the bags of toys and being ready for his next trip. He asked, "Why haven't my bags been readied and filled? Who is responsible for this sloppy work? We will have some disappointed kids out there." Well, the elves all pointed at me so I tried to hide. Santa was ranting and raving as he searched for me all over the North Pole. I stayed one step ahead of him until I slipped on some ice and fell flat on my face. When Santa finally caught up to me, my nose was swollen and glowing. Santa was still mad, but all he could do was laugh. He'd never seen a red-nosed reindeer before, but finally said, "Serves you right"!

When Santa was almost finished for the night, the weather got real nasty. He still had to visit all of the kids in North and South America, and his last stop would be in Hawaii. This last trip was going to take him down the east coast of North America and the weather forecast was for snow and possible blizzard conditions. I think I'll need some help if the weather continues to get worse. He didn't have time to change teams! What he really needed was a light in front to show the way.

Mrs. Claus suggested that Santa put me in front of the two leading reindeer to guide his sleigh. My nose was getting brighter as the cold wind blew harder and harder against my face. The weather was worse than expected. There was a northeaster snow storm in New England, an ice storm in the Mid-Atlantic states, blizzards in the central states, and out west, forest fires filled the sky with smoke. Visibility was terrible all over the country! The worst Santa had ever encountered. He still wasn't too happy with me, but was glad that I was out front leading the way.

I had never flown in such terrible conditions. The blizzard blew us off course, however, I was able to recover using my *GPS*. In Chicago, the sleigh almost slid off an ice covered roof; and navigating through the smoke in the west was a bummer! Santa and all of us reindeer had to put on masks so we could breath. I'm glad no one saw us because we all looked like bandits.

After we cleared the west coast, we headed for Alaska. We visited some American Eskimos up there and then headed for our last stop, Hawaii. After twenty-four long hours our deliveries were complete. Everyone in the world had been visited by Santa and it was time to go home.

When we arrived back at the North Pole, Santa invited everyone except me to share in Mrs. Claus's cookies and milk. For my poor behavior earlier that night, I had to first put the sleigh away and clean the stalls. Mrs. Claus snuck a cookie out to me, and then convinced Santa to let me join the party. There would be plenty of time before next Christmas for me to make up for my bad behavior. All of the reindeer and elves cheered as

I entered the party. I was happy to join them in the celebration. Santa, Mrs. Claus, the elves and reindeer were all forgiving friends and that's the spirit of the season. Peace on earth and good will to all, even to me. And now you know how I got my red nose and the chance to lead Santa's sleigh on a Christmas Eve a long time ago.

Sea Fever
by
William V. Bastow

Since childhood, I have had a deep fascination with ships and the sea. It all began in 1934 when my Dad received his partial payment of the bonus promised veterans of WWI. It was just enough, $200.00, to pay for a round trip passage to England for my mother to see her family. For years she had been saving small change in her "going home box." Then, a relatively affluent uncle gave her another $100.00 so that I could go with her.

That voyage aboard the RMS Georgic opened a world of dreams for this eleven-year-old. My favorite reading matter had been the old *Tom Swift* novels. These were superseded by *Moby Dick, Two Years before the Mast,* and *Mr. Midshipman Easy.*

As a high school freshman, I built my first boat, a ten-foot rowboat for fishing which I converted to sail the following year. A school pal invited me to join the Sea Scouts and I was off and running!

My childhood pal, Naomi, and I were teens when we would pore over a *National Geographic* map of the Pacific Ocean, planning our exploration of those romantic and mysterious islands of Polynesia aboard the Tahiti ketch that I hoped one day to build. Of course, those plans, we realized, would have to wait a few years.

Naomi's great grandfather, in the mid nineteenth century, had been the Master of a sailing vessel sailing between Philadelphia, South America, and South Africa. No, he wasn't a slaver. She wound up with salt water in her veins, if I may be permitted a cliché!

My first adventure as a Sea Scout was on a trip to Philadelphia aboard the 35' power boat owned by the South Jersey Scout Council. It was on Easter weekend in 1939. As we were passing through Maurice River Cut into Delaware Bay, the wind rose, the seas became increasingly rough, and the thermometer plummeted. We were locked into an early spring gale. Had we attempted to come about and return to port, we could well have capsized in those seas. There was nothing for it but to ride it out.

228

We finally pulled into the West End Yacht Club on the Delaware River where the manager, Mr. Duffy, provided us with a hot meal and a place to bunk down. Three of the guys, having had enough of boats, jumped ship and hitch-hiked home. The rest of us jeered them without mercy, calling them quitters and chicken. Let me point out right now, that one of the quitters, my pal Frank, was awarded the Navy Cross for heroism in WWII.

During that war, I wound up in the Army; so that was that for sea scouting. In later years I built a couple of small sailboats, but that was just a stop-gap for the real stuff.

Many years later, with our children grown and off on their own, we purchased an O'Day 25, a sloop well suited for coastal and bay sailing. However, we wanted more, *more* being a 31' cutter, a fine ocean-going vessel capable of facing just about anything with which the seas cared to challenge us.

Sea Fever II had most of the amenities available ashore: a propane stove with an oven, a sink with hot and cold running water, and a tiny freezer which I built under the chart table. The head was about four feet square, but had a flush toilet, shower, and a small sink. A Diesel engine gave us emergency mobility. The only things we lacked were the many expenses attendant to maintaining a house ashore: taxes, utilities... although we did miss the convenience of a car on excursions ashore.

In the spring of 1981, having sold our condominium, we took early retirement and moved aboard Sea Fever. In June of 1982, as part of the city of Philadelphia's celebration of the anniversary of its founding, a tall ship race was held between Caracas, Venezuela and Cape Henlopen, Delaware; the culmination of which was a glorious display of ships under full sail up Delaware Bay and River to Philadelphia. We planned our departure so that we could sail along with them.

Early on the morning of June 16, we left the marina on the Cohansey River. As we entered the bay, we got our first glimpse of those great ships looming out of the morning mist. We had the spellbinding joy of sailing with them as far as the Delaware and Chesapeake Canal where we turned south toward the Chesapeake and the seas beyond. Thus we embarked on the cruise of which we had dreamed some forty years earlier. While we never made it to the South Pacific, we did enjoy an exhilarating four years of memorable experiences.

* * *

Between the Delaware River and the upper reaches of the
Chesapeake Bay, there is a splendid seafood restaurant. Across
the canal is the engineer's basin, an anchorage maintained by
the Army Corps of Engineers. Pleasure boats were encouraged
to tie up at the restaurant dock while dining, then, after dinner,
anchor in the basin for the night. We had taken advantage of
this several times previously on short trips; however, *this* time
would be very different.

Situated on the canal, it was always of great interest to
patrons to hear the stories of passing vessels as they
approached. The restaurant radioed the ships to learn their vital
statistics, and then relayed it to us by loud speaker.

On this trip, as we were enjoying our crab imperial, the PA
system announced the approach of a tug towing a barge
destined for Baltimore.

As it happened, we knew the tug's skipper to be the son of
our close friends and sailing companions, Horace and Marigold.
All eyes were on the tug and its tow as it neared. When directly
abreast of the restaurant, the crew lined up at the rail, laughing
and waving to the diners. Then, as a unit, they turned their
backs, dropped their britches and mooned the diners to the
latter's uproarious glee and applause. A few were shocked, of
course, but all-in-all, it was a moment to remember. As soon as
we were back aboard Sea Fever, we called Doug's parents to
report.

That summer was spent on Chesapeake Bay where we
contributed mightily to the decline in the blue crab population.
On some days, we enjoyed crabs, in one form or another, at all
three meals. We found a spot in the Wye River where we stayed
at anchor for two or three days. I would be on deck hauling in
those tasty crustaceans, while Naomi, down below in the galley,
would be boiling and picking out the critters (a romance that
quickly fizzled!).

At the time of our travels, there were perhaps 20,000
families living aboard their boats. Some, like us, were foot loose,
looking for adventure and new places, while others stayed in
marinas while holding jobs ashore. One couple we met, he, a
retired policeman, she, an un-retired nurse (RN), sailed until
they ran out of money, then anchored while *she* went to work to

230

earn enough for more weeks of sailing. What did *he* do? Do? Hey! *He* was retired!

We patronized marinas only when no anchorage was available. Anchoring was not only free, but was far more comfortable. An anchored boat always faces into the wind, cooling the cabin as any breeze was directed down the hatch into the living quarters.

Those readers who have RV'ed around the country will have experienced the same helpful camaraderie that we did. At one point, in Maryland, we tied up our dinghy at a marina dock to ask the proprietor where we might get propane for our stove. He told us it was several miles away. "Here, take my car" this perfect stranger said, and handed me the keys. On our return, he invited us to a cocktail party he was hosting for his customers. That evening was most pleasurably spent swapping experiences with other cruising couples.

In our sailing among the Abaco islands, and later, we often reencountered friends whom we had met months and miles before. On those many evenings, as the sun "dropped below the yard arm," we gathered in the cockpit of one boat or another to "splice the main brace" and exchange paperbacks and remembrances.

At our marina near Atlantic City, we had become acquainted with a young man who was employed there. We enjoyed talking to Mike since he was a sailor of vast experience. Two years later, we ran into him again in Oxford, MD. He gave us a key to his apartment and invited us to avail ourselves of his TV, shower and laundry facilities.

He also told us where to get the best soft-shell crab sandwiches in the world—a secret strictly guarded from outsiders. Now there's a pal!

When we pulled out of Oxford, we said goodbye since it was unlikely that we would meet this fine young man again. I say "fine" young man in spite of his heavy black beard, long pony-tailed hair, and extravagant tattoos. Being constructed along the lines of a middle line-backer, he gave the appearance of a blood-thirsty pirate. One might expect him to have a cutlass between his teeth. But just wait.

After sailing a year in the Bahamas, we decided to head up to Maine for a look-see. In route north, we dropped anchor for a night at Block Island off the Rhode Island coast. As we approached the dinghy dock, who should be there to secure our line but our old friend Mike! Was this fate, or what? True to form, Mike took us in hand and spent the whole afternoon showing us the island's sights. Then, as we hauled anchor the next morning eagerly anticipating the seas and adventures that lay ahead, we wouldn't have bet a button on Mike's not being on hand to take Sea Fever's line at Camden or Rockport, Maine. Or, for that matter, at a dock in Malaga or Alicante, Spain.

After Maine, what? Wherever Sea Fever's bow points, and for as long as it is fun.

Reflection:

"Life is a circle without ending... never narrow always bending."
Morgan

Stateside Commando
by
William V. Bastow

When Pearl Harbor was attacked, I was a high school senior
and enthusiastic Sea Scout, with the rank of quartermaster,
equivalent to Eagle Scout. That could have qualified me for an
Ensign's commission in the Navy.

Unfortunately, I had been seriously injured in an accident
several years earlier and still walked with a slight limp. That,
coupled with a deaf ear and 20/200 vision, disqualified me for
naval service. The Army, in all its wisdom, assigned me to Basic
Training in the Infantry. Physically, the best thing they could
have done for me. Now, as a trained infantry soldier, I was
assigned to the Western Defense Command in the Antiaircraft
Battalion.

To backtrack a bit, in this thrilling tale: shortly after high
school graduation, as I walked past the school, camera in hand
as usual, the play of light and shadow on the building, with
maple trees in front, prompted me to make a photograph for
posterity. A few minutes later, a policeman muscled me into his
car. Someone had called the cops to report a Jap spy was taking
pictures of Millville High School.

I was ushered into the interrogation room at the police
station and bombarded with questions. (No, there were no
rubber hoses or blinding lights.)

"Why were you taking pictures of the High School? It's
illegal to photograph public buildings in war time." (Untrue.)

"It's my hobby."

"Who's paying you? How much? Who are you taking them
for?

"Just me, for myself."

"Don't you know the penalty for espionage and treason?"

Having been notified that a spy had been captured, the
Mayor strode in! Mr. Goodman burst into laughter. "Bill, what's
going on here? (The previous evening, he had been a guest at
our Sea Scout meeting!)

"You idiots! I know this kid, he's the skipper of our Sea Scout
Ship."

The local paper gleefully printed the story. The editor was the father of one of my boyhood pals.

Well, I seem to have strayed off course again!

Those of us stationed on the west coast were constantly being reminded of our mission: to protect our country from invasion.

Technically, the entire coast was considered a theater of operation. One night, an unidentified submarine was sunk by the Navy. We patrolled the beaches for a time, but no hostiles were found. Later, a body washed up on the beach, but was not identified. So much for the threat of invasion! (But, remember, President FDR had evacuated all Japanese citizens off the west coast at that time!)

On the whole, life was pretty easy, though boring. But most of us felt our training and service were being wasted. We felt that if we couldn't serve a more meaningful duty, we could have been working in a San Diego aircraft factory. However, "Ours not to question why, ours but to Do... or Else."

In San Diego, we were allowed two 48 hour passes a month, and, occasionally, a six-hour pass to attend church. Some of us actually went to church, while others would spend time at "Bradley's Bar" AKA "Bradley's Church of the Inebriation."

We stateside commandoes had opportunities denied to real soldiers. While attending chemical warfare school at Van Nuys Air Base, I was able to go to the Hollywood Canteen. Bette Davis was a co-founder who devoted almost every evening to dancing with service men while having her feet trod on. She seemed to take special enjoyment in it. I have always admired how movie people devoted all that time, talent and money to entertaining the troops.

On my first visit, I heard a voice say: "Would you like a sandwich, corporal?"

I accepted with pleasure the snack given to me by—Oh my God!—Jennifer Jones. But, before I could take a bite, a hand appeared and popped the sandwich into another mouth—hand and mouth belonged to one of my favorite actors: C. Aubrey Smith. Jennifer Jones and C. Aubrey Smith all in one night!

My response to the iconic question "What did you do in the war daddy?" was, "I met Jennifer Jones."

One evening, I went ice skating in Westwood Village. I had gotten to know the rink manager, so he introduced me to Donna Atwood and her husband, Bobby Specht. They were the stars of the Icecapades. She accepted my request to skate with her. Wow! I was skating with one of the world's greatest skaters.

While doing my stuff at another rink, I spotted a pretty girl's clumsy attempt at skating. Gallant soldier that I was, I offered to be her personal trainer. After a futile attempt to train this inept beginner, I retired to the stands for coffee. When I returned, my pupil was no where to be seen. I looked out on the ice to see her in the center practicing her fantastically professional routine. She was a professional skater having a bit of fun at a poor Dogface's expense.

One more anecdote: Shortly before the war ended, at a camp in the Mohave Desert, we were given a three-day pass in Los Angeles. My buddy, C.P. White, had met a girl at a dance in Hollywood and had made a date for our leave.

He called and asked if she could find a date for me. "Yes, she could. Her sister would be happy to come along."

She had told C.P. earlier that she had a sister in the Movies. (In the interest of full disclosure, I must admit that I didn't know how many sisters she had.) I could only believe that I had a date with a movie star.

As the big day approached, all the guys offered to lend me money. You can't expect to please a famous star on a $65 a month pay check.

On the appointed day, we piled into trucks for the drive into L.A., then, the sky fell in! When the First Sergeant ran out of the orderly room, he announce that leaves were cancelled. We were shipping out immediately for Fort Bliss, Texas.

To this day, I never learned which young lady was to have been my date, but, I still like to think of myself as the only guy who ever stood up Donna Reed!

The Anniversary
by
Naomi P. Bastow

The hostess seated the elderly couple and handed them
menus. Cora, observing them from the service area, took a long
pull on her cigarette. "Couple hicks." Cindy, putting a fresh
coffee filter in the machine, glanced over her shoulder. "Oh, I
don't know; they look like a pair of old dears. Probably
celebrating something."

Grinding out her cigarette, smoke escaping with each word,
Cora said sourly, "Cheapest thing on the menu. They'll order the
chicken; wanna bet?"

Cindy shrugged, hesitated, and then wheeled around. "You'd
better watch it, kiddo; they get many more complaints, they're
going to can you." Softening her words with a smile, she added
"Just take it easy, can't you?" and patted Cora's arm.

Setting down water glasses, Cora stood holding a pencil
poised above the order pad, staring out at the hillside. The
autumn trees were brilliant as the last rays of sun touched them
briefly; the lake, with its broken shoreline, reflected the colors
overhead.

This was one of the best tables in the inn, with its view down
the mountain and across from the fireplace where blazing logs
cast light and shadows around the dimly-lit room. How had
these two frumps rated this choice table, wondered Cora,
directing her gaze to the couple studying their menus.

The woman: softly-waved gray hair neatly combed, old-
fashioned dress—her Sunday church dress, no doubt—fitting
her thin arthritic frame loosely, a corsage of gardenias pinned to
her shoulder.

Seeing the waitress eyeing the flowers, the woman smiled
shyly. "It's our fortieth wedding anniversary." Touching the
petals, she murmured "Henry wanted to take me to some place
special..." Her voice trailed off.

A bored Cora said nothing, just tapped her pencil
impatiently against the notepad.

The man: gray-haired and sparsely-built, wore steel-rimmed
glasses and a neat, but ancient, three-piece suit. Probably
married in that, thought Cora, be buried in it too. His work-
worn hands turned the pages of the menu. "Now, Nellie," he

smiled tenderly at his wife, "No looking at the right hand side tonight; just pick what sounds good." Looking up, he said, "But first, I think we'll have some champagne."

Without a word, Cora turned the menu to the last page and pointed with her tapping pencil.

"Oh, Henry," said the woman, "Do you really think we should?"

"I certainly do. Man's not married forty years every day!" He reached across the table and caressed her hand lovingly, smiling.

Old fools! Thought Cora.

Turning his attention to Cora, he said, "We'll have a bottle of Gold Seal extra dry. And, we'll have it in those tall glasses," he paused, "tulip, err, flutes, not those with the wide tops."

"Yes Sir!" said Cora, with deliberate emphasis on the "Sir." Raising her pencil again, she asked, "And what's it going to be for dinner?"

The old gentleman put down the menu, stared straight into Cora's eyes and held them fixedly for a long moment. Then, slowly, and distinctly, he said, "Will you please light the candle and bring the wine?" Then, dismissively, he said, "We'll decide after that."

Cora snapped her notebook shut. "Of course, Sir!" and flounced toward the bar. Now how did the old hayseed know the difference between a tulip and a saucer champagne glass? She wondered contemptuously.

When she returned with the wine and the bucket of ice, the man was lighting the candle himself. The two of them sat looking alternately at each other, then at the view, then again at each other. The soft light seemed to have erased years from the woman's face. Must have been pretty once, Cora thought grudgingly as she twisted the bottle in the ice bucket and poured the champagne.

Lighting a cigarette, Cora watched them from the service area as they raised their glasses and toasted each other. Had it ever been like that with Al and me? She wondered bitterly. At first, maybe—that week-end in Atlantic City....But it didn't last. She shook her head. It never lasts...one day he just walked. Left her with the hotel bill, too!

Cora saw that the dinners were up for the old couple—not chicken after all, filet mignon. Let the old fools wait. Let them sit there mooning at each other. She lit up again while the steaks stopped sizzling.

The old gentleman beckoned Cora. "Are those our steaks sitting there growing cold?" he asked sternly.

"I'll bring them right away," she said indifferently.

"And we'd like coffee with our dinner, please," the man added.

"Right away," snapped Cora.

As the food was placed before them, the man said to his wife, "See if the steak is cooked the way you like it, Nellie."

Hastily cutting into the filet, the woman said, "Oh, its fine, just fine."

Cora was counting her tips when Cindy opened the door and said "Table six is asking for you. He doesn't look too happy, either."

"Oh, for God's sake!" Cora said crossly, stuffing the money into her handbag. "I thought I had those two settled!"

"Yes, is there something you want?"

The man looked at her for a moment, then said evenly, "I asked for coffee with our dinner; and we'd like a little more butter, if you please."

"Yes sir," Cora said stiffly, "and, you want more butter."

Setting the cups on the table, splashing coffee into the saucers, she asked coldly, "Will there be anything else?"

"Not just now, thank you," replied the man. "But yes, you can bring a clean saucer for the lady."

Leaning on the bar, Cora totaled the elderly couple's bill, walked into the dining room and presented it to the man. Smiling sweetly (and, for the first time), she said "I hope your anniversary celebration was a happy one," and to the woman, she said "Was your steak okay, honey?"

The woman smiled warmly, and said, "Oh, it has been a lovely dinner; the view is so beautiful, and with the logs burning in the fireplace...it has been just perfect. Thank you."

Smiling brightly, and speaking effusively, Cora said, "Well, thank you! And, have a nice daa-ay!"

They lingered there in the dusk, finishing their coffee, watching the lights twinkling in the valley below, quietly absorbed in the moment.

When Nellie left for the Ladies, Henry picked up the check and studied it. After a moment, he took a page from a small notebook he carried in his breast pocket. He wrote for a few minutes, laid the tip beside his coffee cup along with the page he had written, picked up the bill and walked toward the cashier.

As Cora approached to clear the table, she saw the man help the woman with her coat; saw her take his arm, and heard him say, "Did you enjoy our evening, my dear?" And, she saw the woman look radiantly into her husband's face and say, "Oh, Henry, it was a lovely evening, simply lovely."

As they passed from view, Cora picked up the note.

"Young woman," the note read, "Here is your twenty per cent tip with the following deductions:

1% for being impatient
1% for being rude
1% for neglecting to light the candle for my wife's pleasure
1% for failing to bring coffee as requested
1% for slopping the coffee
1% for not serving our steaks when they were ready
1% for acting as though you owned the butter cow
1% for the only smile you gave—and did it hurt?
1% for your ungraciousness to my wife on this special night
1% for ditto number

Cora stared at the note in disbelief.
"Well!" she said. "Well, I'll be a son-of-a-bitch!"

Reflection:

"By the work one knows the workman."

La Fontaine

Matilda Trumble Pays a Call
by
Naomi P. Bastow

"*Now* what are you up to?" Amos Trumble regarded Matilda
over his breakfast cup as she assembled doughnuts on a plate.
His eyes widened as she bent to retrieve one that had fallen to
the floor. She held it up to the light to see if it had picked up any
hair or other foreign matter. Apparently satisfied, she blew on it
to make sure, and returned it to the plate.

Matilda glared. "Why, I'm going to take these down to the
new neighbor—a welcome gift, like."

Amos put down his cup. "But, you baked those several days
ago for your club, didn't you? Won't they be stale?"

Defiantly, Matilda tore off a sheet of plastic wrap. "Oh,
they'll be okay dunked in coffee." Her tone said "And *who* asked
you anyway?"

Amos shook his head behind the morning paper and
continued a surreptitious observation. Pretty and plump when
he had courted her twenty years ago, she was now fifty pounds
overweight and un-particular about her appearance. An unkind
observer might have called her a florid-faced slattern.

Amused, Amos remembered when the moving van delivered
its contents to the large Victorian house at the end of the street.
Matilda had scurried to their third floor window to ogle the
furnishings as they were unloaded, and he knew she would
never rest until she got inside that house for a good look.

Matilda pulled a sweater in a hellish shade of puce over her
rumpled flowered housedress. (She had given up ironing right
after the honeymoon, Amos recalled.)

"My dear, did you know that your dress has come
unstitched? There," he pointed at a three-inch gapping seam.

An impatient Matilda scowled. "You can't see it under my
sweater. Anyways, I'm not going to change it now!" She
flounced out the door in a huff, the plate of doughnuts in hand.

In the beginning, known as the Gables, the house had once
occupied several acres some distance from the village. But, over
the years, a disintegrating fortune had forced its owners to sell
most of the land. Now, the house stood in a small garden amidst
modest other households.

Standing before the recessed door, Matilda couldn't make up her mind whether to ring the bell or use the highly-polished brass knocker. Never indecisive for long, Matilda pushed the bell twice and gave three sharp raps with the knocker. Just as she prepared to repeat the performance, the door was opened by a beautifully coifed and groomed woman in her late sixties. She stared inquiringly at the disheveled apparition on her doorstep.

Unabashed, Matilda smiled fatuously and proffered her plate of aging baked goods. "I'm your neighbor from down the street. I've come to welcome you to the neighborhood," then added, "Baked these doughnuts for you myself."

The woman smiled and stood aside. "Then, you had better come in, hadn't you?"

Triumphantly, following her hostess through a spacious hall and into a sitting room, Matilda's plump-prune eyes darted everywhere, taking in her surroundings, missing no detail.

Grace Talbot introduced herself, and adroitly steered Matilda away from a delicate-looking satin-striped chair toward another more substantial one compatible with her guest's avoirdupois.

Settling herself happily, still clutching the doughnuts, Matilda (allowing no time to elapse), leaned forward confidingly, and waded right in.

"How much did you pay for this place, dear?"

Mrs. Talbot stared at Matilda as though she had been transmogrified into a two-headed Hottentot. Her voice was frosty. "*I beg your pardon!*"

Undeterred, Matilda plowed right on. "I said tell me how much you paid, then I'll tell you how bad they ripped you off."

Recovering, Mrs. Talbot said icily: "Do let me take those lovely- looking *fastnachts,* and I'll make us some coffee. Do you fancy *cafe au lait?*"

Matilda surrendered the plate and corrected her hostess. "Those are doughnuts, not fast-a-whatchamacallits."

"Indeed," Mrs. Talbot's voice was as dry as a good martini. "And the *cafe au lait?*"

"Mexican coffee?" Matilda considered; "No, I prefer my coffee with milk...or cream, if you have it."

Raising an eyebrow, Mrs. Talbot repeated even more dryly, "Indeed."

In a short time, the two women, unlike a swan and a turkey buzzard, were seated before an ornate silver service and delicate *Limoges* china. Mrs. Talbot bit off a minuscule bit of doughnut, savoring neither its extremely greasy exterior nor its extremely dry interior, and hastily swallowed some coffee.

Meanwhile, Matilda dipped a doughnut into her coffee and carried it dripping towards her mouth, her pinkie finger elegantly pointing toward the ceiling.

"Good, aren't they? I'll give you the recipe and come over real soon, and teach you how to make them."

Looking as though she had just been offered a quick turn on the Rack, or a couple of days in the Iron Maiden, Mrs. Talbot's voice was strained. "That's magnanimous of you, Mrs. Trumble, but I really couldn't impose on your generosity."

Daintily, Matilda patted her lips with her napkin, and, leaning closer, clutched Mrs. Talbot's knee, never noticing how she flinched. "Now, that's an end to it. We're going to be great friends, Gracie, me and you. Why, I can see, we're two of a kind. Go on, Gracie, eat your doughnut."

Blanching, "Gracie" gazed at the offending confection as though it were covered with roaches, and rose. "I'll just clear this away," she said, hastily leaving the room. And, when she returned, she saw that Matilda's eyes were fastened on a large painting over the fireplace.

"That's your husband, right? Sailor, was he?"

Looking at the portrait of her late husband, she said softly, "Yes, that's my husband. He was the quintessential Naval Officer."

"How's that?" Casting a suspicious glance toward her unwilling hostess, Matilda blandly continued. "My brother was a sailor, too. In the Black Gang, you know, below decks, in the boiler room. Wouldn't it be funny if they were shipmates? ....Might even of been drinking buddies!"

This fantasy so entranced her that she gave Mrs. Talbot a nudge in the ribs for emphasis.

"Quite hilarious," answering insincerely, she moved away from the offending elbow and wondered how to get rid of this meddlesome visitor.

Plumping down heavily onto a delicate Hepplewhite chair,

Matilda planted her hands on her thighs, causing her dress to ride up exposing a generous amount of wrinkled stockings and tattle-tale-gray underwear.

"Now, isn't this nice? What shall we talk about?"

Wincing, Mrs. Talbot sent a prayer heavenward and asked pointedly, "Won't you have to prepare your husband's lunch soon?"

"What? Oh, Amos, he gets himself a sandwich. Or like that."

"Oh, a cold collation?"

"A cold what? No, I said just a sandwich. By-the-way," Matilda interrupted herself, "What religion are you?"

Unsurprised at *anything* this appalling woman might ask, indeed, expecting her very next question to be an inquiry into the scatological functioning of her alimentary canal, Mrs. Talbot pondered.

"My religion." *She must get this busybody out of here.* "While I certainly am not an iconoclast, I guess you might say that I have an affinity for the sapient, the innocuous, and the salubrious....with just a soupcon of the whimsical thrown in." With a quick look at Matilda's dazed face, she hurried on.

"At the same time," she said, "I find it anathema to my philosophy anything that is duplicitous, specious, or sycophantic. Although, I suppose it is tendentious of me to say so." Smiling sweetly, she subsided into silence.

"Good God Gerty!" Matilda alliterated, and then piously added, "I'm a Baptist, myself."

Unable to endure anymore of this, Mrs. Talbot rose. "It was kind of you to call, Mrs. Trumble," and, prevaricating unblinkingly, she added, "I shall return your visit soon, but now I really must get back to my unpacking. You *do* understand."

Rising unwillingly, Matilda found herself on the other side of the recessed door, while, in the pantry, Mrs. Talbot hastily crumbled the doughnuts for the bird feeder.

Later that day, when Amos arrived home, he found a pensive Matilda having tea at the kitchen table.

"Well, my dear, what did you think of the new neighbor?"

Matilda turned a jaundiced eye toward her husband. "I don't know what to make of her. I don't. She's some kind of foreigner, I guess." Pausing, she met Amos' inquiring look with a frown. "I couldn't make out half of anything she said."

Blank Happens
by
Judy Abercrombie

The big conveniences of Jacksonville, Florida, didn't reach us on the outskirts. Our rural co-op wasn't dependable and without power we had no water or lights. We had no city sewer lines, and the garbage men would only pick up full cans if I gave them bottles of my husband's Scotch as an incentive.

Our septic tank backed into tubs and toilets - grease and small boys had to be involved. Then somebody broke the tank's concrete cover. While waiting on repairmen, some drunk probably ran into a power pole, and we had no inside water. Being inventive, I doled out large plastic Subway glasses, and removed the bathroom screens. When using our commodes, it was necessary to avoid the windows, which my oldest son forgot, but remembered after that.

Our water source was an icy, deep well, and we took turns bathing in it.

Nosey, old man Johnson must have watched us; because, his heart gave out that same week. They found him by his kitchen window which faced our backyard.

While the kids and I were away for the day, our Shepard dog fell into the dastardly septic tank. From the looks of him, he'd swam most of the day. That was Fang. He looked like a porcupine when we finally got him out.

My youngest, Michael, wanted to play Tarzan by swinging over the open tank with his brother and cousins. Naturally, he was last, being the youngest. The frayed rope held for five boys, then broke with him. He fell in. We pulled out the *swamp thing*, except he wasn't green. I had to cut his clothes off and bathe him in the icy well-water using Tide. Cold water Tide hadn't been invented yet. However, it worked well with that well-water then.

We all survived and became avid campers, having learned how to rough it outside the city limits.

Things Disappear
by
Eleanore C. McDade

I cannot remember when it all began. We all lose track of things now and then. It's part of life from the time we were kids and misplaced our favorite toy.

Then it advanced to not finding the other shoe, buried deep in the recesses of the closet. A lost sock - that can be quite annoying, especially when the only ones I am able to match up have a hole in the heel or toe.

It wasn't much fun in high school when I misplaced my homework. The assignment I had spent 3 hours completing. I did find it a week later, under the reference book I had been using. Oh, yes, things eventually do show up, at least back then they did.

When I began my first real job, it was very important that I file *things* like important documents such as: who the foursome was for Saturday morning golf at the country club. I had better not misfile that!

Actually, my boss had become paranoid over the filing system prior to my arrival on the scene. His previous secretary filed everything, never to be found again. The only thing he asked me under job qualifications was "Can you set up a file system?"

A "Yes" got me that position. I'm still pretty good at it, however, I am only human and occasionally I do misplace some paperwork in the ominous file cabinet. You know, it couldn't be something simple like the paid electric bill... No! It's the credit card bill which, if I don't find it on time, I'll be paying a $20 late fee!

When I got married, everything was wonderful! I can't remember misplacing anything. Then babies came and grew into little kids who screamed when they lost their rubber ducky in the tub or their *Meme,* translation: totally worn-out crib blanket attached to my child's mouth and fingers. Other children call it different names, but they're all the same, the little blanket, soft toy or piece of cloth they cannot live without until they were three or four years-old.

Kids grow up, but in between, it's "Mom! Where's my this, where's my that!" I can't find this, I can't find that. Thank God, they finally become responsible for their life and their things.

I'm older now, the kids are gone and I'm alone. Yet, the strangest things keep happening to me. Things disappear! I just cannot understand it! I know I put that book on the shelf the other day but, it's gone now! I've looked everywhere for it! I'd use my flashlight, but that too is not where I left it! At least, I thought I'd left it on the shelf by the door. Well, hmmm, I think I'll make some tea. Now, where did I put the tea bags? Oh yes, of course, in the cabinet. Well, will you look at that! My flashlight is on the shelf next to the box of tea! Now, how did that get there?

I push the panic button when I can't find my car keys! I do have a spare in my wallet, but what if I forget that I have it there? I think I should write myself a note that tells me where my spare car keys are, but then, what if I forget where I put the note?

I mislay my cell phone once in a while in the house. It can't fool me! I know how to find it real fast! I just dial up its number! Now, where did I write down that number?

Things seem to disappear faster than before. There are little gremlins playing with my mind. I know they are not mean. I think they just want to test me.

Things disappear! I try not to let it bother me...for you see, after all these years, I've come to realize that with patience, these little lost articles will tire of hiding from me and they will re-appear.

It's kind of like a game now in my life. Where are my slippers? Those little rascals! Oh, there you are, right by my bed! Hmmm... I think I'll just take a nap.

Reflections:

On a daily basis, ask the Lord for direction.

Author Unknown

Going Green
by
Eleanore C. McDade

We read and hear daily about saving the planet. Conserve water, fuel, land, forests. Recycle everything under the sun, plant trees, build a windmill, and clean up the environment.

One day, driving in the forest not long ago, I came across an old rusty garbage truck. It was overgrown with foliage. I was intrigued. Why had it "died" there? Who had it belonged to? No county authority would just abandon its property. It must have been a private company. What critters had taken up housing there? Was it empty of garbage when it made that final run?

In this recycle environment, scrap metal is at a premium. I was surprised a collector had not already removed this heap of metal. Of course, it would have to be hauled off piece by piece. You know how big a garbage truck is... Someone may already have tried and found it to be still full of old decaying garbage. Would this then be called "piece meal?"

I must confess, I still read the "Comics," well, just a few. Brewster Rocket: Space Guy! The July 4, 2008 comic said: "We need the energy a black hole can provide, but no one wants the black hole in their sector." Evil Doctor Mel's response: "What's a little green clay character got to do with this?" Dr. Mel: "NIMBY means 'Not in my backyard!'"

The evil Dr. Mel then shows his black hole to Brewster Rocket and says "I'm letting the concerned environmentalists tour my black hole. Once they get a closer look, it should solve the problem."

The next picture shows everyone and everything in its path being sucked into the black hole. Dr. Mel: "See? Problem solved."

Now, wouldn't it be something if we could put everything we no longer need nor want into a black hole which turned it all into energy that could be funneled into driving planes, trucks, trains, cars, billions of megawatts! The whole world could go green!

At this writing, the only one I know who is living a totally green life-style is Leonardo Di Caprio. He drives a hybrid, powers his L.A. home with solar panels and when in Manhattan, uses a bike to get to his "green" condo. Now here's a guy who can well afford to be chauffer-driven in a Hummer Limo that gets eight miles per gallon. Gulp!

Uh-oh, got to go. The wind has stopped blowing, my turbines have stopped turning and the lights just went out.

The old abandoned garbage truck in the woods.
Photo by Eleanore C. McDade

The Life of a Barn
by
Eleanore C. McDade

Since coming to the mountains I have been overjoyed at the numerous barns that I find on country roads. They are all in different stages of their lives. Now you say, what is the life of a barn?

Just like humans, barns have a life too. Some barely get thru their first year. They can die from wind, fire and man. Many barns live long, productive lives, serving their masters well. They faithfully care for the animals, stock, farm implements, and unwelcome critters, children who play in the rafters, on and on. Only God knows who or what else took up residency at this shelter from time to time.

I pass an old barn quite often in my travels thru the country. It is not a well traveled road. Nevertheless, there stands the barn in its faded red coat, trying to remain straight and tall. Age and the elements have taken their toll. It tries to hold its head up high, but its shoulders of old beams have slowly given way to a stoop.

Yes, the old barn tried for many years not to falter, but wind, rain, heat and cold have weakened its joints and wrinkled its sides of wooden planks. If there ever had been a door, it has long since been gone. The hay loft is open allowing birds to fly freely thru it. Could there be a barn owl somewhere deep in its inner loft? Whoooooo knows? I could find out if I came back in the quiet of the night to listen...

The proud barn remains faithful, protecting whatever its contents may be. Cows give way to a shelter for cars, lawn mowers, bicycles, shovels and rakes. Times change and so do families. Kids grow up, parents become grandparents and finally only a fond memory for the loved ones left behind.

I have come across the remains of many an old barn, gradually returning to the soil from whence it originally came.

Come to think of it, the life of a barn is quite similar to the lives we mortals live. We are born, live our lives, die and return to the soil...dust to dust. Only the memories remain.

So, the next time you're driving in the country and come across an old barn, overgrown with vines and crippled by

249

sagging beams, don't look with disgust and think "why doesn't the property owner tear it down?" For you see, there's life in it yet. The old barn still has a purpose, sheltering critters and perhaps a wise old barn owl.

Unless there's a fire, the barn will slowly crumble into the earth, as Mother Nature allows.

The old red barn after a winter snowfall.
Photo by Eleanore C. McDade

Taxi, Taxi
by
Benetta B. Cook

I was scanning the New York City street for a taxi as I descended the steps of the museum. Just as I reached the sidewalk, one pulled up, discharged its passengers, and I climbed in. I told the young driver, "Bloomingdale's, please."

He looked at me over his shoulder asking, "Where is it?"

Oh, boy--do I have a problem, I thought.

"Continue south on 5th Avenue," I directed him. "Turn left at 59th Street and go to Lexington."

The cabbie explained, "This is my second week driving a taxi. Are you familiar with the Garment District?"

Before I could answer, he continued, "It is a mad house in the 30s along 7th Avenue. If it isn't the pedestrians or another cab, it's a double parked truck unloading fabric or those crazy clothes racks being wheeled in all directions. I barely lasted one day there and vowed I'd never go back. I've been driving on the West Side of Central Park until my last fare."

At this point, we came to a dead stop, caught in a huge traffic jam. "What part of the South is home?" I inquired.

With this, he threw the gear shift into 'park', and turned around to face me. "How do you know I'm from Georgia?" he almost shouted.

"I'm going to broadcast school and thought I had lost my southern drawl. What gave me away?"

"It is the end of some of your sentences that identifies your background," I told him. "Ask one of your instructors to listen and coach you."

Less agitated, he actually said, "Thanks, I'll do that tonight after class."

Just then the traffic began to move and we approached the department store. As I paid him, I noticed a woman practically running out of Bloomingdale's toward us. I opened the cab door, stood, and she darted around me into the back seat. I turned to the driver as she said, "34th and 7th Avenue."

His look was one of pure horror as I mouthed, "You can do it!"

Narrow Escape
by
Benetta B. Cook

Escaping was the only way out. Helen had to do something. The relationship began on a good note, but she just didn't have time now for her friends and they were a priority. After all, this is their senior year in high school. In a few months, many of the girls would go their separate ways. How many more Saturdays would they have together?

Rick lived in Gainesville, where they met at a friend's birthday party. Helen's home was in Dahlonega, about 35 miles northwest. Rick called after the party and they had seen each other several times since. He was getting too serious. Well, what could you expect? He is a junior in college. Yes, she had to tell him she couldn't see him. Mainly this afternoon, but 'Never' as far as she was concerned at the moment.

The phone felt icy cold in her shaking hand as she dialed the long distance number. Finally he answered, and she could hear his voice soften as he realized who was calling.

She is panicked. *Just get it over with,* she thought. "Rick, I've come down with something--I'm running a fever and have a sore throat. "Helen mumbled, "I'm sorry, but I can't go to the movies with you this afternoon."

"Oh, Helen, I'll miss seeing you, but I understand and you need to rest. I'll call you tomorrow. We'll talk about next weekend."

Wow! That was easier than I imagined it would be, Helen thought as she hung up the phone and her heart returned to its normal rate.

Immediately she dialed another number. "Hi, Linda, are the girls still planning to go to the matinee? Great, I'll meet you at the theatre."

It was a romantic comedy and they screamed, laughed, and cried as only teenage girls can. Afterwards they walked to Doug's Drug Store for sodas and hamburgers. They discussed their favorite scenes from the movie, next week's football game, and other school activities.

Just as their food arrived they heard the Greyhound bus come to a stop outside. The store doubles as Dahlonega's bus station. Linda gasped, "Helen, look, there's Rick getting off the bus."

"Stop it, Linda, I told him I'm sick and..." She glanced out the window and there was Rick stepping off the bus with a bouquet in one hand and a box of chocolates in the other.

The smell of the untouched food almost made Helen sick. She was caught in a lie! She couldn't let him see her. What was she going to do?

Linda and the girls met Rick on the sidewalk and stalled him --while Helen raced through the back door of the drug store and sprinted the three blocks home. She shouted to her parents that she would explain everything later as Rick was coming. She had her pajamas and robe on by the time Rick rang the doorbell.

He agreed she looked flushed and attributed it to her fever. All she could think about was how she's deceived him while he was truly concerned about her health.

While Rick talked, Helen became more miserable. By the time her future husband was leaving, the fragrance of the flowers was making her nauseous and mere thoughts of the candy were compounding the situation. As soon as the door closed behind him, she was racing again. This time to the bathroom.

Helen did have a narrow escape, but it wasn't the one she planned that morning.

Reflection:

You are the cause of everything that happens to you. Be careful what you cause.

Author Unknown

Conference Connection
by
Benetta B. Cook

Six months ago, I went to a writer's conference in Chicago; held at the Market Crown Plaza. While there I met with editors from two publishing houses about printing my next mystery. One was really interested, and I recently signed a contract. But that's not the adventure.

At one of the conference breaks, I was talking with several people over coffee in the hospitality suite. One man said, "I was told I could get coffee here, but this group isn't part of the United seminar, is it?"

We told him 'no', but he was welcome to stay.

Everyone was introduced and then he told us, "Your program sounds livelier than mine. I'm coming out of retirement to help the airline launch a new marketing campaign."

Small talk was shared until we returned to our meetings. I though, *He's not bad looking, outdoors type--along the lines of the Marlborough Man. Why can't I remember names? Doesn't make any difference--I won't see him again.*

After lunch, I was stopped by another conference attendee and told Jordan Wiley was looking for me.

That's his name! Wonder what he wants?

At our next break, there he was in the hospitality suite.

He intercepted and guided me away from the others saying, "I'm divorced, have two grown children, and three grandsons. Will you have dinner with me tonight at the Top of the Mart?"

Before I could say anything, he added, "I think we have a future together."

As I was fumbling for words like a teenager, he raised his hand as to ward off any objections, "Just think about it," and away he went.

I had no idea what my program was about that afternoon because Jordan was right about one thing, I did think about dinner and him.

When I left the last writer's session of the day, he was waiting in the hall.

All right, I thought, *this has to end right now, one way or the other.* I looked at him saying, "Come with me."

I led him into an alcove off the main lobby and told him, "Sit down, we need to talk.

"If you are serious, I have some questions. First, do you like animals? I have two cats. "Do you attend church? Because if you don't, we can say good-bye now."

"Last, where do you live?"

"All right," he smiled. "Yes, I like animals. I have a Golden Retriever. He's called *Wheat*. I not only belong to a church, but I'm an elder and I live outside of Seattle, Washington in Port Orchard."

"It'll never work, I live in the Georgia Mountains!"

He started to chuckle, then really laughed, as he reminded me, "The distance is no problem, Elizabeth, I'm with United and can fly anywhere."

Anywhere began with dinner that night at the Top of the Mart, watching the lights of Chicago come to life. Together, our adventure has continued along the east and west coasts. Next week, we are off to the City of Lights, Paris.

Reflection:

Your interpretation of what you see and hear is just that, your interpretation.

Author Unknown

Changing Times
by
Benetta B. Cook

In late August, 1919, U.S. workplaces are overflowing with job applicants recently discharged after World War I. The three Schroder brothers were among the unemployed and not finding work near their Georgia home, they decided to try their luck in the oil fields of Pennsylvania.

Their parents and sisters were seeing them off on the noon train to Atlanta where they would change trains for Philadelphia.

"Let's go," exclaims Jim, the eldest brother, "the conductor has already called all aboard."

"One of you write as soon as you get there," their mother tells them, "I'll be so anxious until I hear."

"Goodbye," everyone is shouting.

"Please send picture postcards of the city," pleads Louise, their younger sister.

"Hey guys, our seats are to the left," says Hank, "and we can each have a window seat. This car is so hot it feels like an oven."

Jim, waving to his parent asks the others, "Did you notice how quiet Papa was all morning? He doesn't look good. Maybe he should retire as Post Master."

"Yeah, and another thing, he's worried we can't find jobs," replies Hank.

Tom stored his suitcase on the overhead rack, fell into his seat, and was thankful he has it to himself. He misses Nancy so badly he is almost sick. His thoughts turn to her.

Am I doing the right thing going away to look for work? I hope she doesn't meet someone else. I wish she could have come to the station to see me off. Oh! When she visited me at college before the war for the Fall Festival I can remember going to pick her up...

"Hank, I'm on my way to Nancy's aunts, I'll meet you at the pavilion in Mohawk Park in about half an hour. Hey, do you mind taking my sax?"

Tom was so excited that Nancy was visiting relatives in Athens, and that he can take her out. Really, he was not supposed to have a date. He and Hank are members of the Festival Dance Band. Since the college rules state students can play in the band to support themselves while at school, the regulations made it clear they cannot dance since the school is a church institution. Tom's philosophy was, I'm going to have fun while Nancy's in town and the college officials will never know.

Tom walked to the Sanders' residence on the corner of Lake Street and Grand Avenue. He had not been in this area of town before and was impressed with the lake, the tree lined streets, and the big homes. His thoughts turned to Nancy and having time, hopefully alone, with her as they walk to the dance.

The Sanders were on the shaded front porch, drinking iced tea. Nancy introduced Tom to her family including her best friend and cousin, Ann. Nancy's uncle was ready to take everyone to Mohawk Park and asked Tom to ride with them in his new Ford.

Nancy was seated next to him and he was glad they could admire the new car because he found himself tongue-tied. She was so beautiful--Tom could hardly believe they were together. Once they reached the pavilion, the Sanders found a table next to the dance floor.

"As often as I can, I'll break away from the band so we can dance. Hank will check on you during his breaks, too," Tom told Nancy before joining the other musicians.

Tom and Nancy realized they were not going to have much time alone, so they tried to bring each other up-to-date on their activities as they danced. Back with the band, Tom observed Nancy had more dance partners than he liked.

At the end of the evening, Tom asks, "Mrs. Sanders, would it be all right if I walk Nancy home?"

"Of course, Tom," answered Aunt Frances. "I imagine Ann and some of her friends would enjoy walking on such a beautiful night, too."

This was not what Tom had in mind and by the time they were ready to leave, their group totaled seven. They discussed who was at the dance, other Festival programs, and what they would do tomorrow. In the morning, Tom would accompany Nancy to church and afterwards, have lunch with the family.

As they approached the lake, Nancy and Tom stop for just a minute to share a kiss.

Sunday went as planned. After lunch, the family remained at the dining table talking, except for Nancy, Tom, and Ann. They had moved to the front porch.

"When will you be coming home?" Nancy asks Tom.

"Not until Thanksgiving. When is that, about six weeks? I wish it could be sooner," he replied.

"That sounds so long. We are lucky I have family here so I could come for the Festival."

"Hey, kids," called Uncle Stan, "it's time to leave for the station--don't want Nancy to miss her train."

Tom saw Nancy off and Stan took him back to the campus. Tom thanked him for being included in the families' weekend, collected his books, and headed to the library.

Monday morning already, Tom thought, *it seems like Nancy was hardly here. Well, I've got to move; it is my turn to go to class. Wish it was Hank's so I could sleep late--tomorrow I can. One advantage to being an identical twin is people can't tell us apart. It's something to go to class, answer role for both of us, and know the professors have no idea which is really present.*

Coming back to their room, Tom called, "Hank, I have some handouts we need to study before next week's test."

"Well, brother, we've another test of sorts to think about. These summons arrived a few minutes ago from the President's office. He wants to see us at four. He's heard we may have been dancing Saturday night."

Hank told the President he didn't dance and was waiting for his twin. Tom softly closed the door as he left the President's office although he preferred to slam it.

Hank jumped up, "Tom, what did you tell him?"

"The truth. What did you think I would tell him? For the truth, I'm suspended for a week, but that's not the worse. The President is sending a copy of the papers to Papa. I have to contact Louise. She has to work with Papa at the post office and intercept that envelope. The suspension is nothing compared to what Papa will do if he finds out.

He'll...

"Tom, wake up. We're coming into the Atlanta station."

Easter Daze
by
Zadie C. McCall

Collectively they were all the same, the Easters of my
childhood. We always dyed eggs, and Mama always saved the
banty eggs for me. In case you don't know about banty eggs,
they are the eggs of a very small breed of chickens, known as
bantams. I can still see those tiny child-sized eggs dyed baby-
blue and pale pink. They were nestled in artificial green grass
and served as a centerpiece for the midday meal.

Mama always made me a new Easter dress. Sometimes I got
new shoes and certainly new anklets to match the dress. Easter
Sundays were chilly in the North Georgia mountains, and you
longed for a beautiful pastel sweater to go with your dress, but
you were not about to cover up your new Easter finery with your
old school sweater or a dull winter coat. So you shivered.

At church we sang "He Arose" with the basses booming out
on the chorus. There was much wiggling around during the
sermon, because we children were eager for the egg hunt to
begin. You knew Mama would fuss if Miz Della Mae Plott shook
her head and *"shushed"* at you, even though Mama said
privately that Miz Della Mae never noticed when her own
grandchildren misbehaved.

But at last came the egg hunt. The sun was warm and bright,
all things had been made new, and Easter was now as it should
be.

After dinner the real fun came. We piled into the car and
went to Grandpa and Grandma Byers' house. In the pasture,
Mama and the aunts, and occasionally a stray uncle, would hide
eggs for my cousins and me to hunt. These egg hunts were much
more fun and much less civilized than the ones at church. Out
there in Grandpa's pasture, it was OK to be loud and boisterous
in the sunshine, and OK to snatch an egg right from under
Oliver 'Jr.'s nose without Miz Fanny to frown at your manners.
Besides when the egg hunt was over, you knew that the eggs
would be divided equally among the cousins and you.

Did I say my Easter's were all the same? Well, not quite. One
stands out among the others. After the family egg hunt, my
cousin Bobbie had one of her wonderful ideas. Bobbie was three
years older than Oliver Jr., Bruce, and I, and we were three

years older than little Naomi. Bobbie, with her skinny legs, skinned knees, freckles, and long brown pigtails, could lure you into all sorts of mischief by calling you *fraidy cat*. So on this particular Easter Sunday, Bobbie and three of the *fraidy cats*, me included, started out to walk the dirt road which made a loop from the highway and crossed Crawford's Creek. We knew we were never to go past the bridge on Crawford's Creek, never to go on the highway, but Bobbie and the three *fraidy cats* went anyway.

About half way down the highway, a strap on Bobbie's sandal broke, and she decided it was too far to go back the way we came and too far to complete the journey to the store and back to Grandpa's from the opposite end of the loop. The only thing to do, Bobbie decided, was to wade the creek and take a shortcut back to Grandpa's through the cornfields. The boys rolled up their pants, took off their socks and shoes, and squealing at the unexpected coldness of the creek in April, made it safely to the other side. Bobbie crossed over, but I was having trouble with my shoes and socks. Oops! In plunked a shoe, and in retrieving it, I forgot to hold up my skirt and got the whole front of it wet. To my horror, all of the pleats came out of my skirt. I had seen the trouble Mama had went to in getting those pleats pinned down with straight pins. She stood for what seemed like hours at the ironing board. But Bobbie told *Fraidy Cat* to stop crying, that we would slip past Grandpa's and go up the lane to her house and dry off. Bruce and Oliver went off to play whatever boys play, and Bobbie and I sat on the end of the porch in the four o'clock sunshine and dried my skirt. Our feet dangled off the edge, and I flapped my skirt up and down to speed up the drying process. It was only a little damp when Mama came out to Grandpa's woodlot and called me. Time to go home.

Mama said, "How did you get so dirty? And just look at that skirt; I was hoping that material would hold a pleat better than that!"

The next day I was out of school with the sniffles. As I played happily with my paper dolls, Mama said, "I don't know why you have to catch every cold that comes along."

What Are The Chances?
by
George Houdeshel

"Are you crazy? Our little club can't come up with a gift suitable for the Queen!!" This was the first response to my suggestion that the Kiwanis Club of Smyrna, Georgia present the Queen of England with a gift on her visit to the United States in September 1957.

As I pressed on with my wonderful idea, the club members were silent. The futility of such a grandiose idea would surely sink into his brain, they thought.

"What would be a suitable gift?," I asked. No suggestions were forthcoming.

Finally, Al, a past-president of our club, said, "Do you know what elaborate gifts, the Queen receives?"

His question left me stunned, so I dropped the subject. I needed time to think about that!

The newspapers were full of "Queen Stories," and one mentioned young Prince Charles. Suddenly, a solution for the proper gift popped into my head. My six year old son, Dean, had a child's football uniform and he was also about the same age as Prince Charles. Prince Philip, the Queen's husband, enjoyed sports. In fact, the Queen's entourage was to attend a University of Maryland football game so that Prince Philip could see first hand what American college football was all about. Wow! We could give the Queen a football uniform for her young son Charles, and one of our club members actually sold them! What a great idea, and one we could afford!!

Maybe we could give the gift on behalf of Kiwanis International? I called Kiwanis headquarters in Chicago and asked if they were planning any activity or gift during the Queen's visit. They were not. Good!! Would they permit our Smyrna club to make a gift in behalf of Kiwanis International? They said they would let me know in a few days. They returned my call and said that if it was acceptable to the Queen's Visit Committee at the British Embassy, they would approve it.

Now, for the first time, I realized how complicated this idea could become! But, I was determined. I called the British Embassy.

The call went something like this: "The British Embassy, Secretary Johnson speaking; to whom do you wish to speak?"

"I'm calling in behalf of Kiwanis International. We would like to present the Queen with a gift during her visit to the United States."

"May I please have your name and from where you are calling?"

"This is George Houdeshel and I am calling from Smyrna, Georgia."

"Would you please spell you name, and repeat where you are located?"

I spelled my name and repeated Smyrna, Georgia. She asked me to "hold."

A very formal voice came on the line. "This is the First Secretary to the Ambassador. I understand that you wish to present a gift to Her Majesty during her forthcoming visit."

"Yes," I replied, "from Kiwanis International at the University of Maryland football game!"

"All of the activities for Her Majesty's attendance at the University of Maryland are being handled by the university. You need to contact them. Thank you for your call."

I called the university and was told that Maryland's Governor McKeldin was in charge of that day's activities. I called the Governor's Office in Annapolis, Maryland , and was told that the Maryland Secretary of State, Mr. McCormick, was handling the details for the Governor. I called Secretary McCormick's office and learned Mr. McCormick was a member of Kiwanis, and the Governor was also a member. Good!! After I explained that I had the approval of Kiwanis International and had spoken with the British Embassy, Mr. McCormick's secretary said I would receive a letter explaining how the gift was to be prepared for shipment to England.

Having obtained the necessary approvals, the Kiwanis Club of Smyrna sprang into action! A *Queen's Gift* committee was formed and assignments for the necessary tasks were made. They were:

1. procure the football uniform
2. package the gift
3. procure tickets to the game
4. make travel arrangements for my wife and I to go to Maryland

5. write appreciation letters to those involved in obtaining the approvals

6. prepare a story for the news media.

Everyone worked hard to insure that all tasks were performed well and in a timely manner.

We had wonderful seats in the stadium very close to the Queen's Royal Box. The gift was presented to the Queen, wrapped and sealed, at a reception following the game. It was a wonderful once-in-a-life-time experience. The little Kiwanis Club of Smyrna, Georgia, had presented the Queen of England with a gift!!

Postscript: I wrote the following letter to the Queen in 2010 and received this letter in reply.

BUCKINGHAM PALACE

11th March, 2010

Dear Mr. Houdeshel,

The Queen wishes me to write and thank you for your letter.

Her Majesty thought it kind of you to recall your memories of her visit to the University of Maryland in 1957, and of your efforts to arrange a gift for The Queen.

Her Majesty was pleased to know that you have such happy memories of her attendance at the University football game which you watched with your late wife, and I am to thank you once again for your thoughtful letter.

Yours Sincerely

Mary Gouise.

Lady-in-Waiting

Mr. G. Houdeshel

263

Dear Queen Elizabeth,   January 22, 2010

I recently read a book about the history of The University of Maryland, and it brought back a wonderful memory - Your visit to the university in 1957 when you and Prince Philip attended a football game.

I had a very small part to play on that wonderful day - I was 29 years old and president of the Smyrna, Georgia Kiwanis Club, {Smyrna is a small town just north of Atlanta).

I was wonderfully excited about your visit and wanted to do something!! Maybe we could give The Queen a gift? But, we were a small club with limited resources and The Queen would be getting elaborate gifts from several sources. Then, a thought, maybe we could give The Queen a small football uniform for Prince Charles. (We had a club member who sold them).

I called Kiwanis International Headquarters in Chicago and asked if we could give this gift from Kiwanis International. After several calls to various officials, I got permission, if I got permission from The University of Maryland. I called the University (I am a graduate - class of 1953) and was given permission, if I got permission from Maryland's Governor Theodore McKeldin.

Governor McKeldin was to be The Queen's Host for the game. I called his office and was referred to Maryland's Secretary-of-State, Mr. McCormick (He would be handling the details for the Governor). I called his office, and after several telephone conversations, was given permission, if the British Embassy in Washington would agree. I called the Embassy, talked to several secretaries, and received their permission with instructions for packaging.

I was very delighted !!!

My wife and I drove to Maryland for the game. We had very good seats and got a good look at The Queen and Prince. We also enjoyed the game (Maryland won!).

I received a very nice "Thank you" letter from your secretary. My wife has passed away, but I thank you so much for a great highlight in my wonderful life.

Love and Prayers

George Houdeshel   236 Buck Snort Road, Blairsville, Georgia   USA

Listen to Your Momma
by
Juanita J. Schneider

The wash tub was half-full when Momma yelled, "Kids, lets get those crawdads up here now! I want you cleaned up; a famous man is coming to town and I want you to see him."

I looked down at the tub of squirming crawdads, and then up at Momma. She was standing on the front porch, wiping her hands on the colorful feed-sack apron tied loosely around her waist. Momma didn't budge from that spot until she saw us walk toward the house, she wouldn't be making a second request!

We had learned over the years to listen and do what Momma asked. She was the mover and disciplinarian of our home, keeping all five of her children in line, learning this ability of motherhood when she was but six years old. Her parents divorced in 1917. Mom had to take over the responsibility of her two younger sisters, ages four and two, while her mother worked to support them.

In unison, we pulled in our crude home-made fishing poles, a long pliable twig with heavy white string tied in a notched-out section at the tip. At the end of the string was a firmly tied hunk of bacon fat that teased the many crawdads found in our cool, fast moving creek that ran next to our home.

"You cousins, come on too; your momma expects you to come along."

The five cousins pulled in their fishing poles. They too had become accustomed to doing what Momma said.

Looking at one another, we walked toward the house with the heavy tub. I asked "Who is this famous person? Who's so important that we should stop fishing?"

My oldest sister nudged us on, "You'll see; Nita, now let's get to the house."

Washing our faces, hands and arms in the small, red-rimmed, enamel wash bowl that was sitting on the back porch linoleum covered table. Grabbing the raggedy towel from the nail hook, we dried off the water. We put on freshly cleaned and ironed clothes.

My brothers and sisters, with our cousins who lived next door, all ten of us, began our walk to Englewood, almost two miles away. Warm weather and lots of sunshine gave us a pleasant walk to Winner Road, the main thoroughfare going into our small town. We loved walking together, always finding something to talk about or stopping along the way saying 'hi' to friendly folks working in their gardens.

The sidewalk was crowded with people when we arrived and sister stated, "You little ones get on up there in front so you can see well".

"Excuse me, sir, excuse me" we said, as we edged our way to the front, poking our heads through to get a clear view.

"How's this going to work, Sis? Where's that famous person?" we asked as the older folks stifled their giggling and smiled down at all these kids that appeared out of nowhere. I wondered why everyone was in such a happy and festive mood.

"Here comes a bunch of cars, is this the famous person Mom was talking about?"

The string of cars, flags waving, slowed down as they neared. We saw a gentleman in a fancy blue suit sitting on the back seat of a shiny black convertible.

Beaming a broad smile the gentleman waved his hat and yelled "Hello all". Looking down at us kids he yelled with a tilt to his voice "hello children, so good to see you!"

Jumping up and down, getting into the festive mood, we yelled back "Hello, hello", as we waved to the happy man. The car moved eastward toward town and he was gone.

We moved slowly away from the road and started walking home. "Was that the famous man?" I asked my sister.

"Yes, that's the famous man, my sister stated once again. That's our President, Harry Truman and the First Lady."

This was his first visit home after the ending of World War II.

NINE YEARS LATER

My friend, Carol Lee, and I usually arrived at high school early so she could find a parking place on the street for her huge 1949 'fast back' Packard. Most mornings we took a walk around the block before the start of classes. One morning we were busy talking and laughing when we noticed someone walking briskly towards us. In unison we wondered out loud, "Is this who we think it is???"

Tipping his hat in our direction the man said "Good morning, young ladies!"

Sure enough, it was President Harry Truman taking his famous morning walk around Independence on this early morning of April 1954.

"Good morning, Mr. President!" I told the President about that day many years ago when Momma had called us in from play, making us clean up to see him pass by after the war ended. How excited and pleased I was that he waved and said hello to us.

He smiled broadly remembering the day. As he started back on his walk to his home two blocks away, he stated, "You girls have a good day."

Smiling and looking to me he said, "Your momma's a smart lady; always listen to your momma."

Reflection:

"The Buck Stops Here!"
    Sign on Harry Truman's Desk

My Special Encounter
by
Rhonda Kay Brigman

I met a little old man, where I stopped in front of his run-down trailer to look at a few things he sat out for sale by the road. He came out and greeted me warmly, and we dickered on prices as I bought a couple small items.

Both being the friendly sort, we talked awhile and he began to tell me a little about his life. His name was Clint. It seems he had cancer and had refused all treatment, with the exception of his pain pills. His family continued to argue with him about taking Chemo, but he declined.

He said he desired to have some quality of life to enjoy, as he awakens every day. Though he appeared not to have much in the way of worldly goods, he did have one very important thing that he counts on daily. To hear him tell it His Lord will see him through that day, and as many days ahead as the Lord deems fit.

He considered himself blessed and wanting for nothing, except for his boy to come back to the Lord. He says the Lord already saved his boy from dying and brought him home safely from Iraq.

He tells me of a time several months ago, when his boy was lost in Iraq while on duty. He received a knock on the door and the Armed Service's men told him his boy was Missing In Action. Though he says he suffered greatly, he knew His Lord would watch over his boy. Just three days later, the Armed Service's men pulled up in front of his trailer again. This time they brought good news, as they told him his boy and two other soldiers had been found alive and well. Though he knew a sniper's bullet, a roadside bomb, or any other deadly injury could have occurred, he was comforted in knowing his boy had been under the protection of His Lord.

Now that his boy had been sent home to him, he had been talking to him about coming back home again. He told me he wasn't just referring to his coming back home safe to his family, but coming back home to His Lord.

He said he had some successful discussions with his son so far, and his son had begun thinking about everything. Though his son was sure his life had been spared, he was still angry at God for things that had gone wrong in his life.

As the little old man continued to speak, he kept apologizing for wiping his tears aside. He smiled at me and gave me a deep look with the most piercing blue eyes. He kept his gaze on me all the while he spoke, as if he was looking into my soul. He thanked me for listening to him and having been an encouragement to him. We gave each other a hug, though we had been strangers before that day.

Though I assured him that he and I had met at this particular time, for this reason or others unknown to us right then, he thanked me repeatedly anyway. I promised him I would pray for him and talk with the Lord about his situation. However, no matter how hard I tried, I could not convince him that I was the one that had received the blessing that day. Maybe, we both did!

I pray this true story blesses you today and throughout your week, and that you remember when you encounter someone at any time, they may need a word of encouragement, a listening ear, and a small amount of your time... even at a yard sale.

Reflection:

"Write it on your heart that everyday is the best day in the year."
Ralph Waldo Emerson

'Til Death Do Us Part ...Really?

by
Rhonda Kay Brigman

As long as history is documented, couples that delve into a more permanent relationship; i.e.: marriage; find they will have many hills, valleys, mountains, and sometimes even deserts and empty plains! We all know what these descriptive nouns represent in a relationship, just as much as we know how our lives intertwine. As two or more lives are intertwined, the resulting cause & affect that erupts between us, and all around us. It is evidenced in the many directions our lives take both collectively together and independently apart. As we proceed down the many roads that ordinary living can bring to each of us, the one thing we can count on is change.

Change comes to each and everyone of us almost on a daily basis. Whether it is in the very small things of life that we hardly even notice, or the major things that can wreak havoc and twist our lives from what we know into what we no longer recognize. Change can be our friend when things turn out for the better... but oh watch out, when that change rears its ugly head, like an attack of a tornado ripping through an event or otherwise normal circumstance. You've heard the old expression, "the calm before the storm?" Well, that's when we feel like things are just going too smoothly and we begin to fear that it just can't continue. However, when we know my new expression: "the calm after the storm"; that's when we feel like a hurricane has torn up every existing avenue we've ever known, and 'battening down the hatches' went flying out the window with it!

When this whirlwind happens unexpectedly, we feel like we have been belted in the stomach and landed on our knees, then we slowly lift our heads and see if the coast is clear once again. We don't always know what we will find as we look up, but we always know it will be quite different from what we knew before. Most people call these times the 'trials' in their lives, and though shell-shocked and at a loss many times, they slowly recover as they stagger on the path that will take them back to some kind of normalcy.

Couples always start out like they are on the same path, though that is not really so. As we date and get to know one another better, we let small glimpses of our 'true personality' shine through to test the potential partner of our life. As that becomes accepted without too much resistance, we then can get past the courtship phase and on into the real joining of our personalities; where we see if we can 'totally be with one another'. As we relax into a meshing of a relationship that allows each person to be who they really are, we then either accept that person or become turned off and wonder how we were ever attracted to them in the first place. If it is the latter outcome, we go on about our way and begin looking towards a new relationship. If we feel we are ready to join back into the dating pool, it's because we have conquered our self-confidence once more. However, if we have decided we will continue with the original relationship and have begun to accept the whole person we are with, (their quirks and all), then we will continue to grow together in hopes of a more lasting and permanent relationship.

We always think relationships should last forever; however, they do not always. Actually, very few of the relationships we encounter throughout our lives will last forever and always. We as individuals grow not only as a child up into an adult, but we also grow in the demands and boundaries of our relationships as we mature. Mature is a funny word, is it not? Not every individual person grows into maturity at the same rate; some never reach full maturity, as it turns out. But that's OK, as not all individuals need nor want fully, matured individuals in their lives. Again, I ask you what is a fully, matured individual? Well, it appears that is simply a matter of perspective like so many other issues in life. Wouldn't many of us feel 'saddled' with a partner that we were attracted to in our high school years now? That is not to say that they would have been wrong for us then; but, simply to say they may not have grown at the same rate and time, as we have to this current date.

Each of us is influenced by the events and 'trials' that occur in our individual lives. That, along with the mental IQ and wisdom of each individual, has an affect on each person's development in their life. Our life choices, including our interests, careers, hobbies, and even the areas and time we give to volunteerism shape the type of life we have. As we look back at our lives, we sometimes can't even begin to realize how we got to where we are today. Today we never even had a clue we would end up on the path of our growth.

The paths of our lives, be it individually or co-relationally, have come to be as it is this very moment, due to our choices, our failures, and our successes. Who is to say what a failure is? Who is to say what a success is? If each of us had not made the choices we did, at the time that we made them, what affect would that have had on where we are at, right this very moment? We will never really know; *or will we?*

That too is yet to be revealed in our lives as we continue to grow and mature, and then even that depends on how long we live, and progress with the years ahead of us.

Life is ever-changing, and I truly believe that is the way it is supposed to be. The one thing we can all count on is *Change*; that is, if nothing else changes to change that event, time or place. Guess by now, you get the idea. Be open to the changes in your life...as they will truly spell out your life.

Reflection:

Divorces are final long before they go to court.

Author Unknown

All Hallows Eve
by
Larry Casey

She gripped the steering wheel tightly, as if the tighter she squeezed the more control there was over the torrential rain slashing against her windshield. So it was no wonder Laura O'Brien breathed a sigh of relief, when finally, she turned onto the long twisting driveway leading up to the family's ninety year old Victorian home.

As she negotiated the twisting dirt road in the driving rain, Laura reflected on how this would be the first Halloween she would be spending alone. Sean, her husband of eighteen years, was in Seattle on business. Because O'Briens' nearest neighbor was a half-mile away the twins, Tess and Phillip were enjoying Halloween with classmates in town so they could "trick and treat."

Laura was jolted back to reality when the car caught a rut in the road. "Have to remember to ask Sean to put some stone in that hole when he gets back this weekend," she told herself.

The other thing that rut brought to mind was the motion light on the garage should have come on by this time.

When she finally came to a stop in front of the garage door, Laura pressed the remote control to open the door and at least light up the garage. Nothing happened. She pressed the button several times and then decided it was useless, because the power was out. Probably caused by the storm.

"Well this is just great," she complained. "Halloween and I don't have any lights in a haunted house."

Legend has it, that eighty-years ago, Clyde Northrup murdered his wife Mildred in a fit of rage over her supposed infidelity to him. He buried her under a chestnut tree in the back yard. As the story goes, Clyde was so guilt-ridden over what he had done, that within six months, he hung himself in the living room. An empty quart of Old Bushmills Irish Whiskey was found near the body by the police.

The legend further informs those interested or otherwise, that old Clyde, when he met his Maker, had his soul sent to roam the empty halls of that house, and reflect on the terrible thing he had done. He was to remain there until a suitable place could be found for him down below. So, according to legend he or his ghost anyway, has been there ever since. That is, until the O'Briens moved in and refurbished the whole place.

All this folklore did not cross Laura's mind at the present time, as she rummaged through the glove compartment, eventually finding the small flashlight they kept there for just such an emergency.

Holding the unread *New York Times* over her head, Laura got out of the car and ran to the door, as she tried to dodge the numerous puddles between the car and the front porch. She was searching through her purse for the door key, made difficult by trying to hold the small flashlight at the same time.

Suddenly Laura stopped, hearing the slight creaking of the door. It was already open. *I know I locked that door when I left this morning.*

The first feeling of foreboding entered her senses. "There may be someone in my house," she said under her breath, not wanting whoever it might be to discover her presence.

Laura went to a hutch in the hallway, and reached for a box of candles she had remembered placing there last Christmas. Lighting one and stuffing the rest in her raincoat pocket, she kicked off her wet shoes and cautiously began a room by room search. She made her way through the downstairs living area, including the closet and discovered nothing.

As she started up the stairs, Laura noticed an odd odor, very faint, but unmistakably, the acrid smell of sulfur. Mentally noting the various appliances, including heating and air conditioning equipment, she could think of nothing that would emit the odor of sulfur. While she was pondering this dilemma, power to the house was restored, and the total darkness gave way to brilliant light. But an instant before this happened, Laura thought she saw a transparent blue-like figure, with no definite shape, rather just floating.

"What was that?" She said aloud. "This is getting a little weird."

Continuing up the stairs Laura sensed the odor becoming stronger.

She checked the three bedrooms and found them empty. It wasn't until she reached the storage closet at the end of the hall that the odor was so strong it made her eyes sting. It was as if a force of evil was surrounding her. She was aware of groans and sighs almost like background music, not really knowing where it was coming from.

Then, just as suddenly as the lights had come on, the hall was once again thrown into total darkness. The transparent form immediately became visible, hovering between the top of the door and the ceiling, constantly changing shape and size. Laura sensed it was protecting or indicating something inside the closet.

With trembling hands, she groped around in the dark until her shaking hand found the doorknob. Tentatively, she turned the knob and slowly opened the door. Laura was mystified at what happened next. She discovered nothing on the lower shelves. While standing on a small footstool, she was able to have a view of the top shelf. Lying on a shoebox, was a newspaper clipping that seemed to be glowing in the dark. Cautiously, Laura reached for the article and no sooner had she retrieved it from the closet than light returned to the house.

She looked closely at the clipping now brown with age, and saw that it was a photograph of a young woman. In the right upper corner was the name *Beatrice* scribbled in pencil.

"This had to have been Clyde's wife!" exclaimed Laura.

Instantly, the house was once again drenched in darkness. The blue transparent form became visible as it began moving. As if mesmerized, Laura began to follow the form that seemed to provide just enough light for her to see where she was going.

The form led her down the stairs, along the hall and into the kitchen, eventually floating to a stop in front of the microwave oven. Laura stood there for a moment and then instinctively seemed to know what to do.

She opened the door of the oven and the form subliminally told her to place the newspaper clipping inside. Laura reached in and placed the photograph, gently, almost reverently in the middle of the oven.

No sooner had she removed her hand than the lights came on. She could no longer see the form, but she felt an icy-cold chill across her body and knew that the form had entered the oven. The door instantly closed and Laura seemed to know what to do next.

Setting the timer for five minutes, she pressed the *start* button. There was a tremendous sound of static electricity, and an explosion as a hole tore through the back of the oven, through the wall and into the back yard. Laura threw open the door just in time to see a bolt of white-hot lightning shooting straight up in the air to a height of what seemed to be nearly a mile. Then slowly, it made a huge arc and headed back to earth.

As it neared the surface, the ground opened up and the bolt of lightning, now fire-engine red, dove directly into the chasm. Instantly the ground closed as if it had never separated. The only thing remaining was a strong odor of burnt sulfur.

Laura returned to the kitchen and cautiously opened the oven door. The photograph of Beatrice was untouched and rested right where Laura had placed it minutes before. As she watched in amazement, the time-worn piece of parchment burst into flames and became hundreds of pieces of black ash.

Later, when Laura had sufficiently recovered her senses, she sat at the kitchen table sipping Chamomile tea, and pondering all that had happened in the last hour. After some reflection, she came to one conclusion: She would tell no one of this event because, number one, no one would believe it. And two, all the evidence is gone. She finished her tea, took a hot shower and went to bed.

Green-Eyed Envy
by
Ellie Dobson

When I was a little girl, I had a favorite aunt. Her name was Aunt Alta.

I went to her house often because she lived nearby. Her home was like a special getaway place for me. Aunt Alta taught me everything I know about cooking, cleaning house and sewing. I spent many hours watching her do all of the above, and as she worked she explained everything she was doing to me.

Sewing was her specialty. Aunt Alta even made her husband's shirts and suits. One summer she had me try on the beginning pattern of a little girl's dress. Every visit out came the dress and pattern and I stood still as she pinned away. First the sleeves, next the sides and finally she begin to pin up the hem, all the while I'm beaming inside thinking this dress was for me. When the dress was near completion, she told me she was making the dress for my cousin Carol, and since we were the same size she used me as a model.

After that statement my heart sank and I regretted every time I had to stand still for that darn dress to be pinned in place. I was so disappointed, and so envious of my cousin Carol knowing she was getting a dress I wanted so much. I was so glad when I could finally visit without that dress coming out.

Christmas morning of 1948, as we opened presents and checked our stockings, I saw a package under the tree from Aunt Alta. Imagine my surprise when I opened the box and there was *the dress*! Aunt Alta had pulled off the same trick with my sister Linda, and my cousin Carol. I was so ashamed of myself for a very long time for thinking the way I did all through the Holidays. Later in life I realized what a clever trick she pulled off.

Reflection:

"Blessed is he who expects nothing, for he shall never be disappointed-"

Jonathan Swift

Biographies

Judy Abercrombie

Judy was born in Chicago where her folks had settled after emigrating from Poland. She was reared in Florida, finally earning her Master's Degree from the University of North Florida by age fifty due to three kids and a full-time secretarial job keeping her from attending college during the day. Her jobs varied from typing Alan Shepard's countdown to teaching junior high biology.

Judy has written articles providing helpful hints for wildlife magazines and homemaker journals. These articles were based on "make-do" and "quick-fix" projects that demonstrated the many uses to which milk jugs, paper towels, pantyhose and petroleum jelly could be put.

Her sports and hobbies in the past were physically challenging and competitive—motorcycle-racing, hunting, fishing and canoeing. She says that age and ailments have slowed her down, forcing her to replace those hobbies with more sedate choices, which leaves her to rely on memories for experiencing the fun times she can no longer participate in. She enjoys playing the banjo and guitar as she participates locally with "The Red Dirt Road Band" as her repertoire expands.

Naomi P. Bastow

Naomi has been writing since she was nine years old, while a student at the Lankenau Hospital School of Nursing she was the editor of classes' yearbook. She earned a BA in education and a MA in psychology and counseling.

While working as a nursing instructor she wrote a food and travel column in several newspapers and magazines, including Cruising World, Traveltips, and Freighter Travel. In 2009 she published her first book titled, Elizabeth and the Old Fool and Other Stories.

Naomi has been married fifty-four years to her husband Bill and they have one daughter. The author hobbies are writing, reading, travel and cooking. She lives with her husband and five cats in the mountains of Western North Carolina.

William V. "Bill" Bastow

Bill is a veteran of WW II, a graduate of Rutgers University. At the age of fifteen he joined the Sea Scouts and developed an intense in ships, the sea, and sailing.

Taking early retirement, Bill and his wife Naomi and boyhood pal moved aboard the 31' cutter sailboat. Sea Fever, and explored the Atlantic coast between Down East Maine, Chesapeake Bay, Florida and the Bahamas. Having "swallowed the anchor" they now reside in the mountains of Western North Carolina.

Bill's previously published work consists of a treatise on the History of the Glass Industry in the monthly Owens Illinois Outlook, plus occasional irate newspaper "Letter To The Editor" or to an offending politician.

James L. "Sonny" Boyer

Retired South Florida Building Contractor, Scoutmaster for Troop 210 in Miami. Sonny relocated his family to the mountains in 1978 after being born into a pioneer South Florida family.

He started his writing at ten years of age, as reporter on a neighborhood weekly newspaper (Echo), during the WWII. He published several articles in the Miami High school newspaper. His love of animals, art and the outdoors rewarded him with an article about an owl published in the Florida Wildlife Magazine while still a teenager.

Sonny published forty-four pages in the seventh edition, volume seven, of the "American Boyer's" that was taken from "Elias Boyer and Descendants", a publication compiled as genealogist for the Boyer family.

His first serious attempt at writing was a historical novel, "The Pot" which was published in 2009, after twelve years of research about the now extinct Calusa Indians. They inhabited South Florida at the time of Columbus. Sonny writes the newsletter for his Church, "The Church Without Walls."

His next book is almost ready and will be about some of his hunting and fishing experiences, with emphasis on how to participate safely.

Sandra Laurie Boyer

Former Delta Airline Stewardess, retired high school biology teacher, member National Honor Society at Dan McCarthy High School in Ft. Pierce FL., graduated St Petersburg Jr. College, B.E.D. from University Miami, science degree from North Georgia College, member of State of Georgia Curriculum Committee for designing science curriculum for Georgia students, 1996 –1997. Chairman of Union County Republican Party 1997- 1999.

After years of grading papers and proof-reading my husbands papers, I decided to attempt my own project with "My Kids," a story about some of my students and experiences during my teaching career.

Rhonda Kay Brigman

Rhonda Kay was born and grew up in Lumberton, North Carolina, until at 1tenyears-old she was moved to Apopka, FL. Following relocation, she excelled throughout her school years and ensuing life for 43 years. Finally with life changes and circumstance, she happily moved to Blairsville, GA in 2005.

Since her retirement, she has been involved in the Georgia Mountain Writers Club, her church, and daily activities of home and hearth. She has been interested in writing since those school days, writing many stories, poetry, prose and articles. She has been published in various newspapers, along with many school related resources such as "The Blue Feather." She continues to be published in local papers such as *North Georgia News, Towns Herald, Franklin Press, Macon County News, Cherokee Sentinel* and *View From The Top Newsletter.*

Her retirement days are busy with many interests, especially writing in various genres such as creative fiction, murder mysteries, poetry and prose, along with some children and young adult works. She plans to publish and market her own work in the near future. You have read a excerpt "Innocence Lost" in the book. Look for "Innocence Lost" on the local book store and library shelves soon.

jillie1@windstream.net   petnannyrkb@hotmail.com

Faye A. Brown

Faye was born in 1942 on Marco Island, Florida. At the age of thirteen she moved with her parents to Naples. On December 4, 1961, she was united in marriage to Clarence M. Brown, and together they lived in Marathon, in the Florida Keys for two years before moving back to Naples where they raised four children. In 1991, she published a booklet entitled "Caroline." In 2003, she and her husband moved to Blairsville, Georgia. This past year, She published a book entitled "Weeks Family Connections." This book is stories of her Weeks and Nunez family who came to the New World, via England; and their lives are interwoven with some of our countries earliest beginnings since 1636. The stories of "Ginger" and "A Kidnapping that Went Awry" are partly fiction mixed with a few facts!

W. Franklin Boulineau

Franklin was born in 1936 on a farm in Jefferson County, Georgia. His growing up years on the farm provided a good education about strong working people and about nature.

He attended two years at Emory University-at-Oxford followed by three years with the Army Security Agency in Japan. Later he earned a B.S. Degree in Biology and a Masters Degree in Chemistry at Georgia Southern University. His last seventeen employed years were as a principal in the Richmond County, Georgia Public School System. Boulineau lives his retirement years with his wife in the mountains of Hiawassee Georgia and is the author Granddaddy Joe. franklinboulineau@yahoo.com

Larry Casey

Larry has written his own anthology containing thirty homilies he has given over a period of fifteen years. In his preparation of these works, he has attempted to contemporize the Scriptures to reflect Christian living in today's secular society. Casey has described events in his personal life that identify with difficult issues each of us confront in struggling to maintain a Christian attitude in our families, workplace, and community.

He is an ordained deacon in the Catholic Church, holding Masters' Degrees in Theology and Social work.

Larry is a co-founder of this Georgia Mountain Writers Club along with Ellie Dobson.

Benetta B. Cook

My professional background is fashion marketing and education with writing experience in advertising, promotions and curriculum development. I do some editing.

She is from Tulsa, OK, married, has three daughters, thirteen grandchildren, and two great-grandchildren. She is a graduate of Oklahoma State University and the University of North Texas. She currently resides in Blairsville, GA with her husband.

Eleanor "Ellie" Dobson

I started off as the Girls Sports Editor in high school. As the years progress, in 1979 thru 1982 I wrote a monthly column for the Elk's club bulletin. I became the newsletter editor for an organization called Parents Without Partners. I also won a Soap Opera writing contest sponsored by the Gainesville Times newspaper, wrote many Letters To The Editor and was published by The Atlanta Journal and Constitution , The Gainesville Times and our own North Georgia News.

I have been published in The 400 Edition, The Black Bear, Southern Poetry, Poems of Great America, Yarn Spinner, and Mountains Meditations.

I have also been teaching a writing class with the OASIS program for ten years, and I am the co-founder of our Georgia Mountain Writers Club. I have taken courses at John C. Campbell Folk School, Long Ridge Writers Group, and many writers workshops throughout the years.

I love watching members and students realize their potential and getting their own books published. I am currently working on two novels.

287

Catherine Fiser

I am presently a retiree, having lived in Florida, before coming "home." Blairsville has been home to me and my husband for twenty-one years.

Once I was a teacher, school librarian, a mother of four and now "Gram" of twelve.

I paint and write and am inspired by the wealth of talent around me. Originally from New Haven, Connecticut I have been welcomed in the South for our fifty-two years of marriage.

Philip W. Gatlin

Phil's parents were from Georgia and moved to Miami in the mid-1920s, looking for work during the Depression. Phil was born in 1937 and grew up in the Allapattah area of Northwest Miami. He was in the Marine Corp. Reserves before going on active duty with the U.S. Air Force in 1955.

Phil worked in various jobs, changing his career path along the way.

Phil moved from the Atlanta area to Blairsville, GA in 2009. He was married to Carolyn Mullaly Gatlin for 48 years before she passed away in 2010. Phil has six daughters, 14 grandchildren and 7 great-grandchildren.

Phil joined the Georgia Mountain Writers Club in 2011 due to his growing interest in writing. He is currently working on his memoirs and a novel.

Paul and Christine Goings

Paul and Christy are a special couple in many ways. They both have Multiple Sclerosis. When you read 'Lucky in Love,' the Goings thought it was important that you know a few things about their life. In 2007 this story was first published in the MS Focus magazine. On numerous occasions, in different ways the Multiple Sclerosis Foundation had helped them out. It was printed in hopes that others may know that even if you have MS, there are good things that can come your way. The editor of this magazine called the Goings and interviewed them over the phone. Chris the editor was able to understand Christy better than Paul because of his peculiar Mississippi southern drawl. She was of great help to the Goings and they felt it only honorable to mention her and the magazine's name. "Lucky in Love' is their story.

James Goode 1920-2008

Truly a member of the "Greatest Generation." Seaman before WW II, joining Charles Chennault and his "Flying Tigers" in Burma as Sergeant in US Army Air Force and ending his career of public service as Chief of Police for Orlando Police Department. Jim retired to the mountains in 1999 where he fought the ravages of Parkinson's disease as he compiled his memoirs into a journal he called, "Soldier Sailor Lawman." Two of those witty tales are included in our anthology as he was a participant in the Georgia Mountain Writers Club.

George Houdenshel

George served in Army Air Corps. He served in Panama in 1946, and participated in Berlin air lift. Receiving an Engineering Degree from the University of Maryland, he was later employed Lockheed Aerospace of GA for thirty years. George engineered the development of Executive Information Systems (EIS) and co-authored two books on EIS, currently President of Smyrna Georgia Kiwanis, Senior Warden of his church and volunteer mentor to Union County schools. He also stays busy serving as Stephen Minister and teaches Bridge for the older adult program Oasis program.

Nadine Justice

Nadine divides her time between a mountaintop cottage in Blairsville and her home in Atlanta. She enjoys a successful career as an Interior Designer. Her design work has been published in Better Homes and Gardens and in Atlanta Custom Home magazines. She grew up in West Virginia and is a coal miner's daughter. She is currently writing a book of memoir stories.

Ralph Kwiatkowski

Ralph served in the US Navy and graduated from the University of Toledo, OH with a BS in Mathematics. He worked many years in the insurance industry as a Large Property Underwriter.

He moved with his family to the mountains in 2002 residing in Blairsville, GA.

He loves to write short-fiction and humorous stories.

Best Wishes

Ralph

Zadie Cunningham McCall

Zadie was born in Towns County, Georgia. She is a retired elementary teacher from the Douglas County, Georgia school system. Interested in the written word from an early age, Zadie helped publish a school newspaper with fourth and fifth graders for seventeen years.

After Zadie's husband, who was also in education, died, she returned to the N. GA Mountains and resides in Blairsville with her 22 year old cat, Sage. (Yes, 22!)

She is mainly interested in writing for children but also dabbles in poetry and short stories. She has published a book, *The Weather on Blackberry Lane,* that is part of the widely used Waterford Early Reading Program. She also has magazine and newspaper credits.

Eleanore C. McDade

Her writing career started when she wrote for her junior and senior high school paper. When she entered the workforce, she wrote a weekly newsletter for the company and also captured and distributed photographs for a monthly magazine. For many years she also wrote the monthly newsletter for an art guild she founded in 1992.

Eleanore is currently writing articles and doing a monthly column for the Institute for Continuing Learning (ICL) in Young Harris, GA. Her writings include poetry, short stories, collaboration in writing a play and a work in progress on her memoirs. She has taken writing classes with the OASIS program.

Jean A. Nethery

Mother of four adult children, published author, world traveler and adventurer. She has visited all but one of our fifty states and 60 countries throughout the world. Recently traveled with her daughter to Italy, to participate in a six day cooking class. Hiking, cooking and nature are three of her loves and at present is composing a cook book, "Muffin Mania," a collection of recipes that contains anecdotes on family and friends that have contributed. She has written travel articles for the 'Boca Beacon' from Boca Grand, Florida, the 'Black Bear' and a feature article in the, 'International Travel News,' about her travels to Tunisia.

Lorraine M. Orth

Lorraine has been writing for years, favoring poetry and short stories. She was a member of our club for many years and has since moved to Cape Cod, Massachusetts.

Juanita Johnson Schneider

Juanita was born and lived in Independence, Missouri. She is the family historian, doing genealogy research the past 30 years. She is in the process of writing several historical books, as well as a book of her childhood. Her attempts at writing poetry have found several being published locally.

Juanita and her husband Richard, married 57 years, have four children, five grandchildren and one great-grandchild. They have lived in California, New Jersey and Florida. They found it easy to make their retirement home in the mountains of Georgia.

Idell M. Shook

Author of "Rivers Of My Heart," a successful book of poetry, published in 2002.

Her poems and stories have been published in the Towns County Sentinel, the Clay County Sentinel and the Georgia Nursing Home Association. In 2001 she was featured on 'Art in the Mountains' on television with David Sellers. She hones her talents by taking classes from the Oasis program and being an active member of the Georgia Mountain Writers Club.

Bruce R. Sims

Bruce R. Sims was born and spent his childhood in the Blue Ridge Mountains of North Georgia. He enlisted in the U.S. Air Force at the age of seventeen, and rose to the rank of Lieutenant Colonel.

He combined a military and civil service career. His assignments took him to the Far East, Africa, Europe, and Puerto Rico.

His travel and interest in people influenced him to get a BS Degree in Geography from FL State University.

He now resides in retirement in his hometown of Hiawassee, GA.

Charles H. Souther

Born in Union County Georgia in 1929. Union County High School 1947. U.S.Army 1948-1951. Army Ballistic Missile Agency 1956 – 1960 instructor. NASA/ Marshall Space Flight Center 1960-1981 Engineering Technician.
Part Time Farmer; Assisting Elderly Relatives; Author of *From the Mules and Wagon to the Space Shuttle.* More than twenty awards for work in the missile and space programs.

Dorothea Spiegel

Dorothea now lives in Gainesboro Tennessee, she is ninety years old. She has written all her life. She has edited newsletters, and had articles published in newspapers in New York, Florida and Georgia. She studied Creative writing at Tri-County College and John Campbell Folk School. She is a member of North Carolina Writers' Network and the Georgia Mountain Writers Club. Dorothea has published several books of her own poems, one titled "From My Desk."

Sylvia Dyer Turnage

Sylvia was born and raised in Blairsville, Georgia. After graduating from Union County High School, she moved to Atlanta to begin employment and to continue her education. Following retirement from a career as a CPA, she returned with her husband, Billy, to take residence on her family's old homeplace in Blairsville.

She is the author of *The Choestoe Story*, a children's rhyming storybook; *Choestoe Songs,* ballads about places and legends of Union County, GA; *The Legend of Clark Dyer's Remarkable Flying Machine,* the history of her great-great-grandfather's invention; *Financially Savvy,* a money management guide for Christian youth; and *Georgia's Pioneer Aviator Micajah Clark Dyer*, an expanded second-edition about her great-great-grandfather. Her stories, poems and articles have appeared in the Atlanta Journal Constitution, North Georgia News, 400 Edition Magazine, Mountain Chronicle News, Union Sentinel, Mountain Meditations and HOPE Newsletter.

Sylvia has two grown children, a son who lives in Blairsville and a daughter who lives in Chula Vista, California. She finds her retirement days happily filled with writing and making presentations around the North Georgia area on both financial and local history topics.

sturnage@windstream.net

Carroll G. Williamson

Carroll was born in Blairsville, Georgia and still resides around the area of his birth.

His first book, "A Place In Time" was published in 2006 by Morris Publishing. The stories are about his families history and were written to entertain his readers . This was his first attempt at writing for writing.

He is currently working on his 2nd book that will contain letters and stories from the Civil War era.

rjw4@hotmail.com

Ode to Ellie – A Tribute

WRITING FOR FUN

Thanks dear Ellie for sharing your life
For helping us with our daily strife
To open anew our imagination and still
On a blank sheet of paper you help us fill

Thoughts come easily at times and yet
Some moments we do seem to fret
Oh my gosh, what do I write next
Soon becoming a fine little text

Our little plot proudly comes near
On a blank sheet of paper it does appear
Thanks dear Ellie for guiding us through
Sharing our memories and thoughts with you

Juanita Schneider
May 2005

In Memory And Honor Of

These members had been with us since the beginning of our club. Their presence is still felt. We appreciate their contribution and insight into the development of our club.

The members we honor have made and are still making an impact on our club. Their seasoned writing abilities have inspired us to continue with the mission of this club.

Kenneth Johnson – Our Mentor
Patti Hamilton
Gene Beinke
Ethel Rose
Lou Laux
Earl Spiegel
Dorothea Spiegel
Lucious Endicott
Robert and Mary Swift
Joan Doolan
Magdelina Houdenshel
Dorah Marshall
Larry Casey

Sponsor Acknowledgement

     We would like to express our thank you to all the Sponsors for their gift, helping make the publishing of this anthology possible for Georgia Mountain Writers Club. As this project was initially begun to celebrate our 10th Year Anniversary since the club formed in 2001, we continue to celebrate our book coming into fruition with thirty of our members' works put in print.

     We recognize each and every Sponsor for their own foresight into our abilities by way of their encouragement and expression of support in our project. We truly appreciate their continuance in believing us to be an integral part of our community.

Business Sponsors:
- Walmart, Blairsville, GA
- Danny Burch Insurance, Hayesville, NC
- Office HELP! and Time to Call Plan B, LLC

Non-Business Sponsors:
- W. Franklin Boulineau Family and Friends
- Faye A. Brown Family
- Shirley Maurer Family
- Elizabeth Lashley
- Jayne L. Robertiello
- Nancy Nethery and Kenneth A. Rogers
- Charles H. Souther Family
- Jean and Arthur Nethery
- Bart Kwiatkowski
- Frank and Jennifer Kwiatkowski
- Dianne Craft Kwiatkowski
- Hubert Dobson
- Phillip and Yasko Rudisil

Georgia Mountain Writers Club
P.O. Box 374
Blairsville, GA 30514
(706) 745-0678

Order Form for: **Reflections From The Mountains**

Additional paperback books are available for $14.95 each.

Please place your order with the requested information. Enclose the correct amount due along with your completed order form and mail to the above address. Be sure to enclose $3.00 for mailing costs.
If you're ordering more than 1 -3 books at a time, please contact us for special mailing arrangements.

NAME: _____

MAILING ADDRESS:

_____

_____

NO. BOOKS ORDERED: _____

BOOK AMT. ENCLOSED: _____

POSTAGE ENCLOSED: _____

TOTAL AMT. ENCLOSED: _____

RFTM2012Rkb

3-1-13